A Mexican View
of America in the 1860s

Matías Romero. *Courtesy of the Library of Congress.*

A Mexican View
of America in the 1860s

A Foreign Diplomat Describes
the Civil War and Reconstruction

Translated and Edited by Thomas Schoonover
With the Assistance of Ebba Wesener Schoonover

Rutherford • Madison • Teaneck
Fairleigh Dickinson University Press
London and Toronto: Associated University Presses

Associated University Presses
440 Forsgate Drive
Cranbury, NJ 08512

Associated University Presses
25 Sicilian Avenue
London WC1A 2QH, England

Associated University Presses
P.O. Box 39, Clarkson Pstl. Stn.
Mississauga, Ontario
L5J 3X9 Canada

The paper used in this publication meets the requirements of the American National Standard for Permanence of Paper for Printed Library Materials Z39.48-1984.

Library of Congress Cataloging-in-Publication Data

Correspondencia de la legación mexicana durante la intervención extranjera, 1860–1868. English. Selections.
   A Mexican view of America in the 1860s : a foreign diplomat describes the Civil War and reconstruction / translated and edited by Thomas Schoonover ; with the assistance of Ebba Wesener Schoonover.
       p.   cm.
   Translation of: Correspondencia de la legación mexicana durante la intervención extranjera, 1860–1868.
   Includes bibliographical references (p.   ) and index.
   ISBN 0-8386-3432-X (alk. paper)
   1. United States—History—Civil War, 1861–1865—Sources.
   2. Reconstruction—Sources.   3. Romero, Matías, 1837–1898—Correspondence.   I. Schoonover, Thomas David, 1936–
   II. Romero, Matías, 1837–1898.   III. Title.
   E464.C672513   1991
   973.7—dc20   90-55960
                                                          CIP

Contents

Dedicated to the memories of

Harriet Rislove Schoonover,
Robert (Bush) Schoonover,
and Werner Biehlig

and to the encouragement in our life, Paco

Acknowledgments

I discovered Romero's ten-volume *Correspondencia de la legación mexicana en Washington* while working on my doctoral dissertation with the generous support of the Civil War Roundtable Fellowship. There was too much material to be incorporated into my book, *Dollars over Dominion* (Baton Rouge: Louisiana State University Press, 1978). Hence I undertook a second project, which has led to two volumes of Romero correspondence, each organized around a different theme and incorporating different series of correspondence, which Romero wrote on a regular basis. I wish to thank Kinley Brauer for his advice and intellectual stimulation. I owe special thanks to David Pletcher, Walt LaFeber, Ralph Lee Woodward, Jr., and Hans-Ulrich Wehler for encouragement at stages of my scholarship, which has kept me at this and other projects that I might otherwise have abandoned.

Many people and institutions have helped in the preparation of this book. I wish to thank particularly the library of the Secretaría de Hacienda (Mexico City), the Indiana University and University of Southwestern Louisiana libraries, and the Archivo Histórico de Matías Romero (Banco de México). I wish to thank my colleague Robert Butler for helping me translate the difficult passages, and Stanley Ross, Bill Evans, Robert Kirkpatrick, and Judy Gentry for reading the translated texts for style and readability. My wife, Ebba, labored with me throughout the entire process of translating, typing, critiquing, proofreading the manuscript, and compiling the index. I wish to thank the National Endowment for the Humanities for its support of my research in Central America and Mexico in 1972–73 and the German Academic Exchange Service (DAAD) for support in the summer of 1975 when I worked at the Ibero-Amerikanisches Institut des Deutschen Kulturbesitzes in Berlin. Finally, I wish to thank my student assistants, Shana Swilley and Mayra Rodríguez, and the student assistants of the History Department for typing and proofreading assistance.

The Universität Bielefeld, Germany, where I spent 1981–82 as a Fulbright senior lecturer, provided me with spiritual and material support during the revision of this manuscript. Although I was a transient Fulbright instructor at Bielefeld, its faculty and staff willingly and eagerly aided my work in any way they could. Their interest in scholars and scholarship enlightened me regarding what a university could and should be. The French magazine *L'information* discovered that European historians consider Bielefeld one of the five best history departments in Europe. I concur.

Introduction

Recently, historian Eric Foner has drawn our attention to a long-neglected source of information about domestic American reconstruction history—the reports of foreign diplomats who, like Georges Clemenceau, were "fascinated contemporary observers."[1] This book, compiled and translated from the writings of Matías Romero, Mexican chargé and minister during the 1860–67 period, offers the insightful commentaries of an intelligent, active foreign diplomat who resided in the United States during the secession crisis, the Civil War, and reconstruction.[2]

The years 1860 to 1867 encompassed vital, dramatic events in both Mexico and the United States—the Mexican *reforma*, the U.S. Civil War and Reconstruction, and the French intervention in Mexico. After Mexico's civil war, *la reforma*, ended in 1860, France, Spain, and Great Britain intervened in late 1861. The British and Spanish soon withdrew, converting the intervention into a unilateral French effort to sustain a client regime under Maximilian, with the collaboration of the defeated Mexican conservative elements from the *reforma*. Historically important personalities President Abraham Lincoln, Secretary of State William H. Seward, General Ulysses S. Grant, Confederate President Jefferson Davis, Mexican President Benito Pablo Juárez, General Porfirio Díaz, Hapsburg Archduke Maximilian, and French Emperor Napoleon III influenced these crucial events.

Naturally, given the comparative power relationships of the United States, Mexico, and France in the early 1860s, Juárez's Mexico wished for material as well as moral support from its northern neighbor—the United States. Under different circumstances, Juárez's government might have accepted aid from the Confederacy. However, judging the Confederate leadership to be responsible for the annexations and expansion in the prewar decades, assuming the south would favor slave expansion in the future, and recognizing the Confederacy was nearing collapse, the Mexican liberals continued to place more short-term and long-term trust in the liberalism of the yankees.

Lincoln's administration assumed that the French under Napoleon III were seeking to take advantage of the American Civil War to undermine U.S. influence in the Caribbean and to lay the ground work for a revived French presence. Still, the United States assigned priority to its Civil

9

War, and later to reconstruction, thereby rejecting any aggressive policy against European intervention in Mexico. The United States did formally protest French interventionist activity that interfered with internal Mexican politics, and by mid-1865 public pressure was building into opposition to the French in Mexico. Some military leaders such as Grant, some economic and political factions interested in loans and arms sales, and many articles in the press commissioned in Juárez's faction contributed to the developing groundswell of U.S. public opinion. In this climate, Seward issued veiled warnings to the French government. Thus, through indirect means for the most part, the United States played a modest role in inducing Napoleon III's France to reconsider its dreams of empire in the new world and withdraw from Mexico. Other important factors influencing the French withdrawal were the financial costs, the deepening European crises, and the determined Mexican resistance.

Matías Romero was not only an active and competent representative of his government (his voluminous annual correspondence with his superiors in Mexico, about five hundred to seven hundred dispatches, averaged more than one million words yearly), but during the time served as a diplomat, he also managed to write frequent, fairly regular summary reports—labeled *reseñas políticas*—of events, personalities, and developments in the United States. Romero considered these political reports essential reading for his government, to help it properly assess the possibilities of soliciting U.S. assistance in terminating the French intervention in Mexico. Collectively, the roughly 125 *reseña* dispatches represent Romero's history of the United States during the Civil War and early Reconstruction years. This book consists of a translation of these documents. While it would undoubtedly be desirable for those students of the interrelationship of internal and external affairs to read, in addition, both the Seward-Romero correspondence and the Romero-Mexican Foreign Ministry correspondence, this volume cannot undertake to aid that task by translating and publishing the immense Romero correspondence with the State Department and his government. The bibliographical essay guides the curious or unsatisfied readers to various sources and to interpretative studies.

The project of translating Romero's *reseñas* was undertaken with three goals in mind. First, I wanted to make available to scholars and others interested in the American Civil War some new challenging material on that topic. Second, the *reseñas* demonstrate the interconnection between U.S. domestic events and U.S. goals in foreign affairs. Some diplomatic historians sense that there is a close interrelationship between domestic and foreign politics and that a society's foreign policy goals are normally extensions of the domestic goals and aspirations of the governing elite.

Other diplomatic and many political historians, however, seem to focus so sharply upon domestic politics that they have little time or inclination to consider foreign policy matters. From my reading of the literature on the U.S. Civil War and Reconstruction, historians of this period have not avoided this pitfall. Third, U.S. diplomatic history, like most other subfields of history in the United States, has traditionally focused on crises, on the big, dramatic events, or on the elite (the great or evil leaders). The Romero correspondence that I translated and published in *Mexican Lobby: Matías Romero in Washington, 1861–1867* (Lexington, Ky., The University Press of Kentucky, 1986) falls into this general category of crisis-oriented material. I have long appreciated modern social and economic history where the common people and routine events, activities, and ideas are treated collectively as the backbone of a society and a society's political economy. Such common events and people also form the foundation of U.S. international history. Akira Iriye, Fernand Braudel, and others have tried to show, in diverse forms, how culture and popular perception and images underlie all societal actions. This volume offers, in a small way, an attempt to present the routine, the commonplace of international relations that Romero himself considered fundamental to the dramatic aspects. His first *reseña* admonished President Juárez and Secretary of Foreign Relations Sebastián Lerdo de Tejada that the information in the series would only supply the Mexican government with the basic knowledge and understanding necessary for developing sound perceptions of events and personalities in the United States and thus, hopefully, guide Mexico toward intelligent policies in U.S.-Mexican relations. Of course, Romero never claimed that such fundamental labor was the end-all of interstate relations. This routine information was, however, the bedrock upon which such relations had to be built. Although diplomacy, illness, and a myriad of other events demanded his time as the U.S. Civil War ended and reconstruction began, he continued to draft the *reseñas* until the end of his mission in late 1867. I hope these documents will offer the opportunity for the reader to appreciate common personalities and events and to understand better the relationship revealed between internal and external affairs.

These *reseña* dispatches cover material of broad interest. They describe strategy, military campaigns, civil and military leadership at war, political leadership on the home front, the economy, judicial affairs, the role of black Americans, labor and urban problems, and civil liberties in both the Union and Confederate areas. They represent the broadest contemporary history of the Civil War that I am familiar with. Since Romero obtained his information from government documents (both North and South), magazines, newspapers, his personal observations, and a wide range of conversations with political, military, media, and business people, his account cannot escape being an important new source of information about the Civil War era. When writing to his government, Romero did not hesitate to interject his own prognoses or interpretations. Despite his awkward style, at times Romero's observations have a succinct, biting quality. Commenting on the U.S. attitudes and politics towards slavery in late 1862, Romero observed that U.S. conduct was "very far from arriving at the point demanded by civilization and humanity." It is an intriguing remark in light of repeated U.S. intervention in Mexico and Latin America since the 1840s in the interest of "civilization and humanity." In sum, while not written in a particularly lively style, Romero's *reseñas políticas* contribute a detached, insightful, and occasionally eye-opening view of this crucial era.

Romero filled important posts in the Mexican government for thirty-eight of the forty-two years of his life between joining the Relaciones Exteriores (Foreign Relations) ministry in 1857 and his death in 1898. Romero's service included two years in Relaciones Exteriores (1857–59), three periods, for a total of twenty-six years, as secretary of the legation, chargé, or minister to the United States (1859–68, 1882–92, 1893–98), three periods, a total of about eight years, as secretary of the treasury (1868–72, 1877–79, 1892–93), and two years in the Mexican Senate (1875–77). As his voluminous private correspondence in the Banco de México and official correspondence in the Mexican Ministry of Foreign Affairs archives testify, he played a key role in inducing North American capital to enter Mexico and in furthering closer Mexican-U.S. relations.

Romero was born in 1837 in Oaxaca, in southwestern Mexico, the birthplace of fellow Mexican liberal leaders Benito Juárez, Porfirio Díaz, and Ignacio Mariscal. Although educated as a lawyer, immediately upon finishing his studies Romero joined the liberal government under President Juárez during the War of the Reforma (1857–61). As a protegé of Juárez, Romero served some time as an unpaid employee in the Ministry of Foreign Relations before being given a salaried post. Thus, although Romero was young when he entered diplomatic service in the Mexican legation in the United States early in 1859, he was not totally inexperienced. Later, when the outbreak of the American Civil War thrust considerable responsibility upon the twenty-four-year-old Romero, he already had acquired four years of experience in the Mexican foreign service, including two years in the United States as secretary of the legation and chargé d'affaires. Romero continued to serve as chargé until mid-1863, when he resigned due to lack of sufficient funds to conduct the lobbying campaign he judged necessary to produce favorable U.S. action against the French intervention in Mexico. He returned to Mexico hoping to serve in the Mexican army against the French. Upon his arrival in Mexico, however, Juárez and Secretary of Foreign Relations Lerdo de

Tejada persuaded Romero to return to the United States. They guaranteed him prompt payment of his salary, adequate funds to maintain an active legation, and the rank of minister. By October 1863, Romero was back in Washington where he remained until late 1867. Returning to Mexico briefly, the pressing need to resolve outstanding U.S. claims against Mexico in order to facilitate Mexico's credit rating with potential American investors brought him back to the United States in mid-1868. After negotiating the U.S.-Mexican Claims agreement of 1868, which arranged for the adjudication of all outstanding claims between the two countries, Romero again returned to Mexico where, at thirty-one, he became Juárez's secretary of the treasury.

Juárez's decision to seek reelection in 1872 displeased Romero, prompting him to resign and pursue an activity he had long advocated—coffee culture in southern Mexico. This phase of his life lasted only three years, in part because of the hostility of Guatemalan President Justo Rufino Barrios, who feared that Romero's presence near Guatemala's frontier portended future Mexican expansion into his country, and in part because in 1875 Romero was elected to the Mexican Senate. In 1877, after serving only two years of his Senate term, Romero accepted Porfirio Díaz's request that he serve as secretary of the treasury. Romero's health turned bad in 1879, compelling his resignation. Battling recurring stomach problems, which had plagued him since his youth, Romero traveled to the United States to consult medical specialists. In 1880 and 1881, while recuperating, he was involved in several railroad schemes with former U.S. President Ulysses Grant, Albert K. Owen, Hiram Barney, and others. Then, from 1882 until his death, Romero served as Mexican minister to the United States, except for a short period from mid-1892 until early 1893, when he returned to Mexico for his third period as secretary of the treasury. Romero died in Washington on 30 December 1898 after an attack of appendicitis.

Romero's correspondence discloses his involvement in a variety of issues, some of which are matters that concerned U.S.-Mexican relations, others of which were very clearly primarily affairs of internal U.S. concern. Those apparent intrusions into domestic American life were undertaken because of the inherent possibility of ultimately influencing Mexican-U.S. relations. Among the chief topics of Romero's correspondence were trade ties, communication links both by sea and by rail, and U.S. military intervention in Mexico. Romero also persisted in meddling in U.S. domestic politics. He supported, or at least sympathized with, various efforts to oust Secretary of State William H. Seward, who, Romero was convinced, successfully opposed firmer, more aggressive steps to compel the French to withdraw from Mexico. Romero generally cooperated with the radical efforts to defeat Lincoln in the election of

1864 and to carry the elections of 1866; he welcomed the early efforts to impeach President Andrew Johnson in 1866–67; and, finally, he sought to influence appointments to the foreign relations committees in Congress in 1866.

Romero himself initiated the project to publish all his official correspondence from the era of the French intervention in order to aid the claims commission investigations required by the 1868 Mexican-U.S. Claims Treaty. Prior to 1868, the United States had published much more documentation on Mexican-U.S. relations than Mexico had, often in response to demands made by Romero's congressional allies while Romero had served as minister to the United States. But in 1868, Romero's nationalism prompted him to wish that Mexicans would learn about the intervention in Spanish from their own documents. Moreover, he believed that the Mexican government should be as interested in the story as the U.S. government. Yet the publication of the ten-volume *Correspondencia* caused him some embarrassment. In the introduction Romero published a disclaimer denying that the occasional expressions of ill feelings toward the United States found in the published official Mexican documents expressed his true deep feelings. These expressions, he explained, were rather due to tension and the importance of the conditions that threatened Mexico. In other words, they were the product of his patriotism and frustration.

The historical significance and the rareness of the original Spanish language edition (only about six copies exist in the United States, and copies are very difficult to encounter in Mexico) of Romero's official correspondence and the significance of these selected documents for U.S. domestic history makes their translation desirable. I have selected about seventy-five thousand words from Romero's dispatches—only about 1 percent of the total—for translation and inclusion in this volume. The full edition contains about seven million words—ten large volumes averaging more than one thousand pages with about seven hundred words per page. The original edition is, of course, still valuable not only in regard to U.S.-Mexican relations but also for U.S. domestic history. However, many specialists in U.S. history cannot read Spanish well enough to examine such a large collection with ease. Moreover, very few bibliographies or historiographical essays even suggest that Romero's published correspondence might be of value to historians specializing in internal U.S. history during the middle period.

To test the accuracy and reliability of Romero's published correspondence, several hundred dispatches from the published edition of Romero's official correspondence were checked against the originals in the Archivo Histórico de la Secretaría de Relaciones Exteriores in Mexico City. This comparison disclosed a degree of accuracy and reliability that made it unnecessary to check each and every dispatch. Generally, when Romero found it desirable to depart from the manuscript text, for whatever reason, he inserted a series of dots in the printed document roughly equivalent to the length of the passage omitted. Only very rarely did he alter a document, and then because of an orthographic or other minor error in the original. Only once did I discover a significant change in the wording of a document. In this case, where the original document read, " . . . . We [Mexicans] desire to have some of the most distinguished soldiers from the United States go to Mexico as much so that they would serve as a species of nucleus for our army as for making more useful the sympathies of that people for our cause . . . ," it became in print, " . . . . It would not be disagreeable to us to have some of the most distinguished soldiers. . . ." The printed version altered the meaning to suggest that the initiative in proposing that American soldiers go to Mexico came from the United States and not from the Juárez government. This is an important point if one recalls the remnants of bitter feelings towards the United States in Mexico and the Mexican fear of further loss of national territory to the "Colossus of the North."[3]

With regard to accuracy and reliability, moreover, much of Romero's alleged and reported activity is subject to external verification. For example, many of Romero's claims are subject to verification in the correspondence of North American politicians, businessmen, soldiers, and Mexican officials and friends. My efforts to verify Romero's assertions have convinced me that he was an honest reporter. The same sort of internal and external checks suggest that he possessed a good ability to evaluate the rumors and allegations that often became known to him. He did not merely accept those stories or rumors that were favorable to Mexico and discount those that were unfavorable. He evaluated, investigated when possible, and exercised a reasonable amount of cynical, critical pessimism even toward stories he wanted to believe. While he was honest and critical, obviously, at times, he misunderstood, miscalculated, misinterpreted, or was misled. Occasionally, he passed along unfounded rumors and baseless stories. Still, the acceptance of bad information did not occur frequently. Endnotes and the bibliographic essay will guide the reader to modern scholarship useful for checking Romero's narratives and interpretations. An intelligent, talented, serious, and prudent person, apparently from both training and inclination, Romero was a trustworthy agent for his government and a generally reliable, accurate source for historians.

Quantitative information taken from Secretary of State Seward's papers and from *El Siglo Diez y Nueve*, the official Mexican government newspaper, reveal Romero as a persistent and accomplished lobbyist and a prodigious worker. Seward compiled statistics indicating that from 1861 to 1865 he addressed 49 notes per year to the Mexican legation in Washington, the third most active correspondence he maintained with a foreign representative. Romero, however, calculated that from 1861 to 1866, counting annexed documents, the Mexican legation received 80 items per year from the secretary of state. Romero's data reveal that he had submitted almost 300 items per year, totaling 500 manuscript pages, for Seward's consideration. Romero's statistics also show that he submitted about 600 items per year, comprising 4,000 manuscript pages, to his own government. Perhaps the average yearly incoming and outgoing correspondence statistic for Romero while serving in the United States best indicate his vigor and activity. On the average, for each year from 1861 through 1866, Romero wrote 2,850 items containing 8,230 manuscript pages, and received 1,860 items containing 4,030 manuscript pages. One can truly speak of Romero laboring for his government.[4]

In translating the documents contained in this volume, I have followed certain guidelines. For clarity, I have occasionally substituted more customary, familiar names for those names used by Romero. For example, Romero referred to "the Confederate Army of the Potomac" rather than "the Army of Northern Virginia." And he used the wording, "the committee to consider the facts relative to the conduct of the war" for "the Committee on the Conduct of the War." Sometimes Romero used names or labels that would not be clear in English. For convenience I have retained several of these to avoid repeating longer descriptions or terms. For example, I will allow Romero's "gobierno supremo," literally, Supreme Government, to mean the Mexican government of Juárez. Likewise, Romero's "this Ministry" shall appear as he used it, as an abbreviated form for the Mexican Ministerio de Relaciones Exteriores (the Mexican Ministry of Foreign Relations). Romero referred to Mexico as "the Republic," a term I preserve when its meaning is clear to avoid the repetitive use of Mexico. Romero used word numbers and numerals inconsistently; I have followed his usage even when it appeared inconsistent. Romero always used a title of address before proper names. I have dropped these titles in all cases where the title was honorific or formal. As examples, Romero used "Mr." very often; I have dropped this in almost every case. I have changed or dropped Romero's formal "excellency," or "your excellency"; he used "His Excellency the Minister, etc.," which I have shortened merely to "minister."

I have excluded the formal ending of Romero's dispatches. Usually I have deleted casual references to documents not discussed further in the *reseñas* and to the mere brief notice of some person or event related to U.S. foreign relations or European affairs. While Romero followed and reported these developments regularly, these details are not central to the purpose of this book.

Romero's style was so stiff, formal, and awkward that it posed translating difficulties; I have taken the liberty of rendering it somewhat loosely while nevertheless striving to maintain as much of the flavor of his nineteenth-century form and style as possible. For example, many of his sentences run on for several hundred words. I have often broken up the longest ones. His use of pronouns would be impossible in English because of the lack of precision. I have substituted nouns for pronouns when necessary for clarity. Explanatory material has been included in the texts in square brackets in order to eliminate the need for narrative or textual footnotes. Material in parentheses comes from Romero's original text. Except for excluding a limited amount of extraneous or repetitive material and the formal endings, the translated *reseñas* are published in full.

While Romero's *reseñas* are reliable and informative descriptions of the times, his views and narrative suffered from occasional misinformation or misunderstanding. Later historical research has often developed broader and more complex understanding of the personalities and events of the 1860–67 years. To facilitate the interested reader or researcher, I have created several hundred endnotes that guide the curious to specific secondary sources on the chief matters under discussion in Romero's various dispatches. A few of the endnotes pursue some of the more esoteric stories or personalities that caught Romero's attention. For those wishing a deeper understanding of Matías Romero and his role in U.S.-Mexican relations, the translations of his dispatches and the endnotes are followed by an essay including general background information on sources relative to his life and career, to U.S.-Mexican relations, and to the Civil War, Reconstruction, and *"reforma"* years.

A Mexican View
of America in the 1860s

Reseñas políticas (political reviews)

1860

Introduction to the pre–Civil War years: The United States until 1860

Matías Romero's *reseñas políticas* represent an effort to describe the routine, the commonplace, in American history as well as the crises and the dramatic events. Romero devoted only modest space to the battles, to the major political activities, or even to the assassination of President Abraham Lincoln in 1865. Romero routinely described labor matters, general economic and social developments, resistance to the draft or war effort, and other phenomena often slighted in histories of the Civil War. To allow the reader to understand Romero's *reseñas* better, each chapter (which encompasses the correspondence for one year) will be preceded by a brief description of U.S. and Mexican domestic events, an evaluation of Romero's lobbying activity, and a few remarks about U.S.-Mexican relations.

In the 1860s Romero reported on a variety of socioeconomic characteristics of U.S. society. He commented on labor conditions and unions, slavery and race relations, westward expansion and the incorporation of new territories, industry and technology, tariff matters, finance and currency questions, and capital formation. Since these matters attracted Romero's attention, it seems appropriate to describe some developments in these areas in the decades before Romero began his *reseñas políticas*.

In the 1840s and 1850s, the United States experienced extensive demographic and economic growth and expansion. Huge areas of North America were incorporated into the United States as the result of the Mexican War and the Gadsden Purchase. These areas and other lands acquired in the Louisiana Purchase, the Adams-de Onís Treaty, and the British-U.S. settlement of the dispute over the Oregon territory were settled, in part due to the natural increase in population, but also as a consequence of a marked increase in European migration to the United States in the years 1845 to 1860. From 1847 to 1856, the number of immigrants was more than two hundred thousand each year.

The economic growth of the country was evident in the rapid increase of production in the iron industries, textiles, and machine shops. Manufactures from household production declined markedly. The evident shift from family, small-scale to industrial, capitalized production was reinforced in the rapid expansion of the use of steam-powered factories and the emergence of an important machine tool industry. The sectors of production that grew most rapidly were minerals, chemicals, alloy metals, and the use of electrical power. There was a clear trend toward adoption of large-scale organizations and managerial techniques. Key developments underscored the transformation of American society. For example, in 1852 Elisha Otis invented the first elevator; in 1858 a machine was perfected for sewing leather soles on the upper parts of shoes; and in 1859 oil wells operated in Pennsylvania. Gail Borden patented a condensed milk process in 1856 that expanded milk production and sales. Borden's profits rose dramatically during the Civil War. A number of other food-processing firms also developed rapidly in response to the needs of the Union army. In 1860 the repeating rifle was patented, an invention that also found ready use in the following five years. Even dramatists, as men of business, were given protection for their labors under the 1856 Copyright Law.

The domestic market flourished under the 1846 Walker Tariff, which was an ad valorem tariff (as opposed to the common protective use of specific tariffs). The Walker Tariff aimed primarily at generating sufficient revenue for the government. The 1857 Tariff reduced the ad valorem rates further and extended the list of foods and raw materials that could enter free of duty. A large free list generated market expansion by lowering costs of production (cheaper raw material and labor costs) and by reducing discontent (lower cost of living) within a disjointed economy in a tumultuous economic expansion.

Labor responded to the trends toward centralized production and management with its own movement toward larger, broader-based unions. National trade unions rose to meet the challenge. In 1852 the typographers, in 1854 the hat finishers, in 1855 the stone cutters, in 1856 the cigar makers, and in 1859 the iron molders, machinists, and blacksmiths formed national unions. In 1860, the New England shoemakers initiated a strike that quickly attracted twenty thousand participants.

Continued heavy reliance upon foreign capital marked economic growth in the 1840s and 1850s. There are indications that this influx of capital was slowing down as the national productive system expanded and adopted industrial production and organization for the national market. In 1857, for example, foreign indebtedness represented $1.4 billion, but in 1860 U.S. citizens owned about 75 percent of the securities of U.S. corporations. This impressive domestic ownership of corporate securities suggests that domestic accumulation was becoming adequate to finance capital expansion. To facilatate domestic exchange, in 1853 the New York Clearing House was created, followed in the next three years by clearing houses in Boston, Philadelphia, Baltimore, and Cleveland. The U.S. government budget produced large surpluses from 1850 until the panic of 1857. Panic and shrunken federal revenues marked the years 1857 and 1858, but a slow recovery took place in 1859 and 1860.

Politically and socially, the struggle over use of national territory for slave expansion and the future of slave power and culture in the United States underscored the 1840s and 1850s. The Compromise of 1850 did not last long and scarcely deserved the name. It functioned more like a truce. The Kansas-Nebraska legislation, the attack upon Senator Charles Sumner, the Dred Scott decision, and John Brown's raid on Harper's Ferry dramatized the constant tension over the role of slavery in the United States and the continuous possibility of dissolving the Union.

In 1859, twenty-two-year-old Mexican diplomat Matías Romero entered the United States for his first foreign service. After a brief period as secretary of legation, he became chargé in 1860 when the Mexican minister returned to Mexico. Mexico had experienced *la reforma*, a long civil war between liberal and conservative factions from 1857 to 1860. Only in 1859 had the Mexican liberals, the faction of Romero and President Benito Juárez, finally driven the conservative faction from Mexico. The *reforma* conflict had exhausted the resources of Mexico, prompting both factions to seek foreign weapons, funds, or troops in an effort to stave off the victory of the opposing faction. Some Mexican conservative leaders retreated to Europe in 1859 and 1860 where they conspired in France, Austria, Italy, and Spain to obtain funds, military supplies, moral support, manpower, and leadership to sustain a renewal of the struggle with the liberals. The conservative appeal to Napoleon III produced the Jean Baptiste Jecker (a Swiss banker) loan in late 1859. Mexico gave bonds worth $15 million in return for about $600,000 cash. Just as the Mexican conservatives sought the solution to their problem abroad, southern filibusterer William Walker undertook one invasion of Mexico and four invasions of Central America in the 1850s in his search for an external solution to the southern slave-owners' dilemma. In late 1860, Walker was captured and executed in Honduras. Other southerners (and their allies) undertook filibustering projects against Cuba or Mexico.

The most dramatic event in 1860 was the U.S. presidential election. A series of political conventions was necessary before four candidates were chosen. The Democratic Convention met first, but it was divided and faced a walkout of southerners. It adjourned to reconvene several months later. The forces of mediation and compromise that feared the disruption of an American experiment met next and created the Union party, nominating John Bell for president. The Republican favorite, William H. Seward, lost his bid for nomination at the Chicago Convention to Abraham Lincoln. The Democrats reconvened only to face another

southern walkout. The northern Democrats nominated Stephen Douglas, while the southern Democrats nominated John C. Breckinridge. In
November 1860, Lincoln won the election. A month later, South Carolina seceded, followed in early 1861 by six other deep South states.

Political Reviews—1860

Romero to MRE, 31 August 1860, in Romero, *Correspondencia* I, 110–11

. . . In the course of this month, a fusion of supporters of [Stephen A.]
Douglas and [John] Bell has occurred in various places. With the Democrats divided, members of the Union party, which does not possess an
absolute majority, fear a victory of the Republican candidate in the
coming presidential election. . . . Perhaps this movement will continue,
thus increasing Douglas's vote. However, between Douglas's supporters
and those of [John C.] Breckinridge there is no hope of fusion.

In New York a committee has been formed to prevent Lincoln's
election. . . . Meanwhile, the Republicans express the greatest confidence in their candidate's success. In a speech in Boston eulogizing the
"Massachusetts School," [William H.] Seward mentioned the irrepressi-
ble conflict between liberty and slavery. The speech greatly alarmed the
Democrats, serving for several days as the focus of their conversations and
the theme of Democratic newspapers. . . .[1]

Romero to MRE, 18 September 1860, in Romero, *Correspondencia* I, 113–14

. . . In the first days of this month, Maine and Vermont held elections
for governor and Congress. In both states a considerable majority of
Republican party candidates were elected. . . . In spite of this, the
various factions opposed to the Republican party in New York, the most
populous state whose vote will be quite decisive in the election, have not
been able to reach agreement. After conferring and bargaining for a
month, they have almost proven that it is impossible for them to cooperate.

. . . Traveling in the western states, Seward has been received everywhere in a truly triumphant manner. He has employed all the facets of
his fertile mind while speaking in favor of his ideas and the election of

Lincoln. Douglas has already visited some states in New England and the South. After speaking before twelve thousand people in New York City on the twelfth, he moved into the west. Until now, Breckinridge has made only one speech, reportedly to defend himself against the allegations of his enemies. Seward is under way toward Kansas, which has been named "The Saratoga of Liberty." . . .

On the eleventh of this month, Secretary of the Treasury [Howell Cobb] opened public bidding for the construction of a telegraph line to the Pacific. Various proposals have been received, but until now they have not awarded the construction to anyone.[2]

The latest reports indicate that Texas's situation is very violent and deplorable. Because a rumor is circulating that the abolitionists were plotting to have the slaves rise against their owners and because there has been some disorder, the Texans are committing very arbitrary actions, bringing Negroes and whites to the gallows without any form of justice and without any other motive than personal vengeance and base passions. . . .[3]

Romero to MRE, 8 October 1860, in Romero, *Correspondencia* I, 116–17

. . . The different New York factions opposed to Lincoln, the Republican party candidate for president, finally agreed to a fusion. Of the thirty-six electors from this state, they decided eighteen will be Douglasmen, ten will be Breckinridge-men, and eight, Bell-men. The adherents of each faction in New York will vote for the composite electoral list. If the electors receive sufficient votes, they will vote for whichever presidential candidate—Douglas, Breckinridge, or Bell—obtained the most votes in the other states. The Republicans also have a list of electors, who will vote for Lincoln if chosen by the people.

Having already concluded his trip through the western states, Seward has returned to his home in Auburn. . . . Almost every day during his trip, he delivered a more or less carefully prepared speech. He was even invited to speak in the slave states and listened to with attention. Douglas still remains in the West. . . .

Recently, the cruisers of the United States have seized two boats loaded with Negroes being carried to Norfolk. . . .

Romero to MRE, 24 October 1860, in Romero, *Correspondencia*
I, 126–27

On 9 October elections were held for governors and legislators in
Pennsylvania, Ohio, and Indiana. In the three states the Republican
party candidates were elected by very considerable majorities. Since these
states, especially the first two, are among the most populous of the
Union, these election results have revealed the large number of voters
converted to Republican ideas within recent years and the strength which
that party currently possesses. Previously in these three states the Democratic party had predominated. . . . The election, which will take place
on 6 November, is beyond any doubt. Lincoln's triumph is certain. . . .
The only way, it is claimed, to neutralize its effects would be if the
coming Congress has a Democratic majority so that the administration
would find its hands tied and would be unable to develop any of its plans.

Some Democrats, nevertheless, still hope that the New York vote,
which remains uncertain . . . could manage at least to stalemate the
vote, thereby forcing the election into Congress. But also in New York,
where the present state government is Republican, Republican ideas have
made great progress. Even though the Democratic element dominates
the capital because the multitude of capitalists established there give that
site a conservative bend, the same does not hold true in the rest of the
state. . . .

Meanwhile, the southern states discuss whether Lincoln's election is
sufficient grounds for them to separate from the Union. The election
alone, some believe, authorizes them to take this step. Others, less ready
to alter their status, insist that they must wait until the new administration adopts some measure hostile to the interests of the southern states.
However, all this will most likely ease after the election, whatever the
results are, since the South has regularly made similar threats before
elections for the purpose of influencing the outcome in its favor by fear, if
not by reason, among the more conservative masses. Later, these southern threats could not be fulfilled, except at the cost of prejudicing its
dearest interests. . . .[4]

. . . Especially worth notice is the method by which this country
arrives at any important objective. After instilling the reform that one
wishes to introduce in the minds of the people, the government has to
concede to the force of opinion. . . .

Oregon has named [James W.] Neswith and [Edward D.] Baker to the
Senate. The former is a Douglas Democrat and the latter, a Republican.

Yesterday, in the Treasury Department, they opened the bids to sub-
scribe to a loan for $10 million, which the government has solicited with
congressional authorization to cover the deficiency of the public treasury.

The secretary accepted the bids of forty-six lenders for varying amounts. No offers for this capital were received from any southern states. . . .[5]

Romero to MRE, 9 November 1860, in Romero, *Correspondencia* I, 135–36

. . . 6 November, the people of the United States elected Abraham Lincoln, Republican party candidate, president.

Since the elections held a month ago in Pennsylvania, Ohio, and Indiana revealed the strength of the Republican party, the Democrats have known the terrible adversary they had to fight. They used whatever means were within their power in order to triumph. The moment it became known that Lincoln was nominated, they made the South threaten very seriously to secede. They multiplied their correspondence discussing the rights of those states to secede, enumerating the supposed advantages of this course, and asserting that this was the desire of each and every inhabitant of the South. The Democrats provoked a monetary panic in the New York Exchange and strained their ingenuity to persuade the northerners that the result of the election could be nothing less than the ruin of the country. However, nothing was adequate to contain the course of opinion. Lincoln's majorities in the northern and western states considerably exceeded the expectations of his party. Of the thirty-three states, the sixteen most populous and most important, that is, Connecticut, Illinois, Indiana, Iowa, Maine, Massachusetts, Michigan, Minnesota, New Hampshire, New Jersey, New York, Ohio, Pennsylvania, Rhode Island, Vermont, and Wisconsin, voted for Lincoln, giving him 176 Republican electors. Since the total electoral vote is 303 and 152 sufficient for election, Lincoln has 24 more than necessary. Of the other seventeen states, Alabama, Arkansas, Florida, Georgia, Louisiana, Mississippi, the two Carolinas, and Texas voted for Breckinridge, giving him 61 votes. Delaware, Kentucky, Maryland, Tennessee, and Virginia voted for Bell, giving him 50 votes, and Missouri went for Douglas, who only obtained 9 votes. The results from California and Oregon are still not in. . . .

Elections for the House of Representatives were held at the same time in New York and various other states. . . . It is still not known which party will have a majority in the next Congress.

To the honor of this people, the election having passed very orderly, everything has undergone a sudden change. The newspapers, which denounced the Republicans yesterday as disunionists and traitors and called their leaders demagogues, now write in a very different tone. They express their opinion and their hope that the triumph of that party is not sufficient grounds to dissolve the Union.

. . . The South Carolina legislature, composed of people animated by the most ardent fanaticism in favor of slavery, might continue to menace the Union with secession by convoking a popular convention to determine the suitability of secession and by inviting the neighboring states to follow its example. All its efforts will fail, however, before the good sense of the people who do not view the naming of a popularly and constitutionally elected president as any basis for the overthrow of a political system under whose shadow the country has progressed in a fabulous manner.

This election represents one of the principal revolutions that could take place in this country. The coming administration has new ideas and its politics are distinct from those followed by the government that preceded it. This country's relations with Mexico will experience a radical change under the new administration. . . .

Romero to MRE, 24 November 1860, in Romero,
Correspondencia I, 141–42

As soon as the South knew that the Republican candidate had received enough votes to be elected president, the previous agitation peaked. South Carolina, which has placed itself at the head of those discontented with the new order that will begin on 4 March next year, has in fact already separated from the Union. Its two senators, [James H.] Hammond and [James] Chesnut [Jr.], have resigned their seats in the U.S. Senate. All employees of the federal government [in South Carolina], with the exception of the postmasters and the collector of customs at Charleston, have also resigned their respective posts, some to take effect immediately, others effective on 4 March. The U.S. flag, removed from all public buildings and from the U.S. vessels in Charleston Harbor, has been replaced by the South Carolina flag amidst gun salutes and great, joyous demonstrations. Popular meetings have multiplied. At these meetings great applause has interrupted vitriolic speeches against the North and enthusiastic speeches for southern independence.[6]

. . . South Carolina's legislature issued the call for a popular convention on 17 December. This convention will determine whether the state should continue in the Union or not. This example has been followed more or less enthusiastically in the other southern states. Next to South Carolina, Georgia has demonstrated the most similar desire for secession. One of its senators, [Robert] Toombs, also resigned his post. . . . The Georgia governor's message to the state legislature . . . adequately reveals the stage to which things have arrived here, the profound hatred that actually divides the North and South, the proposals of those seeking to establish a southern government, and the means by which they expect to realize their plans.

Alabama, Mississippi, and Florida will most likely follow South Carolina and Georgia, and the southern confederation will initially be formed with these five. Already they have published a proposed act of independence, a manifesto to the nation, and some instructions that allegedly were given to an agent of those five states sent to Paris and London to obtain French and British recognition of the independence of the new confederation.

The remaining southern states are very divided. In Tennessee, Kentucky, Missouri, and Maryland the Union party dominates completely. Texas wishes to secede, it is asserted, not to join the confederation, but rather to build an independent nation. Because of its geographical position, its territorial extent, and its large population, Virginia occupies the prime position among the slave states yet hopes to serve as mediator between the North and South. Virginia will propose a constitutional amendment by virtue of which the southern states have representation in the national legislature equal to the other states despite its inferior number of states and population. In Louisiana and Arkansas the opposing factions are balanced.

. . . An event is taking place that could prevent the realization of the secession schemes . . . [when] the federal legislature convenes on 3 December. On that day President [Buchanan] should send Congress his farewell message. . . . Until now, the president has not indicated if he favors or disfavors secession, nor whether he would oppose it or not with force. His cabinet is divided. He and four cabinet ministers believe that the states do not have the constitutional right to separate themselves from the Union whenever they choose. The remaining three apparently are of the contrary view. The action of the southern states will depend in large part upon what the president says in his message and upon how Congress decides to respond.[7]

In California, the Republicans obtained the majority in the election of 6 November. . . .

The insecure conditions of the country, the danger that there might be major disruptions, and the machinations of some businessmen who are enemies of the Republican party, have provoked a panic, which, if it continues longer, could be converted into a real financial crisis. Various commerical houses have gone bankrupt, and the banks of Philadelphia, Baltimore, Richmond, Petersburg, Charleston, Wheeling, and here in Washington have suspended specie payment.[8]

In the Kansas territory, Captain [James] Montgomery, with five hundred well-armed men, has revolted, proclaiming freedom for the slaves. He has seized Fort Scott and moved into Missouri. . . .[9]

Romero to MRE, 9 December 1860, in Romero,
Correspondencia I, 151–53

Of course, a large part of President Buchanan's message was dedicated
to the question that currently agitates this country. In respect to this the
president stated: First, the southern states have just cause to secede from
the Union; second, according to the constitution they do not have the
right to secede whenever they desire; and third, neither the president nor
the Congress possesses the authority to force them to remain in the
Union. There is no other means of preserving the Union, he concluded,
than to reconcile the North and South. He proposed that the North drop
its pretensions and renounce its principles. [10]

. . . The message did not satisfy either party. The Republicans consider it a joke on them, proposing that they drop all their plans after being
victorious at the ballot-box. Expecting Buchanan to recognize the right
of secession that they believe they possess, the Democrats are not satisfied
even though they have the assurance that [Buchanan's] government will
not forcefully resist their separation.

Both houses of Congress have witnessed very heated discussions over
the questions raised in the message. South Carolina's congressmen stated
that they would not take part in the debate since their state had already
seceded from the Union. The congressmen from Georgia, Alabama,
Mississippi, and Florida made similar statements. In the Senate,
[Thomas] Clingman of North Carolina, considering the question inevitable, said that in his state there are two parties, one desiring immediate
separation, the other wishing to wait until the other southern states
initiate the action. Clingman claimed that the first group is growing daily.
The best solution, he argued, would be to divide the national property
and public debt proportionally among the states, permitting peaceable
separation.

The tone of the speeches in Congress, of the sermons, and of the press
in both sections reveals very clearly that the Union is already in spirit and
in reality dissolved. The hatred between the two factions, the diversity of
interests, and the contradiction of principles grow deeper roots each
day. . . . Before the inauguration of Lincoln, at least the states of South
Carolina, Georgia, Alabama, Mississippi, and Florida will have seceded
from the Union.

Desiring to avoid secession during his administration, President
[Buchanan] commissioned [William Henry] Trescot, assistant secretary of
state and a citizen of South Carolina, to go to his home state in order to
obtain the postponement of secession until Lincoln's inauguration.

The house agreed to send that part of the president's message relative to
secession questions to a special committee, composed of one member

from each state, which should propose the actions that it believes suitable within thirty days. The speaker of the house named the committee. The Democrats are very disgusted at the selection because the Republicans predominate on the committee. The Florida congressman asked to be excused from serving on it, because, as he expressed it, his ideas are opposed to any arrangement or compromise. Similar statements were about to be made by other members of the South, when, in order to avoid the loss of this last hope for reconciliation, and because the discussion had heated up so much, it was proposed and agreed upon to adjourn the house for four days. The Senate made the same decision.

Meanwhile, every day the situation grows more disturbed. The panic has now become a financial crisis; everyone wished to withdraw his capital from his businesses and accounts out of fear of losing it. This has occasioned the bankruptcy of many houses and the suspension of specie payment by almost every bank in the country, except those in New York and Boston. Commerce between the North and South has suffered a considerable paralyzation, which has forced northern manufacturers to reduce or suspend production and, therefore, to dismiss all or the majority of their workers. In the severe climate of the North and in the season now beginning [winter], this [unemployment] is a real calamity for persons who have no other means of subsistance than their personal labor. While many factories reduce or suspend their work, those producing arms are unable to fill the orders that they receive daily from the South. All those states want to arm themselves in preparation for any contingency. [11]

The uniformity of opinions and interests desired by secession's partisans does not exist even within the southern states. The very question of slavery divides these states profoundly. The so-called "cotton states," which include Louisiana, Arkansas, and Texas, besides the five cited above wish to reopen the slave trade. However, the other southern states, called border states because they border the free states, principally Virginia, Maryland, and Kentucky, but also Tennessee, even though it does not border on the free states, are and have been opposed to the slave trade. This diversity of opinion lies in diversity of interests. The border states are the breeding place of Negroes and the cotton states, the market. If the traffic in Africans is reopened, the cotton states will buy slaves at a low price, which will enrich them greatly, while, at the same time, the border states would be unable to sell theirs for the inflated price that they currently receive. To this must be added that slave labor is needed more in the cotton states than in the others. On account of this, Virginia has developed an unwillingness to work in agreement with South Carolina. [12]

. . . Missouri, Kentucky, Illinois, Indiana, and Ohio, which use the Mississippi River to export their products comfortably and profitably, have explained that they will never consent to Louisiana, where the mouth of this river lies, separating itself from the Union. To support their pretensions, they recall that the United States did not purchase Louisiana from Napoleon so that when it desired, Louisiana could transfer the river's mouth to a foreign nation, thereby depriving the midwesterners of the natural outlet for their products. [13]

In case the Union is dissolved, the Pacific states, which nature apparently intended to be separated from this nation, wish to create an independent republic, composed of California, Oregon, and the Washington territory, to which they will certainly add the New Mexico territory. [14]

On 3 December a meeting of abolitionists in Boston desired to celebrate the anniversary of the death of John Brown, whom they consider a martyr for liberty. Many Democrats attended the meeting, electing a chairman from among themselves. Thus, the meeting did not produce the effect that its organizers desired. . . . [15]

Romero to MRE, 23 December 1860, in Romero,
Correspondencia I, 161–64

. . . The South Carolina Convention met . . . on 20 December. Its 150 members unanimously approved a resolution revoking South Carolina's adoption of the federal constitution and dissolving all bonds with the United States. It proceeded at once to name commissioners to draft a manifesto expressing the grievances that have obligated South Carolina to take this step, other commissioners to travel to Washington to solicit recognition of their independence, others to go to the various southern states and influence them to follow a similar course, and still others to regulate several points of internal administration. Notice of the convention's actions have been applauded in various cities in the South, which, to solemnize the events, have fired salvos and salutes, sounded the bells, and lit up buildings.

On the day that the convention met, a newly elected governor . . . most decidedly expressed sentiments in favor of his state's independence.

Before the convention adopted the resolution of the twentieth, it received a request from the Georgia legislature asking it to delay action until a general convention of southern states could be convened. However, the secession sentiment was so strong that South Carolina did not even consider the request.

Although all the cotton states are resolved to separate from the Union, they differ regarding the means to arrive at this goal. Some like Louisiana, Alabama, Florida, and Mississippi wish to accomplish it by themselves and entirely independent from each other. Others like Georgia and Texas desire separation to take place in common agreement among all the southern states. . . .

The Florida convention will meet this coming 3 January, Alabama's on the seventh, Georgia's on the ninth, and Louisiana's on the twenty-third. There is no longer the slightest doubt but that all of them will be guided by South Carolina's recent example.

On 14 December various congressmen from the southern states and the senators from Georgia, Mississippi, Louisiana, and Texas signed a manifesto to their constituents. The discussion is exhausted, they are convinced, and the North will make absolutely no concessions to the South. The honor and dignity of the southern people, they claim, demand the formation of a southern confederation. The manifesto advises each state to work for itself independently.

While the Union is collapsing and menaced by dissolution on all sides, the central government, far from presenting the compact and energetic body that would be necessary to contain the disintegration, finds itself in a real crisis.

On the tenth, Secretary of the Treasury Howell Cobb of Georgia, a partisan and promoter of secession, resigned. He left the cabinet to gain greater freedom to develop his disunionist projects. Soon, General Lewis Cass will also resign. Because of his age, his accomplishments, and his long public career, Cass is generally considered the most respected man of the Democratic party. Behind Cass's resignation lies his belief that the government has the right to use force to obligate the dissident states to comply with the laws of the United States. This opinion is contrary to that expressed by the president in his last message. . . .[16] General Cass wants to reinforce the federal troops presently occupying Fort Moultrie, situated in the entrance of Charleston Harbor. The president did not wish to accede to this measure. Secretary of the Interior [Jacob Thompson] also left the cabinet, although not by resignation, but with a temporary leave. He will undertake a special commission conferred upon him by the governor of his home state, Mississippi, relative to its secession plans. Trescot, formerly assistant secretary of state, also resigned his position to go to his home state, South Carolina. The president has been pressured to fill the gaps left in his cabinet because of the resignations. He has named Attorney General Jeremiah S. Black to be secretary of state, Phillip Frank Thomas to be secretary of the interior, and Edwin M. Stanton to be attorney general. The Senate has confirmed these nominations.

. . . Undeniably Buchanan gave these secession plans a major impetus by openly proclaiming in his annual message that the central government could not forcefully restrain the dissident states. Since the Republicans and the great mass of Union sympathizers hold another opinion, some, in the public press, have accused Buchanan of being a traitor, others have asserted that he is demented, others contend that he is senile, and several have proposed that he resign the presidency, turning over power to Vice President Breckinridge. Buchanan approves and indirectly foments secession, his warmest supporters maintain, because he believes that it is the only means by which the South will obtain what it demands because, after secession, the northern states will submit to southern demands in order to obtain their return to the Union.

All these details, the great discredit that has befallen the administration, and the proximity of great dangers threatening the country, have affected Buchanan's spirit to the extent that, in a statement to the American people on 14 December, he admitted himself incapable of confronting the situation. He designated 4 January 1861 as a day of fasting and prayer for the inhabitants of the United States so that providence might remedy so many troubles.

Evidently the present question cannot terminate peacefully. When Lincoln's administration is installed, five or more states will consider themselves independent. Lincoln's government will not recognize them as such and will use force to make them comply with federal law. Thus, conflict is inevitable and civil war follows.

After several days of discussion, the Senate agreed to name a committee of thirteen members with the same object as that of the House Committee of Thirty-three. . . . In the debate preceding that agreement, the tendency of each party was clearly discernible. It was useless, the Democrats said, to attempt to form new compromises because nothing would suffice to make the southern states desist in their secession projects. They also opposed compromise, the Republicans explained, because they have nothing to compromise and nothing to concede to the South. The norm of their conduct, the Republicans stated, has been the constitution, in accordance with which they have elected a president. The people voted in the recent election in favor of the principles of their party, they assert. In view of these facts, they will do no more than compel respect for the constitution and laws.

In both houses numerous plans and projects for negotiations between the two sections have been proposed. The most prominent, and the only one attracting any attention, is the proposal of John J. Crittenden, senator from Kentucky. His plan would divide the United States by a line running along 36°30′, with the territory to the north remaining free of slavery, and with the territory presently to the south, or which might be acquired in the future, permitting slavery. This is nothing other than the resurrection of the "Missouri Compromise." As a consequence of this project, some of the territories belonging to the United States would be slave areas and others free. The Republicans have expressed disapproval of this project. The principal Republican newspaper maintains it is authorized to state that Lincoln will not concede any of the planks contained in the Chicago platform upon which he was elected. All the territories, one plank declared, ought to be free. The Democrats have not said anything in regard to the proposal, although it is highly probable that they will not accept it either. All the territories, while they are territories, the Democrats hold, ought to be open for slavery, and only upon being organized into states, decide if they will or will not continue to permit slavery.[17]

A House of Representatives' solution of the eighteenth declared unconstitutional the laws of some northern states that place restrictions on the return of runaway slaves. The southern states have leveled severe charges against these laws considering them insults from the northerners. The same session saw a bill proposed and rejected that practically attempted to declare "that slaves are a property under the guarantee of the United States Constitution."

In a resolution of lesser importance, Congress authorized the president to issue $10 million in "treasury notes" to cover public expenditures, since the treasury is bankrupt.

The House also approved, and sent to the Senate, a bill authorizing the construction of a Pacific railroad. . . .[18]

Recently a proposal has apparently won the approval of many people. The proposal calls for forming a central confederation composed of Pennsylvania, Maryland, Virginia, North Carolina, Tennessee, Missouri, Kentucky, Ohio, Indiana, and Illinois, excluding the cotton and the New England states. To my understanding, this project is unrealizable. However, like all the other schemes, which are produced daily, it proves that in general, Union sentiment is greatly weakened and that, if the Union dissolves, a large number of political entities will result.

One speaks also of separating New York City from the state and declaring it a free city similar to the Hanseatic cities. This proposal has not encountered much sympathy either.

In some northern states, principally in Massachusetts, the Democrats favorable to the South have created a mild reaction. . . . Moreover, the Democratic party has won the elections for mayor in Boston, Springfield, and other cities.

The monetary crisis in New York has ended because of remittances in specie, amounting to $6 million, received from Europe, California, and Havana. . . .

1861

Introduction to 1861

The secession of southern states dominated the news in the early months of 1861: Mississippi left the Union on 9 January, Florida on 10 January, Alabama on 11 January, Georgia on 19 January, Louisiana on 26 January, and Texas on 1 February. These six states and South Carolina met in Montgomery, Alabama, on 4 February to form the Confederate States of America. President James Buchanan's administration appeared paralyzed before this series of events. When Lincoln was inaugurated on 4 March 1861, his freedom of action had been restricted. The new administration admitted Kansas as a state and organized Colorado, Dakota, and Nevada as territories. It also passed the Morrill Tariff in March (which was later revised in 1862, 1864, 1867, and 1869). The Morrill Tariff reinstated the tool of protectionism and specific tariffs and generally elevated the rate of tariffs. The subsequent revisions generally raised the protective rates.

Lincoln's administration sought grounds for compromise with southern leaders, but only upon the basis of reunification. The southern leadership appeared uninterested in reentering the Union. As tension mounted at Fort Sumter in Charleston Harbor, both sides geared up for the possibility of war. Armies were raised, contracts for supplies and weapons were issued, and attacks were made upon each other's commerce. The Confederacy initiated a privateering war on Yankee commerce, while Lincoln debated closing the southern ports before deciding to blockade the Confederate ports. On land, skirmishes occurred as both sides sought to raise, equip, and train forces. A series of small engagements occurred in Missouri, along the Mississippi, in western Virginia, and in northern Virginia during the summer and fall of 1861. The largest battle resulted in a Confederate victory at Bull Run in Virginia.

Given the popular enthusiasm for military service in both sections in 1861, both sides needed funds more than volunteers. The U.S. government passed the first income tax in August 1861, a 3 percent tax on incomes over $800 annually (an unskilled or semiskilled wage laborer earned about $150 to $300 per year). While the U.S. economy quickly responded to the demand for war goods, successful Confederate privateering decimated the Union merchant fleet. U.S. ships supplied 5 million tons to carry U.S. exports in 1861, but only 2.9 million tons in 1865. Foreign vessel participation in U.S. ship-tonnage needs rose from 2.2 million tons in 1861 to 3.2 million tons in 1865.

The outbreak of war divided European and world opinion. Many intellectuals abhorred slavery, yet placed great value upon self-determination and self-government. The U.S. government appeared in the awkward position of fighting to end slavery and to impose an unwanted government upon the southern population. The Mexican liberal government immediately and emphatically sided with the Lincoln government, convinced that the southern leadership was at heart elitist, paternalistic, and expansionist. The British elite (sympathetic to the southern elite) and working class (opposed to slavery) divided with regard to the American Civil War. The division almost collapsed under the burden of the *Trent* affair of November 1861, when a U.S. war vessel seized two Confederate diplomatic agents headed for Europe—John Slidell and John Mason—from the British mail packet *Trent* in international waters. The U.S. government, however, released the two prisoners. In early 1861, the Spanish acted as if they intended to take advantage of the U.S. domestic turmoil to reconquer Santo Domingo. In December 1861, Spain, France, and Great Britain initiated a tripartite intervention in Mexico. Several months later, the Spanish and British withdrew, but the French—alone at first, then with Austrian Archduke Maximilian as stalking-horse—remained for six years.

The victorious Mexican liberals faced a continuing problem created by conservative maneuvers in Europe to persuade Spain or France to depose the *reforma* liberals and to return the conservatives to power. The secession crisis occurred simultaneously with the sharpening of Mexico's crisis. Romero rejoiced at the victory of Lincoln and the Republican party because he interpreted the Republican party's platform as a signal for a liberal transformation of the United States. Immediately after Congress certified the election returns, Romero traveled to Springfield, Illinois, to congratulate Lincoln and to seek cooperation and aid from the new administration. In particular, Romero hoped to find a sympathetic ear for his request for support in blocking any use of European funds or forces to return the conservatives to power in Mexico. Romero was content when Lincoln's administration appointed a ranking and esteemed Republican dignitary Thomas Corwin, former secretary of the treasury, to serve as minister in Mexico. Corwin's appointment underscored the importance that incoming Republicans assigned to the Mexican post.

Romero immediately began groping for ways to induce the North American political system to take the steps he and his government judged necessary to preserve Mexican authority. The method developed was lobbying: utilization of the press, public speeches, dinners, contacts with politicians, and socializing with the wealthy and powerful. Romero believed that with proper cultivation, individuals with broad followings such as Postmaster General Montgomery Blair and Massachusetts Senator and Chairman of the Senate Foreign Relations Committee Charles Sumner could be won over to the liberal Mexican position. Such political gains would provide concrete links to the ideological bonds that he believed already existed between the two nations. A practical goal was a U.S. loan to pay the interest due on loans made by European powers to Mexico when the conservatives had been in power. As an inducement to U.S. interests, Mexico agreed to negotiate treaties on extradition, postal matters, and commerce. The purpose of the treaties was to facilitate commercial exchange and investment between the two liberal regimes. A loan treaty was negotiated and presented to the Congress. Congress, however, refused to provide a loan unless the European powers guaranteed that the loan would preclude European intervention. When such a guarantee was not forthcoming, Congress refused to risk millions needed for the domestic war in an uncertain situation. Nevertheless, this first formal effort of a U.S. administration to make a loan to another government merits attention. The loan attempt indicated that both the U.S. Republican and Mexican liberal governments were serious about a rapprochement. Apparently, the United States did not again consider a governmental loan to another nation until World War I.

In late 1861, the lack of success in the Union forces' campaigns against the Confederacy prompted a dissatisfied Congress to form the Joint Committee on the Conduct of the War in an effort to obtain a stronger voice in the strategic planning of Lincoln's administration.

Political Reviews—1861

Romero to MRE, 23 January 1861, in Romero, *Correspondencia* I, 280–82

. . . The previously convoked conventions of Mississippi, Florida, Alabama, and Georgia have met and passed ordinances declaring their respective states independent. Louisiana has already elected delegates to the special convention. The disunionists won the election in such a manner that, doubtless, the convention will dissolve Louisiana's tie with the United States.

The Virginia and Tennessee legislatures, the chief ones in the South and with the most Union partisans, have convoked special conventions. Kentucky's legislature, which occupies a position similar to the other two, is currently debating and will probably soon pass a bill calling for a convention. . . . The ardent unionist governor of Maryland, a southern border state with interests similar to Virginia, Tennessee, and Kentucky, has repeatedly refused to convoke an extraordinary session of the state legislature. . . .

. . . The disunionists have gained considerable terrain among the mass of southern people during the present month. The leaders and principal promoters of secession have instilled exaggerated ideas about the tendencies of the Republican party in the southern population, exploiting the natural provincialism that exists in those states and the distrust that generally exists toward the North. The leaders have persuaded the southern people that, besides being abolitionists, which will vitally affect the slave owners and the many people dependent upon slavery, the Lincoln administration will attempt to force the South under the yoke and tyranny of the North, thereby affecting everybody. This task has not been very difficult to accomplish because no Republican paper, nor speeches, nor manifestations favorable to Republican ideas are permitted in the South.

Meanwhile, then, the states that have already declared their independence and those about to declare their independence have seized the existing federal forts within their boundaries. These forts had been built at great cost to defend the country in a foreign war. [1]

In South Carolina the occupation took on a very serious aspect that could precipitate the outbreak of the civil war presently threatening this country. The authorities of South Carolina apparently had proposed . . . that while the federal Congress was making suitable arrangements regarding that state's separation, South Carolina's forces would not try to seize the Union-held forts in Charleston Harbor. The understanding included no federal reinforcements for the garrison of those forts, nor any other change in them. [2]

Shortly after the South Carolina commissioners, who had been sent to negotiate the recognition of their state's independence with the United States, arrived in Washington, Major [Robert] Anderson, commanding the Charleston Harbor forts, moved under his own responsibility from the fort he occupied to another. . . . Upon learning of this, the commissioners accused the president of violating his promises. They terminated all negotiations and returned to their state. Secretary of War [John B. Floyd], a declared partisan of secession, wanted Major Anderson's conduct disapproved and to have him ordered to return to the fortress he had occupied previously. However, the president refused such measures. The secretary of war resigned from the cabinet.

Major Anderson's conduct caused immense excitement in Charleston. The state forces immediately occupied the abandoned fort and also two others belonging to the federal government. They seized the customs house and the post office. They liberated a ship's captain who had been seized by U.S. cruisers and brought to Charleston for trial for participating in the slave trade. This incident very decidedly revealed the position of the disunionists toward the slave trade. Considering the occupation [of federal buildings] a usurpation and believing himself obliged to defend the fort, which remained in federal power at all costs, the president sent reinforcements to Major Anderson. Previously he had opposed this measure. His earlier refusal to send reinforcements had prompted General Cass's resignation. Its adoption now produced the resignation of the Secretaries of the Interior [Jacob Thompson] and the Treasury [Philip F. Thomas].

Two hundred men and some war supplies were sent on a merchant vessel. Upon entering Charleston Harbor, however, a fort controlled by the local authorities fired upon the vessel. The vessel had to retire without unloading the men or supplies. The administration is now deciding upon the proper course to pursue in this emergency. . . .

The movement for compromise has lost much [support] this month. Undoubtedly, the two parties will not be reconciled. House and Senate committees have reported their inability to reach an agreement. The Senate made a major effort to pass the Crittenden resolutions. . . . [When] submitted to a vote they were rejected. Although a notion for reconsideration was agreed to, there is no reason to believe the resolution will fare better when discussed again.

President-elect Lincoln has nominated Senator Seward . . . for secretary of state. Thus, with the authority of cabinet head of the next administration, he addressed the Senate in very conciliatory terms, but without offering concessions on any of the principles that form his party's dogma. Without some concessions there cannot be a satisfactory compromise with the South.

Pennsylvania, Ohio, and Indiana have each elected a Senator to the federal congress to fill vacancies that will occur on 4 March. Three Republican senators elected will replace Democrats. Since, in addition, all the senators from the seceding states who have resigned were Democrats, the Lincoln administration will have a majority in the Senate. . . .

Romero to MRE, 9 February 1861, in Romero, *Correspondencia* I, 289–91

. . . As soon as the Louisiana convention met, it declared that state separated from the federal union. Louisiana's national representatives and senators resigned at once. New Orleans received this news with marked demonstrations of enthusiasm.[3]

The Louisiana government has gone further than the other states that have seceded from the Union. It not only occupied the arsenal and the federal government forts within its boundaries, but also the hospitals, the customs house, the mint, and some coast guard steamships that were on the river to aid the customs work. Another custom's steamer was seized in Mobile.

The telegraph has communicated that the Texas convention has already declared that state's independence. Since this action was considered certain, the news did not produce much reaction. All the cotton states, except Arkansas, are already outside the Union. In contrast, not only has no border state seceded, but . . . apparently none will leave, at least not as things stand in the country now. . . .[4]

On 4 February, Virginia elected delegates to its previously called popular convention. The Union partisans won these elections with a large majority. This has been a terrible blow for those who desire to establish a southern confederation, since Virginia will definitely remain in the Union, at least for now. . . .

The Missouri legislature resolved not to convoke a popular convention, another important step favorable to the Union.

Apparently a reaction to the spirit that unfolded in the South after Lincoln's election, the above events can only be considered a truce in the excitement that has reigned recently, but not a definite arrangement of the problem. Those now called unionists in the South wish to remain in the Union provided the northern states grant the concessions that they solicit, but not otherwise.

The results of the deliberations in the Virginia convention will depend on what a convention currently meeting in Richmond might achieve. The Virginia legislature requested the other states to send commissioners to Richmond. These commissioners will seek to compromise the differences existing between the two sections peaceably and satisfactorily. If the convention agrees on some general compromise, it will be submitted to the various state legislatures. If the compromise wins the approval of two thirds of the state legislatures, it will be included in the Constitution as an amendment. Virginia proposed the Crittenden proposals as a basis for compromise.[5]

The seceded states refused to send representatives to Richmond, alleging the question does not affect them in any way. Some western and northern states sent representatives to attempt every means of conciliation, but declaring beforehand that they did not share Virginia's views regarding the Crittenden proposals.

On the fourth, the commissioners of eighteen states met in Richmond. Once organized, the convention declared its meetings secret and suspended its sessions for two days. Until now, apparently, it has only named a committee composed of one member from each state. This committee should draft the compromise project that it considers most suitable. There is no hope, however, that the convention could reach agreement on any compromise.

This question of compromise with the South threatens to divide the Republican party. Some Republicans oppose any form of compromise and want strict compliance with the Chicago platform upon which Lincoln was elected. In view of southern activity, other Republicans approve making more or less important concessions.

The states already separated from the Union are busy organizing the southern confederation. Alabama had proposed that each state should send delegates to Montgomery so that a congress could meet on 4 February. The six states that already consider themselves independent sent delegates. . . .

The congressional resolution admitting Kansas as a free state passed both houses and was signed by the president. This act produced great rejoicing among the Republicans, who have spent four years working toward this goal. . . . The extreme Democrats of Virginia and Maryland intended to forcibly seize Washington, according to a rumor, and prevent Lincoln's inauguration on 4 March. . . . The [Buchanan] administration wants to be prepared for this contingency. Washington has been placed upon a defensive footing, under the command of General [Winfield] Scott, who has been recalled from New York. A force considered adequate to prevent a disturbance and repel any aggression has been concentrated in the fortifications dominating Washington.[6]

South Carolina sent another commission to the federal government to solicit the sale of Fort Sumter, occupied by Major Anderson. They threatened forcible seizure if the sale is refused. The president replied that Anderson's duty obligated him to conserve and defend the fort at all costs, so the commission returned to its state.

Romero to MRE, 21 February 1861, in Romero, *Correspondencia* I, 297–300

. . . A real crisis exists [that] ought to be resolved within the two weeks between now and Lincoln's inauguration as president.

The disunionists plan on the fifteen slave-holding states declaring their independence and organizing a general government before 4 March. With more than a third of the nation separated, they believe the new administration will have no option except to recognize the independence of the southern confederation, or to concede those southern demands considered indispensable for a restoration of the Union. Nevertheless, in spite of the labors expended, this plan has not been realized yet. Until now only the seven cotton states have seceded. If Arkansas's popular convention, called for 4 March, meets on that day, it will certainly immediately pass the secession ordinance, thereby allowing the eight seceded cotton states to form the confederacy.

The . . . border states remain indecisive about the course they should follow. Virginia's popular convention met on 13 February. Despite a majority of Union partisans, the convention immediately resolved that Virginia would resist any attempt of the federal government to use force against the seceded states and would consider such use of force as a declaration of war. Otherwise, the convention is awaiting the outcome of the [Crittenden] Peace Congress, which gathered in this city at Virginia's request to construct a compromise between the two sections of the country. If the Peace Congress does not achieve a compromise satisfactory to the two sections, the Virginia convention will declare its independence and drag the other six border states with it. Believing that once the new administration is installed, no danger exists of Virginia trying to dissolve its ties with the Union, the Republican strategy plans to prevent Virginia from seceding before 4 March. To this end the Republicans are retarding the work of the Peace Congress, yet always leaving the impression that a satisfactory settlement will be achieved very soon. Tennessee on 9 February and Missouri on the eighteenth elected delegates for popular conventions. The unionist faction won both with large majorities. . . .

On the eighteenth, Maryland's popular convention met in Baltimore. Neither the legislature nor the governor, who has refused to take such a step up to this point, had convoked the convention. After organizing, it adjourned until 12 March. . . . declaring that Maryland would follow the fortune of the southern states and especially of Virginia. Disunionists formed a majority of this convention.

The Kentucky legislature resolved not to convoke a popular convention, closing the door to all secession projects there.

Various compromises have been proposed at the Peace Congress. The plan of [James] Guthrie from Kentucky has received the most attention and has more possibilities in its favor. Based upon Senator Crittenden's proposals, it would divide the United States by means of a line on the 36°30′ parallel of northern latitude, everything to the north being free and everything to the south, slave. It states nothing explicitly about the status of territory acquired in the future but very clearly implies that it could be slave territory. In the future, no territory will be acquired except with the approval of a majority of both the free-state and the slave-state senators. This proposal declares that the constitutional provision for a two-thirds vote of approval must apply to all treaties involving territorial acquisition. This project represents what they call here the southern rights position. Its approval would be equivalent to the project proposed by Crittenden that encountered so much opposition in both houses of the federal legislature. The free state delegates have not directly opposed these proposals because they wish to preserve the expectation of a settlement. However, neither have they approved them. In turn, as a compromise, they have proposed the convocation of a national convention composed of delegates from the thirty-four states, fully authorized to find a suitable settlement. This proposal, offered yesterday in the House of Representatives and rapidly gaining support, aims at postponing the matter and gaining time, which, if wisely used, could resolve the question.

Meanwhile, the cotton states Congress meeting in Montgomery has actively pursued its work. . . . It organized a provisional government that will last one year, selecting former Mississippi Senator Jefferson Davis for president and [Alexander H.] Stephens from Georgia for vice-president. . . . In his inaugural address, Davis claimed that the time for negotiation and compromise had already passed and the Confederacy will admit those states that would desire to join it, but it will never reunite with the North. He found nothing to fear internally because all the seceded states were homogeneous in ideas and professed the same principles. He declared that they were fully prepared to meet any external difficulties that could arise. [7]

The provisional Confederate Constitution also has a clause prohibiting the slave trade. Adopted to attract the slave-breeding border states that are deeply opposed to the African traffic, this step was poorly received in South Carolina, which could not hide its desire to open slave traffic.

The federal Congress has given precedence [to consideration of] matters relative to the condition of the country, but without any decision in anticipation of proposals from the Peace Congress. . . .

[Lot] Morrill, representative from Pennsylvania, proposed a new tariff with radical changes from the current one. After passing the House, it encountered considerable opposition in the Senate. Various revisions [of Morrill's proposal] have been proposed that entirely change the bill. Apparently it will not pass, at least not in the present session of Congress, even with the changes. Morrill's bill aims primarily at augmenting the duty on the importation of iron and steel manufactures to protect those products of his state, which is abundantly supplied with mines of both metals [sic—iron and steel?]. [8]

On 6 February the House authorized the postmaster general to suspend postal service with the seceded states when necessary in his judgment. Mail service for Florida has already been suspended.

In the session of the eighteenth, Congressman Hanson [sic—William Hemmick] of Ohio offered a resolution to authorize the president to use the state militia to compel compliance with federal law and to quell uprisings, and to accept volunteers for this purpose. [Thomas S.] Bocock of Virginia moved to reject that resolution, but his motion lost by a vote of 110 to 66. . . .[9]

The condition of the public treasury is quite lamentable. The secretary of the treasury advised the house finance committee that the government will need $10 million to fulfill its obligations until 10 March and that the department can only count on an income of $1.5 million. The committee proposed that Congress authorize the president to borrow $10 million.[10]

On the thirteenth both houses met to count the electoral votes for president. The ceremony took place very calmly. Lincoln received 180 of the 303 votes. Thus, he was constitutionally declared the president-elect.

On the eleventh, Lincoln left Springfield for Washington. He stopped at various cities that had extended him invitations. He was received everywhere with marked demonstrations of enthusiasm. He spoke various times but avoided expressing his opinion on the situation in the country. In Indianapolis and Cincinnati, nevertheless, he clearly implied he would use force to enforce the federal laws in the seceded states. This statement prompted a very strong outcry from the border states. Today he is in New York. On the twenty-third he is expected in Washington.[11]

President Buchanan called the Senate into special session for 4 March. Customarily the outgoing president issues such a call so that his successor will find the Senate in session. Then the new president can submit his nominations for cabinet posts and other public offices for senate approval. . . .

Romero to MRE, 9 March in Romero, *Correspondencia* I, 310–12

. . . On 4 March, the president-elect of the United States, Abraham Lincoln, was inaugurated. Before taking the oath of office, he read his inaugural address. . . . It is a well-considered document and the terms of its conceptualization permit distinctive interpretations. The most plausible interpretation, nevertheless, suggests the new administration will follow a coercive policy against the states that have declared their independence.[12]

On the fifth, Lincoln organized his cabinet in the following form: secretary of state, William H. Seward; secretary of the treasury, Salmon P. Chase; secretary of the interior, Caleb Smith; secretary of war, Simon Cameron; secretary of the navy, Gideon Welles; postmaster general, Montgomery Blair; and attorney general, Edward Bates. The Senate confirmed these nominees on the day the names were submitted. Of the persons forming this cabinet, Chase and Blair are considered radical

Republicans, that is, opponents of all compromise, and the others are considered conservative or moderate Republicans. [13]

Before Lincoln's administration was installed, that of the seceded states had already been organized. Davis . . . named his cabinet in this manner: secretary of state, Robert Toombs; secretary of the treasury, Christopher G. Memminger; secretary of war, Leroy P. Walker; secretary of the navy, Stephan R. Mallory; postmaster general, H. T. Elliott [sic—John H. Reagan]; and attorney general, Judah P. Benjamin. [14]

The Confederate Congress has passed various laws to organize the executive offices and the mail service, and it declared the navigation of the Mississippi free. Moreover, it named three commissioners to come to this capital to solicit recognition of its independence from the U.S. government. These commissioners, one of whom is John Forsyth, have already arrived here. . . .

The work of the secessionists in the border states has not progressed at all during the last two weeks. On 27 February, the Peace Congress approved some resolutions of [Thomas F.] Franklin, a delegate from Pennsylvania, sending them to Congress with the intention that if two-thirds of both houses approved them, they would be submitted as constitutional amendments to the state legislatures or to popular conventions. The House ignored these resolutions . . . the Senate rejected them. The same fortune had befallen the Crittenden resolutions earlier.

In place of the [Franklin] resolutions and in order to offer something to satisfy the border states, a two-thirds majority in both houses passed a resolution of [Thomas] Corwin from Ohio, which declared that the federal government could never interfere with the institution of slavery in the states where it currently exists. That proposition will be offered as . . . an amendment to the Constitution. This proposal will probably not satisfy the southern states because it affirms a principle that no one has denied until now. The difficult problem is deciding if slave owners have, or do not have, the right to carry their slaves into the territories and to continue to possess them as slaves in the territories. This remains as much in question now as it did before the Corwin proposal. [15]

The secessionists won the elections for delegates to Arkansas's popular convention. . . .

Various efforts have been made in the Virginia Convention to obtain the secession of that state, but until now all have been fruitless. If Virginia would not secede before Lincoln's inauguration, nor immediately after reading his inaugural speech, Virginia should not approve secession now. . . . Virginia's remaining in the Union guarantees a similar course from the other border states, which are all important because of their size and population. . . .

General [David E.] Twiggs, the commanding general [of the U.S. forces] in Texas, recognized the authority of that state's convention. He placed all the federal forts, arms, munitions, and other war material within Texas's borders at the convention's disposition. He ordered forces under his command, consisting of twenty-nine hundred men, to evacuate the state. However, not all the subordinate officers obeyed General Twiggs. Captain [Bennett H.] Hill, commanding Fort Brown, refused to hand the fort over and prepared to defend it against the state forces deployed to seize it. General Twiggs's conduct has been as severely reprimanded in the North as ardently applauded in the South. As soon as the administration received official notice of the events, it immediately dishonorably discharged Twiggs from the U.S. Army. The Georgia government had already named him general in chief of that state's forces.[16]

. . . In the final days, the Thirty-sixth Congress was occupied with the budget and with discussion on the state of the country. The new tariff was one of the most important measures passed during the last two weeks. . . . It will become effective on the coming 1 April. . . .

. . . Within the last two weeks the annual register of the Navy Department has appeared. According to it . . . there are forty-two [sic—thirty-nine?] steamers, which, combined with the sail vessels, give a total of ninety-three [ninety?] vessels [in the U.S. Navy]. Of this total, twenty are new and capable of any service. . . .

The Montgomery Congress legislated the organization of the Confederate army, composed of fifty thousand men.

By a majority of one thousand votes, North Carolina rejected the call for a popular convention.

The seceded states consider Lincoln's inauguaral speech a declaration of war. . . .

Romero to MRE, 25 March 1861, in Romero, *Correspondencia* I, 332–35

On 11 March, the Montgomery Congress approved the permanent constitution of the "Confederate States of America," which is based upon the old U.S. Constitution. Among others, two principal points of difference are the following: . . . the presidential term will be six years and the president cannot be reelected.

South Carolina will have five representatives in the Congress, Georgia, ten, Alabama, nine, Florida, two, Mississippi, seven, Louisiana, six, and Texas, six. Each state will have two senators.

Congress cannot impose duties to protect any branch of industry. The Confederation will be able to acquire territory, but Congress and the territorial governments will recognize and protect slavery in it. A two-thirds vote of the members of both houses will admit new states. . . .[17]

The respective conventions in Louisiana, Alabama, Georgia, and

Texas have approved the Confederate Constitution. It probably will be approved in the other seceded states. The Louisiana and Alabama conventions rejected proposals to submit the Constitution to the people. . . .

In regard to the bill prohibiting the slave trade that President Davis vetoed, . . . evidently the veto was aimed at an article of the bill that proposes to hand Negroes seized from slave vessels over to the benevolent societies charged with conducting them back to Africa, and if Africa would not receive the Negroes, they would be sold at auction in the slave states. Since the Constitution absolutely prohibits traffic in Africans, Davis considered this method of disposition unconstitutional and returned the bill to Congress. Taken under consideration by Congress, the article was rejected by a vote of twenty-four to fifteen.

The [U.S.] tariff of 1857 is in effect in the Confederate States. The Montgomery Congress has proposed another tariff that would significantly reduce the duty on foreign goods and increase the list of free articles. This proposal did not pass Congress but found much favor. It will likely pass when that body reconvenes. While these states are granting these facilities to commerce, the U.S. new tariff . . . greatly increases the 1857 duties. The Montgomery government has revealed more vision and wisdom in this, since presumably this difference in duties will carry all the European commerce to southern points. Northern periodicals are alarmed. They want a special session of Congress to repeal the new customs law.

Arkansas's convention met on 4 March. It was expected to pass the ordinance secession at once. Far from doing so, however, it rejected that proposal by a vote of 39 to 35. Then the convention dissolved, agreeing to submit the secession ordinance to the people next August.[18]

Texas has had difficulties. . . . The secession ordinance was submitted to a popular vote, which approved it 34,794 to 11,235. The convention immediately approved the Confederate Constitution and demanded an oath from Governor General [Sam] Houston. He would not recognize the proceedings of the assembly, claiming that it only had powers to submit the secession ordinance to the people. The convention proclaimed its full authority to implement Texas's attachment to the Confederacy. . . . Reportedly the lieutenant governor of Texas has assumed the reins of government. General Houston will probably not accept this without resisting. . . .[19]

Virginia's convention . . . is still in session. As a condition for remaining in the Union, Virginia has insisted that property in slaves should be recognized and that no violent measure should be taken against the southern states that have seceded. Since the northern states will only accept the first condition with difficulty, sooner or later Virginia and the other border states will most likely secede from the Union and join the southern Confederacy. If the fifteen slave states form the southern Confederacy, the northern states will be obliged to recognize their independence.

Meanwhile, Lincoln's administration has not adopted any measure indicating an intention to pursue a policy distinct from Buchanan's. Caught between opposing forces, encountering difficulties on all sides, and finding its hands tied, until now Lincoln's administration apparently has been busy getting used to the situation. The Washington administration and the Montgomery government have informally agreed to avoid everything that could lead to a rupture. Certainly no rupture will occur while things remain in their present status.

As one of its first measures, if it has not already done so, this government will have to evacuate Fort Sumter, defended by Major Anderson, in Charleston Harbor. The South Carolina authorities have constructed several other forts in the harbor, which is now so well defended that informed people estimate that the whole U.S. Navy would have to be engaged to force an entrance. In addition, Major Anderson does not have provisions for very many days. Since he cannot receive provisions nor reinforcements, nor sustain himself with the few troops at his command, the government will have to order him to abandon the position. Later, the same withdrawal will occur at Fort Pensacola in Pensacola Bay.

The commissioners of the Montgomery government are still in Washington. The administration still has not responded because it has not decided what course to follow toward the seceded states. Since both sides want peace, the commissioners propose calmly to await the development of events. . . .

Romero to MRE, 8 April 1861, in Romero, *Correspondencia* I, 353–55

. . . The last four days have witnessed extraordinary activity in the Brooklyn and Boston arsenals. All available war vessels have received orders to prepare for sea duty. . . . The government has contracted for three merchant vessels, which have loaded very considerable cargoes of provisions and munitions in New York. The vessels have also been outfitted to carry several companies of infantry and artillery.

. . . Some believe this expedition will reinforce Forts Sumter and Pickens. Others argue it will go to Brazos de Santiago [Texas] to aid General Houston, who is attempting to prevent Texas from joining the Confederacy. Still others assume the expedition will blockade the entrance of the Mississippi River. Some even believe the expedition is directed to Santo Domingo. In my opinion, they are most probably sending reinforcements to the different government forts in the Gulf. . . .[20]

Wherever it goes, that expedition will doubtless encounter the strongest and most tenacious resistance from the dissident southerners. They believe the outbreak of hostilities will consummate their independence, because it will immediately induce the border states to join them. Hence, they have wanted to produce violent actions.

The South Carolina authorities have notified Major Anderson, commanding Fort Sumter, that they will not permit him to receive provisions from Charleston, nor to communicate with the Washington government. This compelled the Lincoln administration either to evacuate the fort or to reinforce it by force. Thus, after hostilities have been avoided for so much time, a disastrous civil war now appears inevitable.

The administration has taken some precautionary measures to avoid certain contingencies. One considerable part of the forces evacuated from Texas were brought to this government's fortifications in Tortugas. This improved the situation of that fort in the Gulf of Mexico. Recent news from Texas apparently indicates that state's convention has removed Governor Houston. . . . Houston appealed the convention's actions to the Texas legislature, which, however, approved the convention's proceedings. Houston supposedly still has many supporters who have advised the federal government to send forces to sustain him and to prevent Texas's incorporation into the southern Confederacy.

. . . Reportedly [Mexican] General [Pedro] Ampudia was marching toward Brownsville with three thousand men. Ampudia claims that Texas legally reverts to Mexico once it no longer has the protection of the federal government. No one believes that rumor. . . .

Meanwhile, the border states, and principally Virginia, preserve an attitude that is very far from conciliatory. Virginia apparently plans to propose constitutional amendments that must be approved [by the Lincoln administration] before it will consent to remain in the Union to discuss these amendments. If the amendments are not accepted, then all the border states will jointly secede from the Union and form a confederation that will admit any other states, with or without slavery, that adopt such amendments.

. . . On 27 March Senator [Lyman] Trumbull from Illinois introduced a resolution which declared that in the opinion of the Senate, the proper method of conserving the Union was to compel compliance with the laws, using force and all other means at the disposal of the president to conserve and protect public property in the separated states as well as in any other state. The Senate did not consider this resolution. . . .

The work of the eighth census of the United States has just been concluded. Apparently the total population of the country is 31,429,891, of which 27,477,090 are free men and 3,952,801 are slaves.[21]

Romero to MRE, 22 April 1861, in Romero, *Correspondencia* I, 363–65

. . . Civil war has now broken out.

Because the Charleston authorities decided to deny supplies to the garrison of Fort Sumter, the Washington government decided to provision that fort. The ships, loaded with provisions, departed from New York . . . unaware of their destination. When the vessels departed, a [U.S.] commissioner left for Charleston to explain to the authorities that the Washington government intended to supply provisions to the fort peaceably if possible, or by force if necessary. The commander of the Charleston forces communicated this decision to the Montgomery government. In reply he received orders to attack the fort at once. On the morning of 12 April, artillery fire erupted that lasted almost uninterrupted for thirty-four hours. After this shelling, Major Anderson, commander of the garrison, surrendered unconditionally and evacuated the fort. . . .

Hostilities having commenced in this fashion, both sides have taken more effective measures to pursue the conflict with greater activity. On 15 April, the president of the United States issued a proclamation which announced that because some states, declaring themselves independent, have placed themselves in noncompliance with federal laws, and in order to force compliance with U.S. law and to recover and defend U.S. property, he is calling up seventy-five thousand men from the state militia. The same proclamation called Congress into special session on 4 July.[22]

The secretary of war included the border states in the distribution of quotas for the seventy-five thousand men. The governors from the North and Northwest hastened to reply that their quotas were already filled. However, with the exception of Delaware and Maryland, the border states governors insisted that they could not contribute any force for the subjugation of the South.

. . . On 17 April President Davis's proclamation authorized the issuance of letters of marque [for privateering activity] for hostilities against northern naval and merchant vessels. In reprisal for this step, on the nineteenth, President Lincoln proclaimed a blockade of the ports of South Carolina, Georgia, Alabama, Florida, Mississippi, Louisiana, and Texas.[23]

The Virginia legislature had previously declared its opposition to the

United States seeking forcibly to coerce the southern states. Before the attack on Fort Sumter, the Virginia Convention sent a commission to the president to inquire what policy he proposed to follow with the seceded states. Lincoln's reply referred to his inaugural message. In view of the Virginia legislature's opposition to coercing the southern states and considering the president's proclamation of the fifteenth a declaration of war against the Confederate States, the Virginia Convention in Richmond passed an ordinance of secession on the sixteenth. The convention also arranged to occupy the federal arsenals and forts within its boundaries. Harper's Ferry arsenal, where only one company [of U.S. troops] guarded the many arms and war supplies, was captured the easiest. The U.S. government had ordered part of the armament sent to Washington. . . . The buildings of the arsenal and the remaining armaments were destroyed and burned. Thus, when the Virginia forces arrived at Harper's Ferry, they only encountered a pile of debris and ashes.[24]

Immediately, Virginia forces were directed to the Norfolk naval yard and to Fort Monroe in Old Point Comfort. . . . The federal government has sent reinforcements to both points. If it succeeds in reinforcing them, which appears easy since both points are accessible by sea, the Confederate forces will encounter considerable difficulty in taking possession of them. President Davis is determined to move his office to Richmond as soon as Virginia secedes from the Union in order to invigorate the operations aimed at taking Washington. Menaced by this danger, the Washington government ordered the concentration of a respectable force here. . . . On 19 April, a Massachusetts regiment of seven hundred men came from New York by rail. A large crowd attempted to impede its passage through Baltimore. . . . The soldiers used their weapons, so casualties occurred on both sides. The troops finally opened a passage and arrived in Washington on the same day.[25]

These events greatly excited public opinion in Baltimore, a southern city, where a majority of the people are Confederate sympathizers. There were street rumors, and the governor, always a most decided opponent of secession, attempted to calm the public excitement in some manner. He requested the president not to order more northern troops to pass through that city. Now groups of Marylanders surround Fort McHenry, garrisoned by federal troops, which protects the water entrance into Baltimore.

These steps have not satisfied the citizens of Baltimore. They immediately destroyed bridges and incapacitated the railroads that connect Baltimore with the North. Thus, they completely interrupted Washington's direct land communication to the northern cities. The telegraph has been cut, so for three days no one knew what was happening, especially in the southern states.

The ill will between the North and South has incresed greatly as a result of recent events. If the Civil War continues on the path characteristic of all the countries afflicted by this calamity, it could easily be converted into a servile war. If southern privateers should molest northern shipping and commerce, the northern newspapers have already warned that the U.S. government will be obliged to grant freedom to captured slaves and perhaps to foment slave insurrections.

Previously, Confederate forces had gathered in Pensacola to attack Fort Pickens. The U.S. government ordered some war vessels to reinforce the squadron in the bay. It is already publicly known that the fort has been reinforced with men and munitions. The next conflict is expected to take place at that fort.

The Confederacy has twenty thousand men under arms. In addition, President Davis requested another thirty-two thousand men from the seven states that formed the Confederacy before Virginia seceded. Apparently the Confederacy can easily unite an army of up to one hundred thousand men. . . .[26]

Romero to MRE, 7 May 1861, in Romero, *Correspondencia* I, 375–78

. . . [Recently] both sides have actively continued preparations for hostilities that they apparently will not desire for a considerable time.

The southern states have obtained the advantage of Virginia's adherence to their cause although this can still not be considered a consummated fact. . . . Upon convoking the present convention in Richmond, the Virginia legislature expressly demanded that any secession ordinance would be submitted for popular approval. The secession ordinance passed the convention on 17 April. It will be voted upon on 26 May. The convention immediately passed another resolution conditionally adopting the Montgomery constitution.

As soon as Virginia's separation was known in Montgomery, President Davis ordered Vice-president Alexander H. Stephens to Richmond to negotiate an alliance between the Confederacy and Virginia so that they would be linked while awaiting the popular vote. On 24 April an agreement was signed in Richmond, placing Virginia's forces and resources at the disposition of the Confederate States. Very probably the popular vote will ratify all the acts of the convention, in part because secessionist ideas in general have gained a lot of ground among Virginia's citizens and in part because those who remain firmly Unionists are suffering persecutions that compel them to leave the state or to abstain from expressing and voting in conformity with their ideas. Thus, it certainly appears that Virginia will remain irrevocably bound to the Confederacy.

This development very greatly favors the Confederacy because Virginia will carry with her the other border states, which possess a large territory and a numerous population. When all are united, secession will assume a very different nature, since then it will consist of nearly one-half of the old Union. As Richmond decreed the secession ordinance, hostile demonstrations were also made against the U.S. naval yard and war vessels in the Elizabeth River, which prevented the departure of the war vessels from the naval yard. Then, to prevent their loss to the rebels, some vessels . . . were scuttled and others burned. The arsenal suffered the ultimate fate; a large part of its buildings, machinery, and materials were destroyed. . . .[27]

In the whole state of Virginia, then, only Fort Monroe remains in the hands of the federal government. Fort Monroe occupies a very advantageous position in the entrance of Chesapeake Bay. Recently it has been strengthened in a manner which suggests that it will not be attacked.

The other border states are disposed to join the South. In fact, they have already begun separating from the Union. Kentucky and Missouri have convoked their legislatures. North Carolina's legislature, currently in session, has convoked a popular convention that will certainly pass the secession ordinance. Maryland is in a very difficult position. Located between Washington and the North, it must consider very carefully before seceding from the Union. If it does secede, the U.S. government will occupy it. After the events that occurred in Baltimore on 19 April . . . the governor called the legislature into special session on 26 April. Because of Maryland's precarious position, the legislature, composed of a disunionist majority, has not approved the call for a popular convention, which is the only constitutional method to pass a secession ordinance in Maryland.[28]

Nevertheless, Maryland is, in fact, already in the power of the northern states. Some twenty thousand men are in Washington, five thousand in Annapolis, and other forces, including nine thousand in Baltimore, are at different points in the state. . . .

The Montgomery Congress met in special session on 29 April. On the same day, President Davis offered the customary address during which he announced that all the Confederate states had ratified the Montgomery Constitution. . . . Referring to Latin America, Davis asked Congress to provide funds for commissioners who would obtain recognition of the Confederacy and establish friendly relations with the Latin American states.

Apparently the Confederate states have ceased, for now, their campaign against Washington. . . . Ostensibly they intend to aid Baltimore and to prevent its remaining in federal hands.

Moving from events in the South to those in the North, the fall of Fort Sumter, the action in Baltimore, and the president's proclamation calling out the volunteers have produced an excitement and enthusiasm never before witnessed in the North. Citizens have hastened to enlist and take up arms en masse. Although the president only called for seventy-five thousand men raised by quota from among the states, three states have offered one hundred thousand each. The authorities are positively embarrassed in constraining the popular enthusiasm.

The Republicans want Baltimore occupied militarily. When the president told the Baltimore authorities after the events of 19 April that the remaining forces moving toward Washington would not pass through that city, a terrible outcry was raised against him with part of the New York press even requesting his removal. The other forces arriving in this capital came via Annapolis. Protesting against northern troops occupying Annapolis, Maryland's governor did not want federal forces to pass across that state. . . . He wanted British Minister Lord Richard Lyons to act as mediator between the two sections. Seward replied . . . that in no case would the United States submit this country's internal questions to the arbitration of a foreign power and even less to a European monarchy. [29]

On 27 April another presidential proclamation extended the blockade of southern ports to the states of Virginia and North Carolina. Nevertheless, the blockade still has not become effective. . . . [30]

In his 19 April proclamation the president entreated the dissidents to lay down their arms within twenty days. After this period has transpired, the federals will probably no longer remain on the defensive. The federal government already knows that the present conflict is not a matter of several months' duration but probably will last for some years. To insure an orderly campaign throughout this time, it has augmented the army and navy, enlisting volunteers for three years. The seventy-five thousand men raised by the 19 April proclamation were enrolled for only three months. . . .

. . . A very important transformation of public opinion has occurred. . . . Until now the southern people and ideas have had many northern partisans. Part of the northern press was dedicated to defending and propagating these ideas. After the events just mentioned, the South's earlier support in the North has shifted completely and decidedly to the federal government. The most extreme Democrats, who were their party's candidates for various offices in the recent elections, have declared suddenly and unanimously for sustaining the government. They have enlisted in the government's defense. Some Democrats are very enthusiastic and determined organizers of volunteers to oppose the South's advance. A similar transformation has occurred in the South also. Many of those who were unionists previously are now the most decided disunionists. The local spirit, so unfortunate in internal wars, has risen very noticeably. Until now this country's principal parties were the Democrats, whose strength came from the slave states with many followers in the free states, and the Republicans, who only had majorities in northern states and some western states. Those labels are no longer heard now. Free state citizens are unionists and slave state citizens are disunionists. Future labels will probably be abolitionists and propagandists. [31]

A diplomatic exchange . . . revealed the aggressive policy that the U.S. government proposes to pursue. . . . Apparently . . . the Confederate States had not actively sought recognition from the French, and France had given assurances that it would not proceed precipitously in this matter. [32]

Seward's new instructions contain an explicit and decisive declaration that this government "has not had, nor has, nor will have the slightest idea of permitting the dissolution of the Union now or on any other occasion. . . ."

Romero to MRE, 23 May 1861, in Romero, *Correspondencia* I, 393–96

The Confederacy has received new members. . . . On 6 May the Arkansas Convention unanimously passed a secession ordinance. Arkansas was immediately incorporated into the Confederacy.

On the same day, the Tennessee legislature declared independence, approving a decree dissolving the existing relations between Tennessee and the United States. This decree will be submitted to the voters on 8 June. Meanwhile, in imitation of Virginia . . . Tennessee concluded an agreement of alliance with the Montgomery government. The Tennessee legislature sanctioned this pact. [33]

In fact, then, Tennessee forms part of the Confederacy. . . . On 8 May Kentucky's governor suggested to the legislature that the state convention wanted Kentucky to join the Confederacy. The Kentucky legislature has not seconded this idea. Presumably Kentucky will follow a neutral course in the present disagreement. Recently a governor's proclamation has prohibited U.S. and Confederate forces from entering Kentucky. [34]

Some recent events in Missouri will either precipitate the separation of that state or contribute to affirming its ties to the Union. The governor and legislature of Missouri are clearly inclined toward the former course. On 10 May seven hundred members of the state militia were camped outside the capital city, St. Louis. The commander of the federal forces occupying St. Louis marched against that encampment. He compelled the unconditional surrender of the troops there and brought them back to St. Louis as prisoners of war. Irritated by those events, the inhabitants of St. Louis attempted to free the prisoners by armed force. They fired upon the U.S. troops who returned the fire. . . . The federal government approved the conduct of the commander of the regular troops. . . .[35]

Virginia is in danger of splitting into two states with one remaining in the Union. With few slaves and bordering on the free states of Pennsylvania and Ohio, the western part of Virginia has expressed its desire to remain in the Union. After the Richmond Convention passed the secession ordinance, the twenty-two counties of western Virginia, representing more than two hundred thousand inhabitants, held a convention at Wheeling. During three sessions the desirability of immediately organizing a new state was discussed. Before taking that step, it was finally agreed to wait for the result of 26 May's popular vote on the Richmond Convention's secession ordinance.

Federal forces completely occupy Maryland, including the city of Baltimore. General Benjamin Butler entered Baltimore on 14 May, immediately proclaiming the city under martial law. The governor of Maryland issued a proclamation calling up the quota of armed forces assigned by the secretary of war in order to place them at the federal government's service. In that proclamation, he claimed the force will serve only within the limits of Maryland, or for the defense of Washington. The Maryland legislature, composed in its majority of disunionists, suspended its sessions for several days until the result of the Virginia popular vote is known. Before suspending its sessions, the Maryland legislature sent commissioners to the Montgomery government. The burned railroad bridges connecting Baltimore with the North have already been repaired and communication with the North via Baltimore has been reopened.

People favoring the Union started an insurrection in Zapata county, Texas. The rising was, however, promptly put down. Supposedly Delaware, which also has slaves, will remain in the Union, because its interest in slavery is insignificant with only slightly more than a thousand slaves, and because it is small, weak, and surrounded by free states. . . .

The Montgomery Congress declared war on the United States, expressly excepting Maryland, North Carolina, Tennessee, Kentucky, Arkansas, Missouri, Delaware (some of which states joined the Confederacy afterwards), the New Mexico and Arizona territories, and the

Indian Territory. The same act authorized and regulated the issuance of letters of marque that President Davis has previously decreed.

The Montgomery Congress has . . . transferred the Confederate capital from Montgomery to Richmond.[36]

On 1 June the Confederate postmaster general will take charge of the conduct of correspondence within those seceded states. Mail service has continued under federal direction until now. The Confederacy has published new postal rates, higher than those in the United States. This measure will likely rupture the regular mails between the two sections.

The Washington government has given General Winfield Scott command of military operations against the dissidents. Naturally, his plans have not been made public. Until now, no force has departed from here to invade the southern states. Nevertheless, allegedly the first expedition will be directed against Virginia. The points considered most probable for armed action are: Harper's Ferry in Virginia, Fort Pickens in Pensacola Bay, and Cairo, Illinois. Harper's Ferry is an important point because it dominates one of the country's principal railroads, which also ties Washington with the west. . . .[37]

The insurgents have gathered ten thousand men in Pensacola Bay. They have also fortified themselves in the Warrington [Florida] naval yard. They have constructed parapets and placed batteries to threaten Fort Pickens, which still remains in Federal hands, and the U.S. vessels aiding in the fort's defense. In that situation, an incident similar to Fort Sumter can occur. To prevent the dissidents from placing batteries where they could easily reach and dominate the fort, the president issued a proclamation on 10 May that authorized the federal commander on the Florida coast to remove all dangerous and suspicious persons from the vicinity of U.S. forts.[38]

Situated in the conflux of the Ohio and Mississippi Rivers, Cairo appears the key to both rivers. Illinois troops under federal orders occupied Cairo and were later reinforced. They have constructed various fortifications. Supposedly they have covered all dangers. Apparently intending to capture Cairo, the rebels are concentrating a considerable force in the vicinity. . . . North Carolina unanimously approved the secession ordinance. . . .[39]

Romero to MRE, 19 June 1861, in Romero, *Correspondencia* I, 419–21

On 23 May a majority of Virginians voted for the secession ordinance. Ostensibly the federal government only awaited that vote before invading Virginia. On the morning of the twenty-fourth, a considerable force from this city crossed the Potomac River and occupied the heights of Arlington in front of this city and Alexandria. . . . The rebel forces abandoned those cities, so they were occupied without resistance. Nevertheless, Colonel [Elmer] Ellsworth, who commanded the U.S. occupation of Alexandria, was murdered while hauling down a Confederate flag floating over a hotel in Alexandria. This young, fearless, and very promising leader's death has profoundly impressed the North.[40]

While Virginia was invaded from the North, General [George] McClellan's brigade crossed the Ohio River, first occupying Parkersburg and afterwards Grafton. The southern forces retired from these places without resistance. General McClellan's troops united with those forces organized in West Virginia that . . . oppose secession and plan to form a new state.[41]

On the thirtieth, Virginia was invaded from the northwest. In the morning four militia regiments from Philadelphia arrived at Chambersburg near Harper's Ferry. These movements apparently indicated the intention to attack Harper's Ferry simultaneously from front and rear. The plan of operations also seemed to involve cutting Harper's Ferry's communications with the rest of Virginia. . . .[42]

On 3 June Ohio and Indiana troops occupying West Virginia attacked a few Confederates defending the village of Philippy. The Confederates offered only weak resistance before retreating. . . .

Undoubtedly this government plans other large-scale movements. In addition to the many preparations in the armaments, a cabinet member claimed that soon not a soldier will remain in Washington. The Confederate government has already moved to Richmond, where President Davis arrived on 29 May. Allegedly he will assume command of the forces occupying Harper's Ferry.

. . . The governor of Kentucky has reiterated his declaration of neutrality. Nevertheless, the legislature decreed that the militia should take an oath to the federal Constitution. This act has been taken as proof of Kentucky's determination to remain in the Union. The U.S. government rejected a truce agreement between the commanders of the federal forces and of the Missouri state militia and then removed the federal commander.

A disagreement has risen between the civil and the military authorities in Maryland. General [George] Cadwalader, commander of the federal troops in Maryland, sent [Elias H.] Merryman to prison. The chief justice of the Supreme Court, Roger Taney, who resides in Baltimore, issued a writ of *habeas corpus* in favor of the prisoner, declaring that judicial, not military authority ought to try him. The general refused to hand Merriman over. The judge issued an arrest warrant against the general. Cadwalader did not turn himself in. His authority had been ridiculed, Taney said, and he would appeal to the executive for sufficient force to make himself respected. The question is delicate because of the responsibility of the judge who has intervened and because the Constitution guarantees the right of *habeas corpus*. Southern sympathizers have attempted to use this incident to discredit the government.[43]

One of the presidential candidates in the last election, Senator Stephen A. Douglas, died in Chicago on 3 June. Yesterday the public offices were closed, and Washington went into mourning.[44]

Continually more effective, the blockade of the South is established at a larger number of ports. . . . In turn, the Confederate States have captured various prizes, in total fifty-eight.[45]

Romero to MRE, 5 July 1861, in Romero, *Correspondencia* I, 453–54

. . . Republican [Galusha A.] Grow from Pennsylvania was elected speaker of the House without difficulty. The result reveals a Republican majority in the House that favors an active prosecution of the war, since Grow announced such a program last night in a speech to a crowd that came to his home to congratulate him. . . .[46]

. . . A sizeable majority approved the secession ordinance in Tennessee's referendum. The eastern section of the state, which favors the Union, held a convention in Greenville on 15 June. Delegates to the convention from thirty-three counties approved some resolutions, including one petitioning the legislature for permission to organize a new state. Should that petition be denied, as it apparently will be, then the unionists might resort to arms to organize an independent state and to sustain their position.

In Missouri, federal commander General [William S.] Harney had agreed with the state governor, who sympathizes with the rebel states, that the U.S. forces would not occupy any additional positions. Lincoln's government disapproved this arrangement and removed Harney. Missouri's governor sought a similar arrangement with General Harney's successor, who flatly refused to enter into such an agreement. The governor then called up the state militia, retiring from the capital to a point that he considered more defensible. General Nathaniel Lyon attacked him in Brownsville, taking various prisoners. The governor retired to Arkansas, where he remains gathering forces with the apparent intention of returning to the field. Meanwhile, Missouri is without an organized government and entirely under federal control, thus greatly increasing its likelihood of remaining in the Union.[47]

Since the unionists won the recent Missouri elections for the federal House of Representatives, the majority of Missourians seemingly favor this government. Kentucky election results were similar.

The West Virginia convention has already finished its work, discovering that, according to the constitution, it could not form another state without legislative approval. Unable to obtain this approval, the convention determined to follow another road to the same goal. Declaring the state authorities in Richmond in treason against the people, it deposed them. Then it proceeded to nominate a new governor and to organize a legislature. Lincoln has already formally recognized the newly installed governor. Thus, Virginia now has two governments, each pretending legitimately to represent the state.[48]

A conspiracy in favor of the South was discovered in Baltimore. The federal commander in Baltimore has used the conspiracy to make various arrests among the people discharging municipal and military offices in order to assure his possession of the city. . . .

Although the main bodies of the contending armies are located a few miles apart, no formal battle has occurred yet. . . . Harper's Ferry was evacuated. Clearly the southern forces either did not consider the point worth retaining, or they did not believe themselves strong enough to defend it against a formal attack.

This apparent suspension of hostilities has raised some voices against General Scott and has revived discussion about negotiation and compromise. Nevertheless, reconciliation does not appear probable now. The eyes of the northern states are fixed upon Congress, which supposedly will revitalize and quickly carry military operations to a successful conclusion.

This government has recommended [Nathaniel P.] Banks and [John C.] Frémont, both members of the Republican party, as generals in the U.S. Army. . . .

Offenses against Mexican territory and outrages against Mexican citizens have been committed in the southern states. . . . [Reportedly] illegal proceedings were taken against a Mexican named Bernardo Cruz under the pretext of his having expressed abolitionist sentiments. The Brownsville newspaper, *The Fort Brown Flag*, claims a so-called Mayer Eward has committed various violent and arbitrary acts [against Mexicans]. I await the official reports about this affair in order to make suitable representations to this government. . . .[49]

Romero to MRE, 13 July 1861, in Romero, *Correspondencia* I, 457–58

On 5 July the president sent a message to Congress that . . . recommended the active prosecution of the war. . . . Its description of events to date appears directed toward rectifying and illuminating opinion in foreign countries where the message would place events under a light favorable to this government. . . .

The secretary of war states that currently the U.S. forces on the battle field number 310,000 men. After deducting from this number the 80,000 who enlisted for three months and whose enlistment is now almost at the end, an army of 230,000 men remains. To cover expenses, the secretary estimates the army will need $185,296,397.19 in addition to the funds assigned by Congress in its last session to sustain operations during the present year.[50]

The secretary of the treasury judges the total sum necessary to cover expenditures for the fiscal year 1862 is $318,519,581, including $185,296,390 for the army and $30,609,520 for the navy. To raise this amount, the secretary proposes gathering $80,000,000 from taxes and $240,000,000 by means of a loan. In order to raise the $80,000,000 in taxes, he proposed revising the present tariff so that some previously duty-free articles, among others coffee, tea, and sugar, would carry a duty.

The secretary of the navy claims that last 4 March the United States had only forty-two utilizeable war vessels, mounting 555 cannons. The personnel complement of this squadron amounted to seven thousand six hundred officers and men. . . . The secretary insisted on the need to augment the federal navy. . . . The total naval force today consists of eighty-two [sic—error in figures] vessels manned by thirteen [sic—thirteen thousand?] sailors, distributed in the following manner: in the Atlantic, twenty-two vessels with 296 cannons and thirty-five hundred men; a similar force in the Gulf of Mexico; and in the Pacific, six vessels with 82 cannons and one thousand men.[51]

The U.S. squadrons near India, in the Mediterranean, near Brazil, and off the coast of Africa have been recalled, leaving only one boat at each of these naval stations. . . .

. . . Legalizing and sanctioning the [federal] executive's conduct and providing the necessary means to continue successfully, the recent policy has occupied both houses. The great majority of both houses is eager to concede the executive more than he requests. . . . The president requested four hundred thousand men and $400 million, and the House of Representatives approved a bill authorizing five hundred thousand men and $500 million. The only measure that has encountered great opposition is a presidential proclamation increasing the regular army. Thanks to the secession of the southern states, no more than eight senators or congressmen oppose the government in either house. [52]

At the beginning of this week, Rebel Colonel [Richard] Taylor came to Washington under a flag of truce, carrying some correspondence from Davis for Lincoln. . . . Colonel Taylor's departure without a reply seems to confirm the correspondence as definitely not important. [53]

. . . Supposedly the federal forces in Virginia will soon advance toward Richmond. This has been proclaimed so often that it is no longer believable. . . .

Romero to MRE, 2 August 1861, in Romero, *Correspondencia* I, 488–90

General McClellan, at the time chief of the federal forces occupying West Virginia, obtained two victories on 12 and 14 July that destroyed the enemy army in West Virginia. . . . [54]

McClellan's triumph encouraged the federal force occupying the right bank of the Potomac under General [Irwin] McDowell's command. He decided to march toward the interior of Virginia in order to attack the main body of the enemy army fortified at a point called Manassas Junction. . . . On 18 July part of the army advanced to Bull Run. . . . General McDowell decided to attack with the main body of his army . . . [but soon] the Union army became disorganized. Slowly the U.S. army panicked. . . . [However,] the southern troops believed the enemy's retreat was a strategic move and did not harass the movement. On the night after the battle and on the following morning, those stragglers who had headed in this direction have been arriving in the city. The army, which had been composed of forty thousand to fifty thousand men, is entirely destroyed. . . . Physically and morally speaking, the U.S. government has suffered inestimable losses with the Bull Run misfortune. Had the rebels been aware of the importance of their triumph and had they moved at once on Washington, they could certainly have occupied this city without resistance. They did not, however. In recent days this government has sought to reestablish morale and, as far as possible, to repair the losses. It brought in General McClellan to assume command of the Army of the Potomac. . . . He has emphatically declared his intention to undertake military operations with new vigor and to profit from the lesson learned at Bull Run in order to avoid future repetition of such a fatal misfortune. [55]

The battle of Bull Run has greatly excited and encouraged the contending parties. Discovering its full force, the South has become blindly confident in its triumph. Conscious of its greater strength, the North desires to erase the affront inflicted upon it by its adversary. . . . [Previously] on the defensive, the southern forces have already begun to seize the initiative.

The U.S. government suffered another reverse in General [Robert] Patterson's corps. Composed of twenty thousand volunteers, most of this force had enlisted for only three months. Its enlistment expired on 19 July. This corps's mission was to prevent General [Joseph] Johnston, with fifteen thousand southern troops . . . from uniting with the main Confederate army at Manassas Junction. Johnston arrived in time to participate in the battle on the twenty-first. The southern victory has been attributed in large part to Johnston's assistance. The U.S. government ordered General Banks to assume command of Patterson's corps, reinforcing it with several regiments of volunteers. In spite of this reinforcement, General Banks did not consider himself sufficiently strong to defend Harper's Ferry and withdrew the major part of his force from there.

General Butler's corps, occupying eastern Virginia with its headquarters in Fort Monroe, was prepared to march on Richmond if the federal forces would have been victorious at Bull Run and Manassas Junction. However, since that did not occur, Butler's corps ceased advancing and fortified its position. . . .[56]

This misfortune has already introduced discord among Union partisans. There is widespread recrimination for the Bull Run disaster, going so far as to request the dismissal of the secretaries of war and navy and the postmaster general. . . .

A. U.S. law authorized the president to collect import duties on board U.S. war vessels when ports are in rebellion against U.S. authority and to close ports to foreign commerce.

Another law authorized the government to negotiate and guarantee a loan for a sum not to exceed $250 million to cover necessary war expenses.

Another law imposed direct taxes. A decree authorized the confiscation of private property in the rebel states. . . .

The House of Representatives has already approved, and the Senate will probably approve, the proposed revisions in the current tariff, the objective of which is to increase import duties by twenty or thirty million dollars. . . .[57] In the Senate, Senator [Samuel C.] Pomeroy from Kansas offered a bill to abolish slavery in the states that have seceded from the Union; the bill was not taken under consideration. Senator Trumbull of Illinois presented another bill to punish the crime of rebellion against the United States. The House is currently discussing Trumbull's bill.[58]

Both houses have recently wasted time discussing a semantical problem, whether the goal of the present war is, or is not, to subjugate the South. The House approved Crittenden's resolution declaring that the war's objective was only to reestablish the rule of law among the dissidents.[59]

. . . It is also known that [Robert M. T.] Hunter, previously a senator from Virginia, has succeeded Toombs, who had resigned as Confederate secretary of state.

Up to 4 July, the Confederates had captured forty-one vessels belonging to U.S. citizens. . . . [Some] facts have exposed the inefficient blockade of southern ports. Apparently vessels willing to risk running the blockade can easily enter and leave.

Missouri's popular convention declared the governor's office and the federal house seats vacant. It called for new elections of representatives. It also named a Union partisan as governor. Supposedly these steps will assure Missouri remaining in the Union.

The Maryland legislature met recently in Frederick. Composed mostly of disunionists, it will, allegedly,soon pass a secession ordinance. Nevertheless, the ordinance will be ineffective since federal forces occupy the whole state. . . .

Romero to MRE, 7 August 1861, in Romero, *Correspondencia* I, 494

. . . The special session of the U.S. Congress ended after having sanctioned the president's conduct and having approved the legislation necessary to continue the active and energetic conduct of military operations against the dissidents. . . . The Senate approved the nominations of officials and military promotions recommended by the president. . . . Lincoln has already announced his decision not to make any cabinet changes, thereby removing the fears of those opposed to changes. The outcry against some cabinet members has been reduced to a systematic opposition against Postmaster General Blair. Blair is assigned the main role in the Bull Run defeat because allegedly he had compelled General Scott to offer battle against his judgment and when the general was still not prepared. Blair is also supposedly in open rivalry with General Scott.[60]

In its recent legislative elections, Kentucky has again expressed its adherence to the Union cause. A very large majority of the unionists' candidates won. General McClellan has already received command of the federal Army of the Potomac, headquartered in Washington. . . .

Romero to MRE, 14 August 1861, in Romero, *Correspondencia*
I, 500–501

. . . General Lyon, whose decisiveness and personal effort had single-handedly succeeded in keeping Missouri in the Union, was completely defeated yesterday at Springfield and killed in action. . . . This new blow is quite strong. Perhaps it will decide the fate of Missouri. Prior to the battle at Springfield, the skirmishes in Missouri had favored the federal forces.

Because Hampton had been abandoned by General Butler, who commands the federal forces in east Virginia with headquarters in Fortress Monroe, the rebels immediately seized, burned, and abandoned that city. This government is apparently dissatisfied with the military operations of General Butler since General [John E.] Wool has been ordered to relieve him. General Wool is one of the most reputable soldiers in the regular U.S. Army. He served during the whole war with Mexico in 1846 and 1847. . . .

. . . The general report of the battle of Bull Run assigns the principal cause of defeat to the reinforcements that the southern army received so opportunely from General Johnston's division.

. . . Presumably, . . . Prince Napoleon's visit to this country has had a political purpose. [Prince Napoleon, Napoleon III's cousin, visited the United States in the fall of 1861. When Prince Napoleon decided to volunteer for Union army service, McClellan appointed the Prince to his staff.][61]

Since the New York elections for state officials are approaching, the different parties are organizing the customary conventions. The Republican party proposed a coalition to the Democrats. The coalition would elect supporters of the Union to posts without regard for their previous political affiliation. The Democratic party refused to enter into this arrangement, which will stymie the unity of views and action that seemingly ought to exist currently in the United States if they wish to succeed in the war.[62]

The secretary of the treasury went to New York to arrange affairs relative to the loan decreed by Congress. I have been assured that the U.S. government would attempt to place part of the loan in Europe. The London *Times* advises the English to abstain from taking any part of it. . . .[63]

Romero to MRE, 12 September 1861, in Romero,
Correspondencia I, 523–26

On 29 August the U.S. forces obtained a victory in Cape Hatteras.
Although far from compensating for prior reverses, this victory has,
nevertheless, reanimated the public spirit and infused some confidence
in the army.[64]
On 26 August Commodore [Silas H.] Stringham commanded a squadron of nine ships that sailed from Old Point (Chesapeake Bay) with troops
under General Butler's command. The expedition attacked Forts Hatteras
and Clark, situated in Cape Hatteras, by land and water. These forts
occupy an important position and are considered the key to the North
Carolina coast. After several hours of resistance, the garrisons defending
the forts surrendered unconditionally. . . . Ostensibly, the expedition
had no other goal, since Commodore Stringham and General Butler
returned once this was accomplished. . . .
This expedition's success has revealed a new, more efficient mode of
attacking the dissident states. . . . Since each southern state has gathered
its forces and sent them to the Virginia theater, the coasts of the rebel
states are almost entirely abandoned. . . . Federal expeditions could
cause considerable damage, seize various important positions, and divide
the rebel forces. Moreover, each state, seeing its own territory invaded,
will soon recall the troops it had sent to Virginia for the common
defense. . . .
After the occupation of the above mentioned points, the North Carolina forces abandoned the forts at Cape Ocrakoke near the lost positions. . . . It was greatly feared that the southern army at Manassas would
occupy this capital. Alternatively, it might have crossed the Potomac
River above Washington and attempted to take Baltimore with its numerous Confederate supporters and to arouse Maryland in order to cut
Washington's communication with the North. The rebel army advanced,
placing itself almost directly in front of the federal lines. . . . Very
probably, having united a respectable force at one point, the rebels will
attempt some movement. Otherwise they run the danger of demoralizing
the army and of exhausting their resources to sustain it. On 19 August the
secretary of war ordered the enlisted volunteers to come to Washington,
even if they are without arms or uniforms and even before organizing into
regiments. Apparently Lincoln's government greatly fears Washington
might be attacked. Later, they said the danger has disappeared and
General McClellan was already prepared to repel any invasion.
Since the rebel victory at Springfield, Missouri, . . . the Civil War has
intensified greatly in that state. . . . The guerrilla war continues.
On 31 August General Frémont, commander of the federal forces . . .

proclaimed martial law in all of Missouri. He imposed the death penalty on those caught with weapon in hand and decreed the emancipation of the slaves of those [persons] rebelling against U.S. authority. This is the first revealing measure taken with respect to the freedom of slaves. Presumably before long it will be imitated in other parts. Assuredly this measure has earned federal approval. Meanwhile, Missouri's former governor, moving with the rebel forces, proclaimed Missouri's secession from the Union and its annexation to the Confederacy. The Richmond government immediately accepted this act.[65]

Shortly Kentucky will also become a prisoner of the Civil War. The Kentucky legislature, with a majority of unionists, met recently. Still, the governor is a declared disunionist. In his last message he recommended a policy of neutrality that he has pursued until now. At the same time, he sent some commissioners to Washington to achieve neutrality. They have requested the necessary orders from the president to withdraw the U.S. forces being raised in that state out of Kentuckians. . . . Lincoln absolutely refused to retire the forces. Meanwhile the federal army from Cairo occupied Paducah, considered the focal point of the Kentucky secessionists. . . .

On 26 August southern forces surprised an Ohio battalion commanded by Colonel Tyler near Summerville in West Virginia. The battalion managed to withdraw. . . . General Jacob D. Cox, who had moved up the Kanawha River to Fayette, retired to Gallipolis (Ohio) after encountering the combined Confederate forces of Generals Henry A. Wise and John B. Floyd.

The rebels have obtained new advantages in Arizona and today they possess the whole territory. . . . Texas volunteers threatened the U.S. forces concentrated in Fort Fillmore. Major [Isaac] Lynde, commander at Fort Fillmore, surrendered unconditionally. . . . I consider these events of interest because they occurred on the Mexican border.[66]

On 3 August the U.S. steamship *South Carolina* bombarded the city of Galveston, Texas. The foreign consuls residing in Galveston, among them a Mexican vice-consul, have sent a note to the commodore protesting the bombardment.

. . . Each side tries to keep its effective strength secret from the enemy. Nevertheless, reportedly the rebels have three hundred thousand men in Virginia. The U.S. government has concentrated a considerable force in Washington. . . . Several mutinies have occurred among these troops for various reasons. These mutinies threatened to disorganize the whole Army of the Potomac, but General McClellan managed to end them. This danger has disappeared, at least for now.[67]

Popular enthusiasm to enlist in the federal forces has declined very much recently. Among other things, this is attributed to the inadequate feeding and clothing of the troops because the contractors have not fulfilled their contracts to provide these things. This has raised a strong outcry against the secretary of war, who is accused of favoritism in granting contracts to his friends without concern for the public interest. Despite all these charges, the active organization of the army continues.[68]

This government has initiated strong measures to defend itself from the assaults and action of southern sympathizers in the northern states. It has prohibited the circulation of several periodicals that openly defend that cause. It has imprisoned several ladies from Washington who allegedly have corresponded with the rebel chiefs.[69]

Washington's mayor (whose fate here lies in popular election) refused to take the constitutional oath recently decreed by Congress. He was removed from office and sent to Fort Lafayette in New York Harbor, which serves now as a federal prison.

A so-called peace party is forming in the North, which sustains southern interests. It is still not very large. The future course of the war will cause it to increase or decrease. Now even the New York Democratic party, which refused to join the Republicans in the coming state elections, met recently in Syracuse and resolved to favor an active prosecution of the war.[70]

In accordance with article 6 of the law of 13 July, vessels in U.S. ports that belong to citizens of the dissident states have been confiscated. In New York alone they have confiscated fifty boats so far. . . .[71]

This government obtained a significant boost during the past month when the secretary of the treasury arranged a loan of $150 million with New York, Boston, and Philadelphia banks. The bankers first expressed a lack of confidence, even resistance, to making this arrangement with the government. But finally they agreed, stipulating that $50 million be issued each month. This operation elevated the government's credit and lends it the most decided support of the whole commercial circle and of the most influential men of the three largest northern cities. At the same time the bankers have desired a popular subscription for part of the bonds just like Napoleon's loan before the campaign in the east. . . .[72]

President Davis issued a proclamation on 14 August, in conformity with the law, ordering all U.S. citizens to leave Confederate territory within forty days, counting from that date.

On 2 September the Confederate Congress approved another bill to confiscate property belonging to the enemies of the Confederate States. All this property would be placed in escrow to satisfy claims originating from the federal government's action against the property of Confederate citizens. Supposedly, in New Orleans alone, goods valued at $50 million will be confiscated in keeping with that law.[73]

The rebel Congress has prohibited the exportation of tobacco from ports other than Confederate ports, in the same terms by which they had prohibited cotton [exports]. . . . The president approved a bill authorizing him to name two more commissioners to Europe and to assign the three already there as he pleases. He also approved a bill authorizing him to aid Missouri to repel the present invasion and to admit it into the Confederacy.

The appropriation bill to raise funds for the prosecution of the war against the United States has been published. The first section arranges for the issuance of $100 million worth of treasury notes, redeemable six months after the conclusion of peace. The second section arranges for the issuance of an equal quantity of bonds carrying 8 percent interest and payable within twenty years. The fourth section imposes a .5 percent war tax on all persons owning more than $500 capital.[74]

Recently an unconfirmed rumor circulated that Davis has died a natural death. . . .

. . . Prince Gortchakov instructed [Edward Baron de] Stoeckel, minister of Russia, . . . to use his good offices to obtain a reconciliation between the contending parties. The note is drafted in terms very friendly to this country. . . .[75]

Romero to MRE, 23 September 1861, in Romero, *Correspondencia* I, 538–40

The Maryland legislature should have met in Frederick early last week, evidently to decree secession. Presumably, the many southern partisans in this state have asked Davis for some troops to aid them to revolt against U.S. authority. Since the legislature had not seceded from the Union and joined the Confederacy, Davis said he could not possibly do anything in favor of their plan. Given Davis's decision then, and since the disunionists were a large majority, the members of the legislature decided to approve the secession ordinance on the very day they met. Aware of these developments, this government decided to arrest several members of the legislature in order to prevent a quorum. At the same time, they arrested several other prominent people in Baltimore, among them [Henry] May. . . .

Some difficulties have arisen between this government and General Frémont, commander of the Military Department of the West. . . . The president disapproved Frémont's decree insofar as it referred to freeing slaves. . . . People from St. Louis, Frémont's headquarters, have made some charges against him. Colonel Francis Blair, Jr., brother of the postmaster general and an influential member of the House, has made these accusations. He was recently sent to prison for insubordination. The government sent Montgomery Blair, postmaster general, as an agent near General Frémont. Recently, Montgomery Blair returned without revealing the result of his mission. Supposedly, General Frémont has received orders to come to Washington to explain his conduct. . . . These differences could assume a very serious aspect because General Frémont, the presidential candidate of the Republican party in 1856, is a very popular man and known for his ideas on slavery. The avowed aboltionists and radical Republicans have taken his side.[76]

Southern forces commanded by General Pierce [sic—Nicholas B. Pearce] attempted to take Lexington, Missouri, which was defended by Colonel [James A.] Mullingan. . . .

More symptoms of the war are about to explode in Kentucky. The legislature approved a resolution ordering the southern forces to evacuate the state. The governor interposed his veto, but a two-thirds vote approved the resolution a second time. Upon receiving the news, Bishop General [Leonidas] Polk, commander of the rebel forces stationed in Columbus, replied that he would not comply with the decision unless the federal forces abandoned their positions in the state. Then the legislature named General Anderson commander of the state volunteer forces, intending to organize an army and force compliance with its decision.

. . . The government has already gathered a very considerable force in and around Washington. According to trustworthy sources, this force amounts to over a hundred thousand men. The U.S. forces have also constructed numerous fortifications. The belief reigns that the rebel army will not take the offensive now. The two armies are almost in view of each other. Each day increases the probability of a general engagement soon.

Last week another maritime expedition with land forces under the command of General Butler departed Fortress Monroe heading south under sealed orders. . . .

The U.S. government has continued rigorous measures. It has arrested various suspicious persons. It has suspended the circulation of various periodicals and sent several editors to prison. Since up to $1 million of new bonds have been sold every day, the public loan has been a greater success than expected.

During the past week the periodicals have been very occupied with a decree issued by the captain general of Cuba governing the arrival in Cuban ports of vessels under Confederate flag. The Confederates claim this decree is formal recognition of Confederate independence. The Spanish minister in Washington, they also claim, has received orders to recognize southern independence without delay. . . .[77]

Very recently . . . Braxton Bragg of Louisiana replaced Leroy P. Walker of Alabama as secretary of war in Davis's cabinet.

On 1 August, in Mesilla, Confederate Colonel [John R.] Baylor incorporated the Arizona territory into the Confederate States. . . .

The Republican party won the recent California elections. Therefore, the next legislature there will have a Republican majority. . . .[78]

Romero to MRE, 12 October 1861, in Romero, *Correspondencia*
I, 558–61

. . . The Confederate forces under General [Sterling] Price have captured Lexington, Missouri. . . . Colonel Mullingan, with twenty-five
hundred federal troops, defended Lexington. . . .[79]

. . . General Frémont's enemies complained loudly because the commander of the Military Department of the West . . . did not aid opportunely in the defense of Lexington.

The surrender of Lexington signifies for the federal government the
loss of two-thirds of Missouri, the isolation of Kansas, and the impossibility of navigating the Missouri River above Lexington.

Shortly after this event, General Frémont left St. Louis to assume
command of the Army of the West in order to regain Lexington. Upon
arriving in Jefferson City, he learned that Confederate General [Ben]
McCulloch had joined Price. Since, besides possessing a force reportedly
very superior to his, the two Confederates were in a favorable position,
Frémont suspended his march for several days. . . . Later the rebel forces
abandoned Lexington and retreated southwards. Presumably it was not
the difficulty in defending that city, but rather that the military strategy of
the southern leaders requires such a step in order to appear stronger in
other places. In any event, the secession cause has gained considerable
ground in Missouri. Supposedly, General Frémont left Jefferson City
yesterday to catch up with the dissident forces.

The dissension between General Frémont and Colonel Francis P. Blair,
Jr., has remained heated. After being placed at liberty, Blair was em-
prisoned again. Both have leveled accusations and reciprocated recriminations before this government. This dispute can only discredit the
cause they would defend. . . . These difficulties convinced a New York
newspaper that Frémont would be relieved. This report produced a very
disfavorable reaction in the west. The secretary of state hastened to deny
the report, assuring that the government was not considering relieving
the general of his command, nor even less, of trying him.

A letter from the president to Mrs. Frémont also indicated what little
impression the accusations against that general had made on the government.

In Lexington, the fugitive governor of Missouri, [Claiborne F.] Jackson, called together some members of the old legislature. They quickly
adopted an act of secession for Missouri.

. . . Both parties are making preparations and will soon convert Kentucky, like Missouri, into a theater of bloody and disastrous war. Supposedly, the Bishop General Polk has marched towards Paducah, which is
defended by federal forces, and Confederate General [Gideon] Pillow has

crossed the Mississippi near Belmont in order to attack the federal forces in Cape Girardeau. Meanwhile, the Kentucky legislature continues to adopt extraordinary measures favorable to the Union. It has approved a bill authorizing the negotiation of a loan of $2 million to cover the necessities of war. . . . It passed a resolution requesting the state's federal Senators Breckinridge and [Lazarus W.] Powell, both of the peace [secession] party, to resign their seats. If they do not, it threatens to ask the federal Senate to investigate the conduct of those men and to expel them if the investigation exposed them as enemies of the government. Reportedly, Breckinridge, the southern Democratic party candidate in the past presidential elections, is in Virginia now, organizing a force to join the Confederate army.

Late last month, the federal Army of the Potomac moved its positions into Virginia. . . . On 28 September the dissident forces abandoned the hills near Arlington, [which] were immediately occupied by federal troops. Upon occupying Munson's Hill (the principal hill), the federal troops discovered that at most, ten thousand enemy troops had been there. This proves that the Confederate approach was not intended to attack the federal lines, but to observe the Union movements from up close and to attract federal attention to that point.

[If] the Confederate leaders . . . evacuated Munson's Hill . . . to lure the federal forces to another previously selected, more advantageous position, they have been fooled. With the Bull Run disaster very fresh in his memory, General McClellan has acted very prudently. He has not ordered another advance.

The occupation of Munson's Hill cost some federal blood. Two battalions advancing from opposite directions mistook each other for enemy forces and opened fire. . . . To avoid a repetition of this disaster, General McClellan has ordered the organization of a "signal corps" composed of six hundred lieutenants. The signal corps is charged exclusively with assigning unerring means of recognition to the different battalions during night marches.

While occupying Munson's Hill, federal troops completely destroyed the houses and property found in the vicinity. This prompted General McClellan . . . to declare that such crimes will be unfailingly punished with the death penalty in the future.

Recently, the federal forces claimed victory in two skirmishes in West Virginia. Confederate Genearls Floyd and [Robert E.] Lee have already joined forces. . . . In spite of this, . . . General [William S.] Rosecrans, commanding the federal forces in West Virginia, considers himself strong enough to hold his present position.

On 4 October the southern forces attempted to recover Fort Hatteras on Cape Hatteras in North Carolina. . . .

Another military department, composed of the so-called New England states, has been organized and placed under General Butler's command. General [Joseph K. F.] Mansfield replaced Butler in command at Cape Hatteras.

Four thousand men from Texas have invaded New Mexico. On 9 September New Mexico's governor called upon the people to repel the invasion.[80]

. . . Command of the Confederate army on the Potomac . . . has been transferred from General Beauregard to General Johnston.

Several northern citizens petitioned the secretary of state to adopt some measure against [William Howard] Russell, London *Times* correspondent. They accuse Russell of having slandered this country in letters directed to his newspaper. . . . The federal government, Seward replied, has never concerned itself with what the foreign press published about the United States. Seward claimed there was no danger that Russell's reports would impair the national credit.[81]

Among the foreigners incorporated into the U.S. Army are the Duke of Paris and the Count of Chartres, nephews of the Prince of Joinville. . . . They joined Prince Napoleon on McClellan's staff. Since both men, members of the Orleans family, have been banished from France, this incident might possibly sway Emperor Napoleon's attitude in a manner very unfavorable to this government. . . . Moreover, in reply to the charge against Russell, Seward expounded a very significant idea in these terms: "The United States government does not depend on the favor or the goodwill of foreign nations, but rather on the will of the American people."[82]

The question of slavery has returned recently to agitate matters. In a meeting in Massachusetts early in the month regarding state elections, the most forceful champion of the cause of humanity in this country, Charles Sumner, . . . presented the immediate abolition of slavery as the salvation of the country. . . . Being authored by a Massachusetts senator who occupies the very important post of chairman of the Senate Foreign Relations Committee lends the speech extra political significance.[83]

. . . [Judge Samuel R.] Betts pronounced . . . the first judgment . . . in the cases regarding vessels seized for attempting to run the blockade. This decision declared the English bark *Hiawatha* a fair prize. The vessel had left Richmond loaded with cotton and tobacco. Since doubts existed regarding the legality of the federal blockade, this decision and the support of the judicial branch are assumed to have sanctioned it. . . .[84]

On several occasions the European press has reported that this government proposed to [Guiseppe] Garibaldi via the U.S. legation in Turin to serve in the U.S. Army and that he has offered command of it. Also, in another incident Colonel [Arthur] Rankin, a member of the Canadian shadow parliament, was arrested in Canada for violating the English neutrality laws, since he was raising a battalion to serve in the U.S. Army. . . . The administration's newspaper explains [that] . . . the federal government has not authorized anyone to recruit troops in Canada, nor has it offered Garibaldi command of the army. Rather, as a naturalized citizen of the United States, Garibaldi had informed the U.S. government that he contemplated visiting this country and that he desired to enter its service. If this were so, this government replied, they would gladly and appreciatively accept his service and would make him a brigadier general, the same rank given to Lafayette in the revolutionary army. Garibaldi decided not to offer his services to the United States at this time. . . .[85]

Every day . . . the ill will that England holds for the people of this country becomes more evident. The London press has bitterly censured the U.S. government for not communicating the recent decision to require passports for entrance or departure from this country to Lord Lyons and the other members of the Washington diplomatic corps. The St. Petersburg cabinet's note to the U.S. government expressing Emperor Alexander's sympathy for the Union cause . . . has prompted the London press to express unrestrainedly its apparent odium and scorn for this country's institutions.[86]

The Portuguese government has published a decree against privateers, renewing the prohibitions against arming vessels or receiving privateers in its ports and dominions. Supposedly, the labors and influence of the U.S. minister in Lissabon produced these pronouncements.[87]

Romero to MRE, 28 October 1861, in Romero, *Correspondencia* I, 573–76

The bad luck pursuing the federal forces since the beginning of the rebellion was evident again on 21 October at Balls Bluff on the right bank of the Potomac River a few miles above Washington. On the morning of the twenty-first, part of General [Charles P.] Stone's division . . . crossed the river without encountering any resistance. Upon approaching the village of Leesburg, the rebels under the command of General [N. G.] Evans attacked and completely defeated these troops. Colonel [Edward D.] Baker, the Union commander, was killed in the action. When the federals retreated to the river, they found themselves without the boats that had brought them. Since the enemy was pursuing them closely, many surrendered and others dove into the water to swim across. However, many drowned in the attempt. The official government newspaper admits to nearly seven hundred casualties among thirteen hundred troops involved in the action.[88]

Colonel Baker's widely lamented death has produced a profound impression. He was distinguished in the Mexican War, a senator from Oregon, and one of the most prominent members of the Republican party. His funeral will be very solemnly celebrated on the twenty-fourth.

General Banks's division had crossed to the Virginia bank of the Potomac River and obtained a victory in the vicinity of Bolivar, near Harper's Ferry, a few days earlier. Baker's defeat forced Banks to retreat to his old position on the Maryland side.

In the west . . . General Frémont has continued his march toward the Missouri rebels without word of any important armed contact yet. Until recently, the secretary of war was visiting the camp of General Frémont in Missouri. Upon returning to St. Louis, the secretary suspended the fortification of that city, the payment of contracts signed by General Frémont, and the salary of officers appointed or promoted by the same general. The newspapers uniformly agree that the cabinet has resolved to remove General Frémont from command of the Military Department of the West. An attempt would be made to name a successor to General McClellan, commander of the federal Army of the Potomac, they claim, and further, General Scott is considering retiring from active service, using a privilege conceded by a law from the last session of Congress for retired military personnel.

Early this month, a fleet of cannon launches armed in New Orleans attacked the U.S. squadron blockading the Mississippi River. [89]

Early this month an engagement occurred on the island Santa Risa in Pensacola Bay. A force from Pensacola successfully attacked the New York Zouaves stationed on that island. . . . Soldiers from Fort Pickens immediately reinforced and aided the Zouaves, compelling the invaders to return to Pensacola.

The rebel forces in Virginia have placed batteries at various points on the Potomac River bank below Washington. These batteries have completely interrupted and blocked river navigation that Washington uses to receive provisions and other material for the federal army from New York. In the future, supplies will come via Baltimore and Annapolis. [90]

In Fortress Monroe, a maritime expedition of thirty-one transports is prepared to sail, . . . but the destination is unknown.

As soon as news was received in Washington that [James M.] Mason and [John] Slidell, Confederate ministers to the courts of Paris and London, had departed Charleston on the steamer *Nashville* . . . this government ordered three light steamers from New York to pursue the *Nashville*. . . . [91]

Mocking the vigilance of the blockading vessels, the English steamer *Bermuda* entered Savannah with a very large cargo of arms and munitions.

Upon learning that the Richmond government has liberated some Union prisoners after demanding an oath from them not to take up arms against the South, the U.S. government freed an equal number of dissident prisoners under an oath to sustain the U.S. Constitution. This arrangement is the first prisoner exchange. . . .[92]

After celebrating an alliance with the Confederate States, the Cherokee Indian tribe has already organized a cavalry regiment to place at its service.[93]

A problem similar to the one between General Frémont and Colonel Blair has arisen in West Virginia between Confederate Generals [Henry A.] Wise and Floyd. . . .[94]

Confederate General Twiggs, who commanded the garrison at New Orleans, has resigned because of illness. Reportedly President Davis has considered naming General Polk, the protestant bishop of New Orleans, as secretary of war.

West Virginia has submitted the question of whether those counties wish to remain part of Virginia or to organize into another state to a popular vote. A large majority favored the second course in the recent election.

The greatest activity prevails in the U.S. naval yards. More than ten thousand workers are employed in Washington, Philadelphia, Brooklyn, Charlestown, and Portsmouth, building comparatively few new boats. They work principally at repairing the old ones and at converting recently purchased merchant steamers into war vessels.[95]

The Haiti Immigration Committee has been busy sending free Negroes to Haiti. In the past week, three vessels carrying four hundred colonists departed from New York. . . .[96]

The southern newspapers are busily occupied in . . . declaring Confederate independence a consummated and assured fact and proclaiming the war's only goal is to acquire natural boundaries for the new nation. . . . Maryland, West Virginia, Kentucky, and Missouri are encompassed within these limits. Located in Maryland, Washington will share that state's fate. . . .

Lord Lyons circularized the English consuls in the southern ports. Accompanying the circular is a note from the secretary of state containing an important explanation regarding how vessels that had arrived before the blockade commenced will be permitted to leave the blockaded ports. . . . Reportedly some Texas secessionists have formed a camp near Fort Yuma, [Arizona] at the conflux of the Fila and Colorado Rivers. Furthermore, suspicious groups of armed men were apparently directed from this camp to Baja California.

The *Baltimore Sun* recently claimed that the Richmond government has sent secret agents to the states of Nuevo León y Coahuila, Sonora, Durango, and Chihuahua to induce them to separate from Mexico and to join the Confederate States. . . .

The colossal work of connecting New York with San Francisco via a telegraph to the Pacific coast has been completed already. Telegrams from San Francisco were received on the twenty-sixth. . . .[97]

Romero to MRE, 9 November 1861, in Romero, *Correspondencia* I, 591–94

. . . General Winfield Scott has resigned from command of the U.S. Army. On 31 October he requested permission to retire, alleging his illness made it impossible to fulfill the duties imposed by his position. The real reason, others believe, lies in the president's poor response to his suggestions. In case of disagreement, the president preferred General McClellan, who exercised immediate command of the Army of the Potomac.[98]

The president immediately accepted General Scott's resignation. Then the president and the whole cabinet went to the general's quarters to read him the decree accepting his resignation, which was phrased in terms very laudatory of that commander. The following day, the secretaries of war and treasury accompanied Scott to New York. Supposedly he will soon embark for Europe where his family resides. On the day that Scott retired from command of the army, General McClellan was named to succeed him. All this government's hopes for success now rest on McClellan's military aptitude and skill. This commander, who is still quite young, has been promoted very rapidly. Only eight months ago he held no military rank because he had left the service in 1857. Earlier he had formed part of the U.S. scientific commission sent to study European progress in the art of war during the Crimean War. Since then he has expressed sympathy for French tactics. Now, reportedly following the French system, he wants to divide the army into several corps. Under his direction everything could experience a radical reform. Allegedly he is also considering completely changing the base of military operations that have been pursued against the South until now. . . . The day following General McClellan's promotion, a committee of Philadelphians presented him a sword of honor in the name of that city, his birthplace. . . .

At this ceremony, the general . . . claimed the present war could not last long. This judgment does not agree with the evaluation of more disinterested viewers. Last week the *New York Tribune* published a report from General [Lorenzo] Thomas, adjutant general of the Union army, which had been presented to the secretary of war relative to the condition of the Military Departments of the West and of Kentucky. The report created a great impression. Apparently it was obtained in an illegitimate manner. Intended to be highly secret because of its nature and destined for the private information of the president and secretary of war, this document presents affairs in those areas under the darkest light. According to the report, General Frémont's subordinates accuse him of ineptitude and of attempting to favor his friends at public expense. The army is greatly demoralized, they charge, possessing neither wagons nor means of carrying its baggage, and Frémont's military leadership has placed the department in great danger of falling under Confederate control. With respect to Kentucky, General [Lorenzo] Thomas said that General [William T.] Sherman, commander of that department, gave him very discouraging reports. The young people were generally disunionists, Sherman informed Thomas, and the older men, although favoring the Union, did not wish to fight against their sons. Sherman also noted that he could not count on organizing many battalions in the state. Rebel General [Simon B.] Buckner was advancing toward Louisville, Sherman added, while he had no means of resisting the advance. Finally, Sherman observed, a two-hundred-thousand-man army would be required to save the state. . . . The report's publication was more unfortunate for the federal cause than the defeat at Bull Run, the New York *Times* declared, since it indicated the weak points in the western department to the enemy and placed General Frémont in conflict with his subordinates.[99]

This report apparently has persuaded the president and his cabinet finally to agree to remove General Frémont. The order for General [David] Hunter, second in command of that department, to assume command of the department arrived at its destination just as the army approached the rebels and on the eve of battle. Supposedly, the order was very poorly received. As a consequence, many officers considered resigning from the corps. Conceivably, this measure might create a movement in the western states in favor of Frémont. Even before this, those states were jealous of and discontented with the east and north. On 30 October a maritime expedition . . . left Old Point. . . . [Despite a storm threat] the expedition arrived safely at its apparent destination, Port Royal near Charleston. If this is true, then presumably the expedition's goal is to attack that city by land and sea.

In addition to diverting the dissidents' attention to other areas and dividing their forces, this U.S. expedition aimed at capturing one or more southern ports. The expedition would also raise the blockade, thus permitting the exportation of cotton to silence the cries of English businessmen who have asked their government not to recognize the blockade because it is not effective. Thus, since the Richmond government will surely not permit the exportation of cotton through ports under federal control . . . seizure of a southern port will shift England's animosity to the rebels.[100]

Immediately upon learning where the expedition was headed, the Richmond government sent General [Pierre G. T.] Beauregard to

Charleston to organize the resistance. Beauregard is one of the most renowned Confederate military leaders. At the end of last month, General [Benjamin F.] Kelly of the federal army occupying West Virginia attacked and defeated the dissidents at Romney, forcing them to retreat towards Winchester. Confederate General Floyd, with four thousand men, attacked General Rosecrans's position at Gauly Bridge on 2 November. Floyd was thrown back and forced to retreat.[101]

. . . The official report of Balls Bluff . . . has inspired a polemic contest between the friends of the dead Colonel Baker and General Stone, who had ordered the attack. The former want the whole responsibility for the ill-fated action to fall on the latter, while Stone's supporters insist Colonel Baker exceeded his orders and was the victim of his own boldness. . . . On his own behalf, nevertheless, General McClellan maintains he neither ordered the attack on the enemy nor the crossing of the river.

On 6 November local elections were held in New York, Massachusetts, Michigan, Wisconsin, New Jersey, and Maryland. The unionists won solid victories in all of them. The old labels, Democrats and Republicans, have disappeared for now. In Baltimore, General [John A.] Dix proclaimed . . . that he would not permit people who had taken up arms against the federal government to vote. Everywhere the elections passed peacefully and the government expressed satisfaction with the results.

At almost the same time the central authorities of the new Confederacy held general elections. . . . The current president and vice-president will most likely be elected since they are the only candidates, thus underscoring in another manner the uniformity of the South. . . . A circular . . . from [Christopher] Memminger, secretary of the treasury under President Davis, responding to a petition from cotton planters to have the government purchase the harvest or make an advance against its value, has stated that the government cannot accede to either alternative because it needs money to prosecute the gigantic war that is under way. In one form this expressed the financial condition of this country. Also noteworthy, Memminger recommended the planters sow grain instead of cotton at the next planting time. . . .[102]

Meeting in Macon (Georgia), the southern commercial convention has . . . not opposed those hostile [Confederate] measures aimed at destroying the North's mercantile influence. One member very judiciously observed that, if such measures were adopted, reconciliation with the North would be impossible. . . .

Before the maritime expedition departed Old Point for the South, the secretary of war instructed General Sherman, commander of the expedition, relative to [captured or runaway] southern slaves. Here Sherman was authorized to use the service of any person, whether fugitive from labor or not, who offered his service to the federal government and who could be occupied in any useful capacity. This appears to encompass slaves belonging to loyal (unionists) and disloyal (disunionists) owners. . . .

Since Washington's water communication with the North has been cut, and since only the railroad connection that passes through Baltimore, one of the most sympathetic secessionists' cities, remains, the fate of the government and this city have begun to inspire alarm. The New York *Times* . . . asked the government to move to a more central point with less danger of being without communication, or of falling under rebel control.

The citizens of Hyde County, North Carolina, convened at Hatteras on 12 October. They approved an act describing the injuries that they have received from the secessionist government and declared their independence from it. The North, which has always believed North Carolina had a unionist majority, has tried to inspire that state to follow this example. Toward this end, a meeting yesterday in New York expressed sympathy for the [Hatteras] people and offered them aid, assistance, and funds.[103]

The U.S. steamer *South Carolina* seized the Mexican goleta *Soledad Cos* out of Veracruz loaded with coffee and cigars . . . for attempting to run the blockade and enter Galveston. . . .[104]

Romero to MRE, 24 November 1861, in Romero, *Correspondencia* I, 605–9

. . . Early in the month, federal forces gained an important victory over the South Carolinian forces defending Forts Walker and Beauregard in the entrance of Port Royal. The naval expedition that left Old Point at the end of October . . . attacked the enemy positions that were abandoned after a battle. . . . Word of this victory produced the greatest enthusiasm in the northern states. . . . This victory is considered important because it increased this government's standing in the insurgent states and because the point occupied offers good facilities for a permanent base while at the same time menacing Charleston and Savannah. The white natives of Port Royal and the inhabitants of Beaufort, a nearby village, abandoned their homes. Some burned their houses. All managed to evacuate [some of] their slaves. Nevertheless, many slaves managed to remain and welcomed the northern forces whom they considered their liberators.[105]

Only U.S. naval forces were involved in the battle of Port Royal. . . .

The federals have labored to reinforce the rebel fortifications and construct new ones, indicating no intention to intern themselves in South Carolina for the present. Since this government supposedly proposes to send up to sixty thousand men, the transports are returning to carry more troops.

 . . . There will probably be no plan to recover that position, which can be very advantageously defended with its reinforcements and aided by the U.S. Navy vessels.

 . . . General [Thomas W.] Sherman directed a proclamation to the inhabitants of South Carolina. Northern radicals have ridiculed this proclamation for its unconciliatory terms.

The success of this second expedition has caused the Lincoln government to consider organizing others. In Boston an expedition is being prepared to sail under the orders of General Butler. . . .

Two days after receiving the news of the Port Royal victory, the U.S. Navy corvette *San Jacinto* arrived at Fortress Monroe. It carried Mason and Slidell, who had been underway to the courts of London and Paris as Confederate ministers. . . . They had departed Havana in the British mail steamer *Trent* on 7 November, proceeding from Veracruz and heading for Saint Thomas, from where they intended to take the steamer for Southampton. The *San Jacinto* overtook the *Trent* in the Bahama Straits and boarded with an armed force to seize these commissioners. Mason, Slidell, and the *Trent's* captain protested against the force exercised against them, but they had to submit in the end. [106]

The prisoners were imprisoned in Fort Warren in Boston Harbor. The news of their capture produced great satisfaction in the northern states, filling the newspapers for several days. The conduct of the *San Jacinto's* captain has been universally approved. Apparently this government will not return the prisoners, even if England should demand that. No official decision has been adopted yet regarding the captain's conduct, nor has the English minister taken any step in anticipation of official information about the affair. Although all act as if it will not be a very serious business, a thousand conjectures exist regarding what decision the British government might adopt. This incident will prompt England to choose immediately the course it intends to pursue toward the United States. If England's intentions are hostile, they will certainly take advantage of this occasion, which could not be more favorable for them. Otherwise, England will probably be content with verbal satisfaction.

When the goleta *San Francisco* arrived in New York, it carried former Democratic California Senator William M. Gwin, whose sympathies favor secession. In San Francisco he took passage on the steamer for Panama. Before arriving there, he was arrested by General [Edwin V.] Sumner, who came aboard the steamer with five hundred men of the

U.S. regular army. Upon arriving at the isthmus, Gwin petitioned the Panamanian authorities to free him because the U.S. forces could not exercise jurisdiction in foreign territory. However, General Sumner refused to turn the prisoner over, disembarking his force in a hostile array and carrying Gwin to New York, where this government ordered his imprisonment in Fort Lafayette. The New Granadian minister of the administration of General [Tomás C. de] Mosquera witnessed these incidents. He arrived on the same steamer as General Sumner and his prisoner. Despite this grave affront to the sovereignty of a friendly nation, the incident has scarcely been talked about. It is unlikely to occasion major complications because of the weakness of the offended country.[107]

Thurlow Weed and Archbishop [John] Hughes of New York departed for Europe early this month as confidential agents of this government to work to prevent the Confederate commissioners from gaining ground in Europe. Edward Everett [of Massachusetts] will leave shortly with the same objective.[108]

On 9 November General McClellan divided the western states into five military departments. . . . He also demoted the officers promoted by General Frémont.

Frémont's removal did not produce any of the dangers feared. Abandoning Springfield, his successor countermarched all the forces to St. Louis. . . . The difficulty of defending Springfield and the southern part of the state against the southern forces prompted this withdrawal. General Hunter revoked almost all of Frémont's arrangements and disavowed Frémont's agreement with the rebel forces regarding the exchange of prisoners and the means of concluding hostilities in that state.

. . . The rebels have burned Warsaw [Kentucky] to prevent its serving as winter quarters for the federal forces.

. . . A battle took place at Belmont on 6 November. . . .

On 8 November General [William] Nelson's brigade engaged the dissident forces under the command of General Williams [sic—Lloyd Tilghman] in Paducah, Kentucky. . . .[109]

Meeting in Russellville, forty counties from southern Kentucky decided to disregard the state legislature and the federal government by refusing to pay taxes to either [the state or federal governments] or to organize troops for the service of the Richmond government. . . .[110]

The symptoms of unionism continue in eastern Tennessee. . . . The inhabitants there apparently have destroyed the railroad bridges that placed Richmond in communication with the South. . . . General Dix, commander of the federal forces in Baltimore, ordered the troops at his command to occupy the counties of Accomac and Northampton in eastern Virginia.

Before Port Royal's occupation, the governor of South Carolina directed the enclosed message to the legislature. The state has spent $1,889,371 on the war, the message reveals, and it has nineteen thousand men on the battlefield [i.e., Virginia], in addition to three thousand on war-footing in Charleston and twenty-one companies of cavalry at various points on the coast. According to this report, 10 percent of South Carolina's white [male] population enlisted in the war. Emotions [in South Carolina] were very excited after Port Royal's occupation. In different parts of the state, allegedly the black flag had been raised as a signal to exterminate the invaders and to indicate a war without quarter.

Because thirteen members of the crew of the privateer *Savannah* are being tried in Philadelphia, and because [William] Smith has been sentenced to death, the Richmond government has ordered an equal number of prisoners chosen by lot from the highest ranks in its control to be used in reprisal. The highest ranking prisoner will be treated in the same manner that the U.S. government treats Smith. This reveals how far the Confederates are prepared to go with reprisals. [111]

The South now possesses fifty-five privateers of which thirty-six are steamers. . . .

The Confederacy held elections at the beginning of this month. The persons currently serving as president and vice-president were elected unanimously for a six-year period. [112]

. . . Supposedly the Union has already enlisted the five hundred thousand men permitted by act of Congress. The southern forces amount to four hundred thousand men. . . .

Colonel [John] Cochrane of the U.S. First Rifle Battalion spoke very spiritedly while distributing winter clothing to his troops. Among other things, in the present war, he claimed, the southern slaves ought to be armed to fight in defense of their rights and of the cause of humanity. His audience applauded this idea. The secretary of war, having also been invited to speak, briefly stated his full agreement with Colonel Cochrane's ideas. . . . That speech has reopened the slavery question that has so divided the citizens of the North. Supposedly the speech was taken immediately to the cabinet, where three secretaries favored and the others opposed Colonel Cochrane's proposal. The president decided for the opponents. Doubtless as soon as Congress meets, the same question will rise up in its midst. [113]

Arriving from Panama, the steamer *Champion* brought a report . . . of an incident in Guaymas between natives and foreigners during which the U.S. consul had been imprisoned and three U.S. citizens have been murdered. . . . [Supposedly] the local authorities had arrested a U.S. citizen who, arriving in Manzanillo from California with a steamer loaded with ammunition, was sentenced to death for introducing contraband war material. . . . [114]

Romero to MRE, 9 December 1861, in Romero,
Correspondencia I, 631–35

. . . The president's annual message . . . is considered a statement of
conservative policy because it does not propose radical measures.

Under the circumstances, the president has acted very moderately in
exercising his discretionary powers, since he has allegedly only used them
when absolutely necessary to defend the constitution and the government
against rebel attacks. He also left several decisions to Congress in situa-
tions where he could have acted himself, but from which he abstained
because he did not consider action absolutely necessary. Certainly the
most philosophical and best-written part of the message is the final
section, in which he very ably defends the supremacy of labor over
property. In their defense of property the rebel states are expressing
aristocratic tendencies. In Virginia a constitutional amendment has been
proposed that restricts suffrage only to property owners.[115]

. . . Davis rejoiced at this year's abundant harvest and also because the
severed communication between the South and the rest of the world has
led to the development of manufacturing industry in the South. He
rejoiced also for the victory of southern forces over the U.S. Army. He
asserted that secession was final. He proposed the construction of a
railway line from Danville to Greensborough, so three complete lines
would bind the northern and southern states of the Confederacy together.
While condemning the United States for conducting a savage war without observing the practices of civilized nations, he said that military
operations will remain paralyzed in the winter. He revealed that proof
had been gathered to demonstrate the blockade's complete ineffec-
tiveness. This proof will be presented to those foreign governments that
wish to hear it.[116]

. . . Bills about slavery . . . have been presented almost daily. The
slavery question, which will certainly occupy much of Congress' time, is
currently one of the most complicated. Without exaggeration, except for
the abolitionist party, which is still in the minority, no two persons seem
to entertain the same idea about slavery. This divergence is observable
even in official areas and among the commanding generals of the military departments. Some, like General [James H.] Lane, claim that
slavery has caused the war and thus want the war directed against that
institution. Consequently, those slaves who join the war effort should be
freed and the government ought to accept as many as possible. Meanwhile, others, like General [Henry] Halleck, contend the war is not
against slavery. They forbid receiving fugitive slaves in their camp. They
order the slaves who have already fled to their camps returned to their
owners. Such arbitrary treatments are meted out to the unfortunate

Negroes in some places. Even here, at the seat of the government, all the Virginia Negroes who fled here have been placed in prison without examining whether they were free or slaves. They are held crammed and naked in one dirty cell. The senate's attention was called to this scandal. The senate passed a resolution asking the administration to explain why they are holding these individuals prisoners. Before this report was requested, the secretary of state had instructed the commander of the U.S. Army . . . to order the punishment of those people arresting Negroes who are under federal government protection.[117]

The completed investigation revealed that the abuse stemmed from the lower military authorities of the District of Columbia. Supposedly the radical senators and representatives will organize a faction to oppose the government for adopting conservative ideas.

The slavery question has been fermenting since before Congress met. In addition to General Cochrane's speech, . . . Senator Sumner delivered a grand oratorical tour de force on 27 November at Cooper's Institute in New York. He demonstrated that the only remedy against southern insurrection consisted in the abolition of slavery. General Lane, soon to take his senate seat, spoke in similar terms at a serenade his friends offered him on the day of his arrival [in Washington]. Everything indicates that slavery will not survive the war unharmed. A motion has already been made to emancipate the Negroes in the District of Columbia with indemnification for their owners. This measure, apparently soon to be adopted, will be the first step toward emancipation. The West Virginia convention proposed that the new state be a free state. Supposedly, Delaware and Maryland could easily adopt similar measures [liberating slaves], with the federal government indemnifying the slave owners.

Both houses have passed resolutions that sanction and approve the conduct of Captain [Charles] Wilkes, who took Mason and Slidell from the English steamer *Trent*. The secretary of the navy thanked him . . . for his service to his country.

Captain Wilkes, speaking at a dinner in his honor in Boston, contended he could have seized the captain of the *Trent* and had not done so only as a favor. Everywhere he has been honored with public demonstrations, which suggests that his conduct will not be disapproved, whatever Britain might demand, principally because this government has repeatedly sanctioned his actions in various official documents.

. . . The federal forces at Port Royal occupied the island of Tibec without resistance. The island has an important location in the mouth of the Savannah River. . . . The federal forces also occupied the island of Santa Elena near Hilton Head in the Beaufort River. The village of Beaufort, still unoccupied, remains in Negro hands.

Shooting has broken out in Pensacola Bay between Fort Pickens and the U.S. war vessels on one side and the Warrington arsenal on the other. . . .

The plantation owners on the South Carolina coast near Port Royal are burning their houses, cotton, and crops and carrying their slaves into the interior to prevent their falling into the hands of the federal forces. If it should come so far, the southern papers suggest all proprietors should follow this example. The secretary of the treasury issued instructions to regulate the manner of disposing of all property found inside Confederate lines that has been awarded to the U.S. government.

To strengthen the blockade and hermetically seal southern ports, this government has resorted to sinking stone-filled whale boats in the entrances [of southern ports]. . . . They have already sent out two expeditions destined for Charleston and Savannah.[118]

The Confederate Congress agreed to move the Confederate capital to Nashville, Tennessee. . . . Some contend that the decision reflects the Confederate government's insecurity in Richmond, which lies almost on the border of the rebel states. Others attribute it to Nashville's advantageous position exactly in the center of the Confederacy and at the junction of several important railroad lines. Nashville is also on the Cumberland River, still navigable some two hundred miles above Nashville, which empties into the Ohio. . . . [Since] the [proposed] change has greatly disgusted Virginia, . . . it will probably not be implemented. . . .

Another reason for the decision to move the capital could be the very serious danger for the secessionist cause of losing eastern Tennessee, [which] would remove one of the two communication lines of the Confederacy. Reports of the destruction of five railroad bridges on the Tennessee railway . . . have been fully confirmed. . . . On 1 December . . . in Morristown, [the] three thousand Tennessee unionists, under the command of the minister Parson Brownlow, defeated the Confederate forces sent to pursue him. . . . The victory was so overwhelming that the press requested Parson Brownlow be made a major general.

Some published fragments of General Beauregard's report on the battle of Bull Run have generated a polemic in the southern papers. In his report, Beauregard claimed that he wanted to follow the federal army after the defeat and that he proposed to President Davis immediately marching the southern army to Washington and into Maryland. Davis did not permit either option, and the South lost an opportunity that surely will not present itself again. The publication of these details has created some dissatisfaction in Louisiana and South Carolina against President Davis.[119]

Another change has occurred in Davis's cabinet. Benjamin's promotion to secretary of war left the post of attorney general vacant; it was conferred on Bragg. The civil war in Missouri continues to spread devastation. . . . General [Sterling] Price, commander of the dissidents in Missouri, indicated that he is weaker than generally supposed. He called on the citizens to enlist in his ranks, claiming that with only fifty thousand armed men the state could be saved. . . .

The civil war continues to spread in Kentucky. The convention meeting in the southern part of Kentucky . . . approved a declaration of independence and an act incorporating itself into the Confederacy. The Richmond government immediately accepted this act. Joint resolutions recently expelled Senator Breckinridge and Representative [Henry C.] Burnett, who participated in this convention, from the U.S. Congress.

The southern cause is losing ground in Virginia. The western section seems definitely to have seceded. . . . The forces that left Richmond to fight the unionists could not obtain their objective and had to retire to their winter quarters. The secessionist governor of Virginia directed a message to the legislature, revealing that Virginia actually has seventy thousand men under arms and has spent $6 million on the war since April.

. . . In the village of Hatteras . . . the appointed governor has . . . fixed the day for elections for the U.S. House of Representatives and called upon the people to obey the constitution and the federal government. This has rekindled hope among the unionist parties in the rebel states. The northern papers rejoice that the U.S. flag floats in all but two rebel states. . . .[120]

Romero to MRE, 31 December 1861, in Romero,
Correspondencia I, 673–75

Although both houses have witnessed a multitude of petitions requesting the abolition of slavery, the slavery question has not returned to stir things up. The most important law approved until now imposes an import duty of twenty cents per pound on tea, five cents per pound on coffee, and other duties on sugar and molasses. . . . The papers have blamed Congress for viewing the situation with unequalled apathy and for not proportioning the resources needed to conduct military operations.

This country and England have settled their difficulties arising from the seizure of Mason and Slidell from the *Trent*. . . .Although the English minister considers the settlement satisfactory, his government might not consider it so. England had demanded the return of the prisoners and an apology. However, the latter has not been conceded, at least not in the expected form.

This proposed settlement of the Mason and Slidell incident has further embittered the opinion of this people toward Great Britain. They feel humiliated by the return of the prisoners and they believe England intends to declare war on the United States in any event, if not over the *Trent* affair, then on another pretext. The English also attribute this [belligerant] intention to the United States. Since England has led abolitionism until now, [yet] in the present conflict has inclined toward those who seek to perpetuate and extend slavery, it has faced the accusation of perfidy and bad faith. England's course has alienated the sympathies of its best friends in this country. The tone taken by the English press with respect to the United States within a few days of this report [on a settlement to the *Trent* incident] has not failed to contribute to this result. Thus, a rupture between the two is not a remote possibility. The United States desires the break after the Civil War, which is not, however, very near its end. Presumably, England will not so complacently await a break.

The financial condition of this country raises serious concern. The banks have not received the secretary of the treasury's plan well. Rather than continuing to cooperate as previously in facilitating the necessary funds for the government, the banks apparently threatened to cease furnishing funds. The secretary of the treasury was in New York a while ago. His mission did not obtain satisfactory [resolutions]. Meanwhile, expenses run more than a million dollars daily, and the resources of the government are exhausted. This state begins to alarm the farsighted people who know the fatal consequences that could result from the lack of revenue. . . .

Meanwhile, the banks have simultaneously suspended specie payment. The U.S. treasury also adopted this measure shortly thereafter. The seemingly satisfactory reason currently given to justify that course and to calm public uneasiness is that, fearing a foreign war, foreigners have been selling their stocks and bonds in the businesses of this country and removing the specie from the country. The foreigners are also removing their deposits from the banks. The specie in the banks early last week amounted to little more than $30 million. At the end of the week it had decreased by about $10 million, although apparently the whole amount [the $10 million] had not been exported. Then, to prevent the withdrawal of the remaining $20 million in specie from circulation, the decision was made to cease specie payments. The gold premium over bank notes is now 2 percent.

On 11 December a ravenous fire began in Charleston. It continued for two days, destroying a large part of the city. . . .[121]

On 12 December seventeen whale boats loaded with stones were sunk in the channel to Charleston Harbor. . . . Learning of the Union intention in this respect, the English papers charged barbarity for resorting to these means. The same means were used previously to close the port of Savannah. The northern states cannot hide their joy in seeing disasters fall upon South Carolina, the birthplace of the insurrection. Besides the Charleston fire and the closing of its [chief] harbor, South Carolina has federal forces in Port Royal and the adjacent islands.

The southern forces defending Galveston Island have abandoned their position and retreated to Houston in the interior of Texas, . . . [which move] apparently produced displeasure in Texas.[122]

. . . General McClellan's health has deteriorated during the last few days although this apparently has not had anything to do with the suspended military operations this month.

General Butler's expedition, organized in Boston, . . . occupied Ship Island, directly in the mouth of the Mississippi. General [John W.] Phelps . . . immediately issued a proclamation to the inhabitants of the insurgent states regarding the slavery question. He claimed the slave states that entered the Union after independence had been illegally admitted and other similar things that produced a considerable reaction here. The proclamation led to his immediate removal.[123]

The same General Butler is organizing another expedition in Boston. . . .

General Burnside has been organizing another large-scale expedition in Annapolis. . . .

A bill pending in the U.S. Congress would authorize the expenditure of $50 million for the construction of armor-plated war steamships, similar to those made recently in France and England.[124]

Early this month a case similar to the English steamer *Trent* occurred in the Gulf of Mexico. Thomas S. Roget of Texas and [J. W.] Zacherie of New Orleans left Matamoros for Havanna on the English goleta *Victoria*. A U.S. steamer captured them and conducted them to Fortress Lafayette where they remain as prisoners. This case may well have the same solution as that of Mason and Slidell. . . .[125]

1862

Introduction to 1862

After the Spanish and British withdrew in early 1862, the French continued a unilateral campaign to force a conservative solution upon the divided Mexican society. One French objective was revealed when a letter from Napoleon III to General Elie F. Forey, the French commander in Mexico, was made public in 1862. Napoleon argued that the French government intended to prevent further U.S. penetration southward. Underscoring the "Latin" civilization of the former Spanish and Portuguese colonies, Napoleon intended to block Anglo-Saxon economic and political expansion south with a revitalized "Latin" [French] barrier. His objective would be served if a conservative, French-influenced government prevailed in Mexico. The French advance was temporarily halted when Juárez's forces defeated Foley's army at Puebla on 5 May (the *cinco de mayo* remains a major Mexican and Mexican-American celebration).

The liberal Republican party took advantage of the outbreak of war and the absence of southern mercantilist opposition to implement a host of development-oriented legislation. In February 1862, the Republican-dominated Congress passed a currency law that placed $450 million of paper money in circulation by 1865. In May 1862, Congress passed the Homestead Act (which had been defeated in 1860, in part due to solid southern opposition) and created the Department of Agriculture. In July 1862, it passed the Morrill Land Grant Act, encouraging agricultural and mining education and development of the west, and the Pacific Railroad Act, establishing a transcontinental railroad to link the Pacific coast to the eastern United States and facilitating the settlement and development of the west.

The land war assumed a major role in the public imagination in 1862. The early months saw a series of engagements in the west, in Missouri and Kentucky, and on various rivers. The most important river engagements were the fall of Forts Henry (on the Tennessee River) and Donaldson (on the Cumberland River) in February 1862, and the fall of New Orleans at the mouth of the Mississippi River in April. A large, bloody battle took place at Shiloh, Mississippi, in April 1862. After Shiloh, the western theater remained comparatively calm until the fall when major battles were fought at Perryville (October) and Murfreesboro (December).

The eastern theater remained relatively quiet until General George B. McClellan was compelled to advance in March. McClellan opted to transfer his forces to the peninsula east of Richmond and advance on the Confederates from that direction. Confederate General Robert E. Lee sought to undermine the transfer of the Union army to the peninsula by directing General Thomas "Stonewall" Jackson into the Shenandoah Valley from March until June. The peninsula campaign lasted five months but included only a few major engagements, the largest being the Seven Days' Battle in July. Lee, after shaking the confidence of the U.S. forces during the Seven Days' [Battle], transferred his army to threaten Washington and Maryland in order to compel the withdrawal of McClellan's forces. The second battle of Bull Run in August was followed by an invasion of Maryland and another indecisive battle at Antietam in September. Strategically these maneuvers compelled McClellan to move his army to the Washington area.

The heavy casualties with few lasting results and the uncertain purpose of the war greatly reduced enthusiasm in both the North and the South. In both armies, desertion ran at about 10 percent. The Confederate government instituted a draft in April 1862. All southern males between eighteen and thirty-five years of age were subject to a call for three years of service. Lincoln resisted efforts to make the abolition of slavery one of the Union war objectives. As volunteering declined and other forms of disillusionment and resistance increased, Lincoln recognized the potential domestic and foreign value of emancipation. He used the "apparent" victory of Antietam, because the on-marching Confederate advance was stopped and the Confederate forces retreated to Virginia, as an excuse to offer the preliminary emancipation proclamation. Major foreign groups were eager to support some sort of crusade to terminate the hated institution of slavery and to find public justification for their continued support of the U.S. government.

The year 1862 had begun with a significant radical Republican intrusion into the political strategy of the Union—the demand for the removal of Secretary of War Simon Cameron. Edwin Stanton replaced Cameron in January. The year closed with seven radical leaders meeting with Lincoln to urge the removal of Secretary of State Seward and his replacement with Secretary of the Treasury Salmon Chase. Lincoln revealed that he held letters of resignation from both; the radicals did not want their fair-haired Chase out of the cabinet, so they retreated.

Romero insisted that the tripartite intervention was not primarily seeking the repayment of European loans, nor even the return of the Mexican conservatives to power, but rather conquest and empire. He sought to persuade the Lincoln administration and Congress that the loan would effectively counter the French, Spanish, and British violation of the Monroe Doctrine. The loan would also encourage Mexican liberal resistance to the European powers. Romero continued his lobbying of Senator Sumner out of recognition of the Senator's powerful position, Postmaster General Blair, and Representative Jacob Cox of Ohio.

Negotiations on extradition and postal treaties moved toward completion because these two treaties involved low-cost matters of obvious, mutually shared liberal interest. The commerce treaty between Mexico and the United States bogged down because, while both sides saw advantages in the pact, the Mexicans judged that they could use the commercial treaty as leverage to extract a loan or, at the very least, an outspoken U.S. opposition to the intervention. In the midst of a civil war of uncertain duration and intensity, the Lincoln administration and the Congress were not prepared to pay such a price. Despite expressions of deep sympathy for the Mexican liberals and condemnation of European intervention, Montgomery Blair finally had to talk to Romero in terms of steps that would allow Juárez to continue to resist until the Civil War was terminated and the United States could intervene in Mexico with force.

As the prospect of a major Mexican diplomatic victory in the form of a loan or some equivalent activity faded, Romero sought to locate alternative avenues of influence and support in the United States. He established confidential access to State Department materials, most likely through Edward Plumb, Robert Chew, and Henry Roy de la Reintrie, all of whom served with the State Department during the 1860s. In mid-1862, when the tripartite intervention disintegrated (Spain and England withdrew) and it became evident that France expected more than mere repayment of the French-held loans and investments, the Lincoln administration tried to resolve a domestic military problem and to alleviate the crisis in Mexico with one dramatic act. Aged and infirm General Winfield Scott was considered a hindrance to the proper military conduct of the war, yet he retained a reputation as a great soldier. The Lincoln administration sought to shuffle Scott off to Mexico as a special minister to compliment Corwin's political role. Scott's appearance would lend military weight to the U.S. mission in Mexico. Scott's appointment would underscore the U.S. commitment for the French while simultaneously removing the aged general from Washington and permitting the promotion of men like General George B. McClellan. Ultimately, Scott refused the Mexican mission.

Another Union scheme occupied Romero during 1862, Many in the North wished to remove the blacks—both slaves and free—from the United States. The matter became urgent as the war lengthened into mid-1862 because such men did not want the war to be interpreted as a war to free the blacks. Nor did they want the blacks free to live in the North. Various schemes surfaced to colonize the blacks in Africa (some had already returned to Liberia), the Caribbean islands (Haiti or elsewhere), Central America, Brazil, Ecuador, or Mexico. Proponents of the projects to colonize blacks in Mexico, Central America, and the Caribbean usually pointed out that ridding the United States of blacks could be an act of great benefit for the Union. Assuming a wise selection of locations, the blacks sent into these regions would straddle the main transit lines linking the Atlantic and Pacific oceans. Thus, the black colonists would strengthen U.S. influence in areas of vital importance. These blacks would also serve as economic, political, and cultural wedges in these areas. Blair, claiming to speak for the Lincoln administration, mentioned the prospects of obtaining colonizing sites in Mexico. Like the Central American diplomats, Romero proved very skeptical. Ultimately, he made it clear to Blair that the blacks could only enter Mexico if they surrendered their U.S. citizenship and became Mexicans. However, whenever U.S. protection of the black colonists was rejected, the U.S. interests urging the colonization projects lost interest in the schemes.

Political Reviews—1862

Romero to MRE, 21 January 1862, in Romero, *Correspondencia* II, 14–18

The often speculated change in Lincoln's cabinet finally occurred, although in an unexpected manner. Secretary of War Cameron . . . resigned on 13 January. The president immediately nominated Edwin M. Stanton of Pennsylvania to replace him. . . . Cameron apparently did not even resign, but the president removed him. . . . I judge two reasons are most likely. First, the president and Cameron hold divergent views on the question of slavery. The latter favors emancipation and wants to arm the Negroes to make them contribute to the war against the South. Lincoln opposes both measures. The second reason relates to Cameron being discredited because of the contracts he signed for armaments, clothing, and food for the army. Since the last session, the nature of these contracts has attracted the attention of the House, which named a committee to investigate and to report on the contracts. . . . The fears regarding the abuses committed in these transactions were confirmed and many other previously unknown frauds were uncovered. Cameron's departure is also attributed to the antagonism between himself and General McClellan regarding how to pursue military operations.[1]

Stanton's nomination as secretary of war suggests the president proposes to change policy in a conservative direction. Stanton is and always has been a Democrat. . . . His nomination encountered some opposition in the Senate but was approved thirty-eight to two. Stanton's nomination apparently has not greatly impressed the Republicans. . . .

Following the resignation of Cassius M. Clay [U.S. minister to Russia], who has expressed a desire to return to this country in order to participate in the military operations, Cameron was named U.S. minister to St. Petersburg. Cameron's nomination encountered very violent opposition in the Senate from Democrats and radical Republicans. After two days of heated debate, it was approved twenty-eight to fourteen.

Similar to the French protest and probably instigated by the English government, the Austrian government instructed its representative in Washington to protest against Captain Wilkes's conduct while capturing the *Trent*. Seward responded that the United States had already settled this matter in the way Austria desired. . . . Russia and Prussia have made manifestations of the same nature.[2]

In the Senate session of 9 December, Sumner, senator from Massachusetts and chairman of the foreign relations committee, made a speech . . . that the press praised greatly. He attempted to demonstrate that the United States had returned Mason and Slidell in order to win the principle of freedom of the seas that it has always defended. Great Britain, belligerent in almost all the European wars of the last two centuries, has always supported unlimited extension of belligerent rights on the high seas against neutral rights. Meanwhile, the United States, having remained neutral until now except on two occasions, has sought to restrict belligerent rights. England is now converted into a defender of neutral rights because a case has arrived in which it is a neutral.

With its position of the *Trent* incident, the United States claims England has renounced its old pretensions and recognized the doctrine that the United States has defended. Allegedly, the United States consented to return those prisoners in order to be consistent with its principles. No one would have doubted the sincerity of this explanation, if the prisoners had been placed free immediately after their arrival in this country. However, since the prisoners were not freed until after the English demands and threats had arrived and after Captain Wilkes's conduct had been approved in different ways, it is not venturesome to believe that reasons distinct from their old principles motivated the United States.

. . . The House approved a bill to abolish the congressmen's franking privilege, which costs the treasury from four to six million dollars annually. It also approved a bill authorizing the expenditure of six million dollars to build and repair forts on the north coast and on the Canadian border. On 6 January, representative [Roscoe] Conkling of New York very bitterly censured the military authorities for the defeat of the federal forces at Balls Bluff on 21 October 1861.

During the Senate debate on the House-approved bill, Hall [sic—John P. Hale of New Hampshire?] proposed to amend the bill that authorizes the secretary of the navy to expend $50 million in the construction of armor-plated steam war vessels. He would grant the authority to the president because the secretary of the navy does not inspire confidence and because of the investigations [into waste and corruption] being conducted by the House committee. This investigation tarnished Welles's reputation because he had given preference to a relative to purchase vessels, and because of the commissions that he had assigned. After some discussion, which on one side pointed to the fact of government squandering and on the other side defended Welles's honesty, the Senate agreed to request a report from Welles, . . [which] completely vindicates Welles's good name and his zeal in the interests of his country. . . .[3]

As chairman of the judiciary committee, Senator Trumbull of Illinois has proposed a bill that would confiscate the property of dissidents and would grant freedom to their slaves. . . .

Both houses have approved a bill that proposes to collect $150 million in direct taxes yearly for the duration of the war. . . . Except for this measure, . . . Congress has not done anything to provide the government with urgently needed resources. The banks have refused to advance more money until they are given satisfactory guarantees. They have sent representatives to this city to arrive at an understanding with the congressional committees on finance and with the secretary of the treasury. Several conferences have been held, but apparently without achieving a satisfactory result. . . . Some bankers favor the secretary of the treasury's plan to contrive financial resources while others oppose the plan. Meanwhile, treasure notes have forced specie to disappear from circulation. Fearing things will get worse, some House members have proposed a bill to impede the exportation of specie. Meanwhile the premium between metal and treasury notes, which was 2 percent at the time of my last review, has risen to 5 percent.

A short while ago more English forces arrived at Portland [Maine], destined for Canada. Since the St. Lawrence River is frozen, they could not move to Quebec. This government permitted them to pass across U.S. territory to reach their destination. This decision has been credited to the government's desire to gain Great Britain's goodwill, which recent events have noticeably reduced. Maine's Senate ostensibly viewed this permission disfavorably. . . .[4]

General Burnside's expedition left Old Point with several war vessels, transports, and a landing force of about twenty thousand men. . . .

The other expedition, prepared in Cairo under the command of

General [Ulysses S.] Grant, also departed down the Mississippi River toward New Orleans. . . .

General Butler has been in Washington arranging the departure of another expedition. . . .

General [Thomas W.] Sherman's forces, which occupy Port Royal, advanced on the Beaufort River and engaged the rebels. Whether this expedition's goal was Charleston or Savannah was unannounced; it already seems too late to capture either of those cities. . . . At the beginning of the month, Fort Pickens again opened fire upon the rebel batteries in Pensacola. The fort's artillery fire again incended the naval yard at Warrington. . . .

Yesterday the telegraph announced two complete victories in Kentucky for unionist forces over the dissidents under the command of General [Felix] Zollicoffer, who died in the first action at Sommerset. . . . Supposedly this victory has given an immense advantage to the federal army in Kentucky because it has broken the fortified line of the southern army. . . .

The Army of the Potomac remains in its old position. During the past month it has not been in an engagement, nor even a skirmish. Its strength is calculated at two hundred thousand men, the U.S. force in Kentucky at one hundred thousand, and the U.S. force in Missouri also at one hundred thousand.

General McClellan continues to enjoy the president's confidence. Congress has named a committee to investigate the conduct of the war. McClellan appeared before that committee to explain what he had accomplished until now, what inconveniences he has faced, and what he intends to do in the future. Allegedly, his explanations satisfied the committee. General Frémont, who is now in this city, also testified before that committee.[5]

Confederate General Pillow resigned the command he held in Memphis because of differences with the Richmond government.

The rebel Congress has approved a law prohibiting newspapers from publishing military news and items relative to the operations of campaigns.[6]

. . . The president refuses to submit the documents relative to the European intervention in Mexico to Congress because he considers it incompatible with the public interest to publish these documents at this time. . . .[7]

Romero to MRE, 4 February 1862, in Romero, *Correspondencia*
II, 40–43

. . . General Burnside's expedition, from which so much was expected, experienced a storm that will neutralize all the advantages it
might otherwise have gained, . . . since the southern forces already knew
which points the expedition menaced and had ample time to reinforce
and fortify them.

. . . Another expedition is preparing to go south . . . under the orders
of General [Samuel] Heintzelman, now commanding a corps of the
Army of the Potomac. The second expedition, under General Burnside
[*sic*—Butler], is ready to depart from Old Point for Ship Island, near the
Mississippi Delta.

These expeditions have not lived up to their original expectations.
Until now these expeditions have only managed to occupy the area near
where they disembark, without attacking the principal cities, even though
Charleston and Savannah were unprepared when General [Thomas W.]
Sherman landed at Port Royal. Moreover, when summer and the unhealthy season arrive in the ports, the federal troops will find it almost
impossible to hold their positions. . . .

Despite Europe's outcry against blockading southern ports by obstruct-
ing the channels, a second fleet of whale boats loaded with stone has
sailed to finish the operation.

. . . The departure of an expedition headed down the Mississippi
under General Grant's command has not been confirmed. Therefore,
Columbus is under no immediate danger of attack. Since the Richmond
government has transferred General Beauregard to Columbus, the South
must lay great importance on possession of this city. Having previously
commanded the rebel army on the Potomac, he is one of the ablest
Confederate commanders.

The State Department has issued instructions relative to the blacks
imprisoned in this city for no other reason than their color. If they are not
charged with a crime within ten days, they are to be released. In the
future they can only be arrested on specific charges. This will belatedly
end one of the greatest arbitrary actions in the annals of civilized countries. These acts were committed in this city with the knowledge and
acceptance of the Union government and they were only revealed when
two or three senators accidentally visited the prison.[8]

. . . Debate over the expulsion of Indiana Senator [Jesse D.] Bright for
having written a letter to Jefferson Davis has occupied the Senate almost
exclusively. Bright's letter recommended a person who wanted to introduce improvements in firearms. Senator [John P.] Hale voiced an opinion
on the secretary of navy's conduct in conceding a 2 percent commission
to [Edward D.] Morgan, who purchased several vessels for U.S. service.

Hale believes the $80,000 commission should be returned to the treasury and Morgan should be assigned a modest salary while in government service. Probably this incident has prompted newspapermen to state that Welles will leave the navy department and will be succeeded by General Banks. One ordinarily well-informed person has assured me that Secretary of the Interior [Caleb B.] Smith will be named to the Supreme Court and that [David] Davis of Illinois will replace Smith in the Interior Department.[9]

Neither federal house has done anything yet to allocate resources to the government. . . . Naturally, this has caused considerable unquietness and made this government's situation more difficult each day. Monthly expenses are not less than $45 million. As things go, it is more likely to increase than decrease in the future. Senator [James F.] Simmons presented a resolution yesterday to establish a national bank.

The House has approved a bill . . . to prohibit U.S. citizens from engaging in traffic in Asiatics, called coolies. It will probably pass the Senate with few modifications. . . .

Kansas Senator General [James Henry] Lane left a little while ago for Leavenworth. He intended to lead an expedition being organized to go south, allegedly to foment insurrection among the slaves. Before General Lane arrived in Leavenworth, General [David] Hunter, commander of the Military Department of Kansas, hurriedly departed with the expedition under his orders. This has greatly disgusted the abolitionist senators. . . . The Senate asked the administration for information about these events and particularly what orders had been issued.[10]

The end of the present Civil War is still very remote. Nevertheless, this government is already occupied with how to treat southern territory when the South is subjugated. Supposedly, the cabinet is divided on this matter. One view favors dealing with them as states, recognizing their constitutional rights as such. The second view wants to treat them as conquered territory, as if they were federal territories.

On 6 January, the Virginia governor sent a message to the state legislature proposing the adoption of some resolutions from the Georgia legislature about pursuing the present war with the greatest vigor and activity until the United States recognizes the independence of the southern states without condition or reservation. The resolutions and Governor Letcher's message, which quotes from the Declaration of Independence, level the same charges against this government that the thirteen colonies made against the government of George III of England in 1776. This very clearly reveals how unreconciled the southern spirit is and, by the same token, how remote the present Civil War in this country is from the end.[11]

The Tennessee legislature has gone still further, . . . declaring that if the Union government should send commissioners to Richmond to discuss reconstructing the Union, the Confederate government should dismiss them immediately.

. . . *De Bow's Review*, considered a semiofficial source for Richmond government policy, explained why the rebel army has preferred the defensive and revealed the blindest confidence in the South's strength and ability to conserve its independence. . . .

Romero to MRE, 19 February 1862, in Romero, *Correspondencia* II, 56–58

After encountering so many obstacles at first, General Burnside's expedition has obtained better success than generally expected. While passing from Pamlico Sound to Albemar Sound, the expedition attacked and captured Roanoke Island. . . . Commodore [Louis M.] Goldsborough, commanding the U.S. naval forces, moved at once against Elisabeth City on the North Carolina coast. The defending forces evacuated that city. . . .[12]

Tennessee. The U.S. squadron organized on the Mississippi under Commodore [Andrew Hull] Foote ascended the Tennessee River to Fort Henry, which surrendered unconditionally. . . . Shortly later, General Grant, who commanded the expedition against western Tennessee, defeated the rebels . . . at Fort Donelson on the Cumberland River. . . . Among the prisoners were Generals Pillow, [Albert Sydney] Johnston, and Buckner, who are among the leading southern commanders. . . . Certainly the federal forces will not remain idle after the victory but will use it to obtain still greater advantages. The federal steamers have climbed the Tennessee River to Florence, Alabama. They have received marked demonstrations of sympathy everywhere, which has renewed the Union government's confidence in the desire of the South's population, now subjugated by the rebels, to conserve the Union.[13]

The advantages acquired by this government do not stop here. The Kentucky dissidents suddenly abandoned their camp at Bowling Green, where they had united a sizeable force to hold the Union forces in check. Federal troops quickly occupied Bowling Green. Rebel General Polk also abandoned Springfield, Missouri, which Union General [Samuel R.] Curtis occupied at once.

These events have so satisfied this government and the northern people that already a widespread belief suggests the civil war will be over within ninety days. Nevertheless, this does not appear very probable to me. . . .

General Stone . . . was arrested for treason and sent to Fortress Lafayette. . . . The secretary of war also ordered the arrest of Joes, correspondent of the *New York Herald*, for attempting surrepticiously to obtain secret reports on military operations for his newspaper.[14]

The secretary of war ordered the reestablishment in its old vigor of the right of *habeas corpus*, which the secretary of state had suspended. In the future, the secretary of war instructs the War Department to order arrests.

The congressional . . . debate on the section of the treasury note bill proposing legal and compulsory circulation has chiefly occupied both houses during the past fortnight. At first a strong opposition arose against that section. However, after the government employed all its resources to maintain this provision, Congress accepted it. The bill authorized the government to emit $150 million in treasury notes that draw no interest and that have no fixed time for redemption. Their legal and compulsory circulation makes them real paper money. The opponents considered that section one of the rudest blows that the credit of this government could receive. [15]

The Senate Committee of Foreign Relations reported in favor of recognizing the independence of and naming a chargé to Haiti and Liberia [two black Republicans]. The Senate still has not discussed this matter. [16]

Sumner presented resolutions relative to the [political] character with which to consider the southern region when it again obeys this government. These resolutions propose considering the southern states as territories and declaring slavery abolished in those states by the very act of insurrection.

The Senate committee on the District of Columbia reported in favor of a bill to abolish slavery in the District. [17]

The Delaware legislature presented a bill to abolish slavery in that state, indemnifying the slave owners from the federal treasury.

Seward sent the Senate communications regarding the presentation of U.S. citizens to the French emperor. Since presentation was a favor of the emperor, this government decided that U.S. citizens must abide by any terms that he chooses to concede them. . . .

Romero to MRE, 11 March 1862, in Romero, *Correspondencia* II, 85–88

After the fall of Fort Donelson, the southern forces evacuated Clarksville on the bank of the Tennessee River, thus opening up the navigation of that river to Nashville, capital of Tennessee. Since the dissident troops in Nashville were demoralized and did not consider themselves strong enough to resist the armored war steamers, they abandoned the city. As occurred in Clarksville, the Union troops of General [Don Carlos] Buell soon occupied Nashville. The rebel governor of Tennessee moved to well-fortified Memphis on the Mississippi. He called the legislature into session there. Because of these movements, Tennessee, which was previously entirely in rebel hands, is now in possession of this government. Lincoln hastened to name Senator Andrew Johnson the provisional governor of Tennessee, first giving him the rank of brigadier general. Much is expected from this nomination. . . . Johnson, previously governor of Tennessee, is senator for that state now and has great influence there, especially among the unionists. . . . [18]

The evacuation of Nashville followed that of Columbus, which, after the evacuation of Bowling Green, had been the only point in Kentucky remaining in rebel control. Intending to establish themselves in Columbus permanently, the [Confederates] had constructed fortifications that prompted the newspapers to call it the "Sebastopol" of the west. A large part of Columbus was burned before the dissidents vacated it. Now it is in federal hands.

General Curtis managed to expel the rebel forces of Generals Sterling Price and McCulloch from Missouri. Now he is pursuing them into Arkansas, where he has seized Lafayettesville. [19]

Thus, the capture of Fort Donelson led to this government's acquisition of control of one whole state and the recovery of two that previously were divided and where the rebels possessed very advantageous and well-fortified strategic points.

Abandoning Columbus made Memphis the next point on the Mississippi that the federal army in the west will be directed toward. . . .

The Army of the Potomac is preparing to advance. . . . General Banks's corps crossed the Potomac River late last month, occupying Harper's Ferry, Martinsburg, Charleston, and Leesburgh. The Confederates have concentrated in Winchester under General Jackson. There the Confederates have the advantage of being able to move by rail in a few hours to Manassas where the principal rebel fortification near the Potomac is located. . . . If all goes well at Manassas, the insurrection could be considered nearing its end, since the federal army will move to Richmond without delay. The public can scarcely contain its growing impatience for the Army of the Potomac to move.

General Burnside occupied Winston and Edenton in North Carolina, destroying the railroad bridges that connect that state with Richmond and Norfolk, Since Burnside threatens Norfolk, President Davis has declared that city in a state of siege and suspended the right of *habeas corpus*. [20]

President Davis finally recognized this large chain of Confederate reverses. . . . He confessed that events have revealed a Confederate government that has attempted more than was within its reach. In addition to the demoralization derived from the reverses, the southern army faces the inconvenience that the enlistment of its men *mostly for one year* expires this month. All do not seem disposed to reenlist for the duration of the war. The unionist spirit has begun to awaken in Richmond and in other places. Posters have already appeared in the streets, and allegedly secret organizations of unionists exist. These signs have alarmed the authorities and led to the arrest of various people. Davis issued a proclamation on 1 March, declaring martial law in Richmond and its vicinity.[21]

Nevertheless, Davis has not expressed alarm in his most recent messages. He has spoken as if Confederate independence were fully assured. The recent defeats, he claimed, will only further harden the spirit of the southern people who have demonstrated such zealousness for their independence and who will be disposed to make new sacrifices to conserve it.

The facts confirm these words. On 8 March a naval battle took place near Fortress Monroe, revealing the South's great determination. In this battle the Confederate fleet carried the honors of the day. When abandoning the Norfolk naval yard, the federal forces had sunk the frigate *Merrimac*, one of the best in the federal navy. The Confederates managed to refloat, . . . repair, arm, and armor it. . . . It sailed against the federal squadron in Old Point. It sunk the frigate *Cumberland*, captured the *Congress* of the same class [as the *Cumberland*], and damaged the remaining ships, obliging them to retreat. . . . It will surely return soon to do battle against enemies it can fight so advantageously. This news produced the greatest alarm in Washington here because it was feared that the *Merrimac* might bombard Fortress Monroe, or go to New York, sink the merchant vessels, and bombard that city.[22]

. . . Until now southern policy has purposely remained defensive. A large part of the country favors taking the offensive. Since the former policy has produced such bad results, a change to the offense will not encounter any difficulty.

On 21 February, a bitter indecisive fight occurred between forces from New Mexico and from Texas at Valverde, ten miles from Fort Craig in New Mexico. . . .[23]

The new Confederate Congress opened its sessions in Richmond on February 18. Nineteen senators and eighty-seven representatives were present at the first session. The next day they counted the electoral votes for president and vice-president of the Confederacy. All 109 votes favored Jefferson Davis for the first office and Alexander H. Stephens for the second. . . . Thus, the permanent government of the Confederate States was organized. . . .

The federal secretary of war recently issued two orders. The first directs two commissioners to examine the grounds for detaining people in military prisons and either place them at liberty or bring them to court. The second orders military possession of the telegraph lines, prohibiting newspapers from sending messages which reveal military movements and prohibiting newspapers generally from publishing news about military movements. This latter measure is absolutely necessary. Thanks to the telegraph and to the many newspaper reporters in the war theaters, it is truly impossible to keep even the most current and delicate military operations secret. Some papers have criticized the order as an attack upon freedom of the press.[24]

The State Department has repealed the president's order that no one can leave this country without a passport issued or visaed by the State Department.

. . . The Italian government has complimented this government for the fine solution to the Mason and Slidell incident.

On 1 March, the president . . . asked Congress to adopt a resolution declaring that the U.S. government should give the necessary financial aid to any state adopting the gradual abolition of slavery. The abolitionist and moderate press have received this message with the greatest enthusiasm, since it suggests the president has finally decided for the abolition of slavery. Since the constitution only permits the states to legislate on the matter of slavery, the president has placed himself on constitutional terrain. The proposed resolution merely offers an inducement to encourage the states to abolish slavery. . . .[25]

On 25 February, . . . the secretary of the treasury explained that this government spent $1,500,000 daily, the budget deficit amounted to $26,430,557.83, and the floating debt has reached more than $40 million. Congress decided to pay the creditors with treasury bonds.

The House Finance Committee presented a bill to establish a direct tax . . . to raise the government revenue required for the necessities of war and to pay the interest on the public debt, which has increased very much. Congress still is not debating this measure.

The Senate is debating a bill to confiscate the property of persons who have participated in the southern insurrection and to grant liberty to their slaves. . . . Those opposed to any compromise defended the bill, while those seeking a conciliatory course in order to arrange a settlement or compromise are opposed to it.

In New York City on 21 February, Nathaniel Gordon, captain of the boat *Erie*, suffered the ultimate penalty for the infamous crime of slave trading. Since the atrocious crime was encouraged more than castigated under the Democratic administrations, this is surely the first case demanding inflexible compliance with the law. Gordon's death deeply disturbed New York. Unprecedented steps were taken to save his life. However, with a firmness that honors him, the president denied the pardon requested by millions of citizens. . . .[26]

In a battle lasting three days near Sugar Creek, Arkansas, the federal army in the southeast, commanded by General Curtis, obtained a victory over the combined rebel forces of Generals [Earl] Van Dorn, McCulloch, Price, and [James] McIntosh. . . .[27]

Commodore [Samuel Francis] Dupont occupied Brunswick, Georgia, and Fernandina, Florida.

General [Joseph] Hooker's corps, opposite Aquia Creek . . . crossed the river and occupied the previously abandoned rebel position.

By abandoning its battery positions on the Virginia bank, the South raised the blockade of the Potomac. . . .

Romero to MRE, 21 March 1862, in Romero, *Correspondencia* II, 99–101

. . . The Confederate forces have abandoned their positions in Centerville and Manassas. . . . They obviously do not consider themselves sufficiently strong to defend the terrain that they selected and have fortified for nearly a year and upon which they have obtained their principal victories. Centerville, Manassas, and Winchester are now in federal hands.

The evacuation of Manassas created the greatest impression here. General McClellan has been most bitterly censured for permitting the escape [withdrawal] of the flower of the Confederate army with all its trains and munitions.

. . . Apparently the government decided that all federal armies would make a simultaneous forward move on this past 22 February. For unknown reasons, the corps of the Army of the Potomac did not move on that date. Allegedly, after the order was issued, the generals met to discuss the possibilities and convenience of such a movement. Supposedly, four generals favored and eight, including General McClellan, opposed the movement. The president overruled the decision of the generals and instructed them to conduct the movement. He divided the Army of the Potomac into four corps, placing a general who had favored the move at the head of each corps.

On 11 March, after the evacuation of Manassas became public, the president removed General McClellan from command of the whole federal army, while retaining him in command of the Army of the Potomac. Moreover, he established two military departments in the west, one for the Mississippi and the other for the mountains, conferring the commands upon Generals Halleck and Frémont respectively.

. . . The location of the Confederate forces is entirely unknown. General McClellan has neither pursued them nor moved from Manassas yet. On the fourteenth he explained his reasons for not moving forward and offered actively to pursue the military operations. He recalled his earlier promise of a short campaign.

Since General McClellan is a Democrat, the radical Republicans oppose him. Should he become more successful, they fear he might attain the presidency in the next election. From the beginning, they already charge, he conducted his military campaign more with an eye on political success than on the public interest.[28]

The federal army of the west continues to move south, overcoming the obstacles opposing it. On 13 March, General [John] Pope's troops attacked and captured New Madrid on the Mississippi River. . . .

The dissidents have fortified Island Number 10 lying in the Mississippi River between New Madrid and Memphis. On 16 March, an attack was commenced on that position . . . , but it has not fallen yet. . . .

On March 14, at Newburn, North Carolina, General Burnside's expedition obtained another victory over the dissidents. . . .

There are no more details of the action near Fort Craig, New Mexico, on 21 February. . . . The federal forces abandoned Albuquerque and withdrew to the Union fort. . . . Thus, the dissidents seemingly have gained ground in the New Mexico territory.

President Davis informed the Confederate Congress that he has suspended Generals Floyd and Pillow for having retreated from Fort Donelson.

The dissident governor of Virginia issued a proclamation calling the state militia and volunteers to arms to fill the additional forty thousand men contingent requested by the Confederate government.

. . . Senator Hale presented a bill . . . to emancipate the slaves living in the District of Columbia and to abolish slavery there. . . .

Senator Hale presented another bill . . . to authorize the government to order an armored ram and also some armored steamers, and to procure the completion of the armored battery proposed by Stevens. . . . The success of the armored steamers in the waters of Old Point produced this reaction. The armored steamer will completely revolutionize the navies of the world.

The House has been almost exclusively occupied in debating the bill to levy a direct tax. That law burdens industry and property very heavily. . . .

The House Committee on Territories presented a bill to organize the Arizona territory. The House will probably approve the bill because many members of both houses have purchased land or mining stock and thus wish to organize the territory to increase their property's value. The same people want this government to order some force to Arizona to end the incursions of barbarians.

The president signed a joint resolution declaring that the U.S. Army or Navy are in no way obligated to seize fugitive slaves, nor to return them to their owners. With this action the infamous fugitive slave law has received the first death blow. . . .

Romero to MRE, 14 April 1862, in Romero, *Correspondencia* II, 132–36

. . . Several skirmishes occurred near Winchester between the forces of General [James] Shields and rebel General Jackson. Each side claimed victory in a formal battle on the last day. Its results, nevertheless, were inconsequential. General Shields was wounded. . . .

General Burnside occupied Beaufort, North Carolina, without resistance. The Confederate steamer *Nashville*, which was in Beaufort, managed to escape from the federal pursuit, thus generating complaints against the secretary of navy. One detachment from General Burnside's expedition occupied Washington, North Carolina, after the dissidents had evacuated and burned the city.

Commodore Dupont, who commands the squadron off the coast of South Carolina and Georgia, has undertaken several expeditions to different points in Florida, taking Jacksonville and St. Augustine without resistance. . . . This government has organized a new military department from the places it occupies in South Carolina, Georgia, and Florida. General Hunter was named commander of this department. . . . General [Thomas W.] Sherman, its previous commander, has returned to Washington. . . .[29]

The union military operations against Island Number 10 in the Mississippi River . . . ended on 8 April, when the Confederate defenders evacuated that island. Commodore Foote occupied it at once. . . .

Most rebel forces in the southeast have been concentrated in Corinto, Mississippi, to prevent this government from obtaining possession of the Mississippi valley and the capability of moving down to New Orleans. General Beauregard and other leading Confederate officers have moved to Corinto. The federal forces under General Grant arrived at Pittsburg's Landing, Tennessee, a few miles from Corinto. General Buell was expected with considerable reinforcements to attack the Confederate positions. General Beauregard was determined to attack his adversaries before the expected reinforcements arrived. On 6 April, a hard battle occurred at Pittsburg's Landing, in which the dissidents obtained very important advantages. . . . The following day fortune favored the federals, obliging their opponents to fall back on Corinto. . . . The battle is described as the hardest and bloodiest of the present campaign. . . .[30]

This government has received such favorable reports with the greatest joy. The president . . . suggested the people should give thanks to the All Powerful. . . . The secretary of war had ordered a hundred cannon salute be fired in the arsenal of this city in honor of the victory and the chaplains of each unit to offer prayers of thanksgiving for the victories.

Reportedly with a hundred thousand men under General McClellan's command, the Army of the Potomac embarked at Alexandria for Fort Monroe early this month. From Fort Monroe it advanced over land towards Richmond. The rebels fell back on the previously fortified Yorktown. . . . General McClellan arrived before the enemy's positions on the fifth. . . . Encountering very strong works, he decided not to assault them but preferred to adopt formal siege operations.[31]

The armored steamer *Merrimac*, which the Confederates have renamed *Virginia*, has reappeared, repaired and reinforced in its armor. . . .

From the first corps of the Army of the Potomac, which has occupied Manassas and which will probably march on Richmond from there, they have organized the new Department of the Rappahannock, which was placed under the command of General McDowell.

General Mitchell occupied Huntsville, Alabama, and cut one of the railroads that places Richmond in communication with the South of the Confederacy. . . .

From the official documents that Davis sent to the Confederate Congress, it appears that the Confederate army contained 465,000 men on 1 May, of which . . . 170,000 are in Virginia.

. . . The [federal] House just finished debating the bill on direct taxation that the Senate has passed. At the conclusion of the debate, [Thaddeus] Stevens, chairman of the finance committee, stated that the government's daily expenses were more than $2 million. A proposed tax of $2 per slave was rejected.

The Senate approved and the president signed the resolution, initiated by the executive and adopted by the House, that would grant financial aid to those states wishing to abolish slavery.

The two chambers also approved a bill to abolish slavery in the District of Columbia, indemnifying loyal proprietors. In addition, Congress appropriated $100,000 to subsidize transportation costs for Negroes who wished to emigrate.

The current congressional position against slavery will be changed. Senator [Henry] Wilson presented a bill on the return of runaway slaves that significantly moderates the barbarous rigor of the 1850 law that is currently in effect. The Senate approved Sumner's resolution, stating that color should make no difference in carrying of the U.S. mail.

Representative [Isaac N.] Arnold of Illinois presented a bill to declare liberty a national [force?] in the United States and slavery a devisive [force?]. This resolution forewarned that slavery would remain abolished in all present territories or those acquired in the future, regardless of how acquired, in all places purchased by the United States to erect fortifications, storehouses, arsenals, naval yards and buildings of this type, in all vessels on the high sea, and in all remaining places where the federal government exercised supreme jurisdiction of executive power. . . .

Representative [Albert S.] White [of Indiana] offered a resolution, which was approved, to name a committee of nine individuals to examine and to report whether a plan for gradual emancipation of African slaves and for the extinction of slavery in Delaware, Maryland, Virginia, Kentucky, Tennessee, and Missouri was feasible and whether promoting the emigration of the emancipated Negroes was desirable.[32]

The secretary of the navy submitted a communication to the chairman of the Senate Committee on Naval Affairs in which he proposed to construct a navy of armored vessels because, beyond doubt, wooden vessels cannot offer [effective] resistance to armored vessels. This matter is considered so important that, as soon as news of the naval combat between the armored steamers *Merrimac* and *Monitor* arrived in London, Parliament moved to suspend work on the vessels under construction until experience would reveal the most advantageous manner of constructing ships.

. . . Democratic congressmen caucused late last month. . . . The result of the reunion must not have been of great importance because no one talks about it anymore.

. . . This government has just significantly moderated its rigorous prohibitions about trading with the rebel states. The secretary of the treasury issued a circular authorizing the administrators of various customs [houses] to permit the shipment of noncontraband items from loyal citizens of the northern states to loyal residents in Union-occupied parts of the South.[33]

. . . Davis recently organized his cabinet as follows:

Secretary of State. — J[udah] P. Benjamin of Louisiana
Secretary of War. — George B. Randolph of Virginia
Secretary of Navy. — S[tephen] R. Mallory of Florida
Secretary of the Treasury. — C[hristopher] G. Memminger of South Carolina
Postmaster General. — Thomas H. Watts
Attorney General. — [John H.] Reagan of Texas.

Southern papers claim Davis has gone to Memphis to take command of the Confederate army in the west. However, this report is unconfirmed.

Early last month, the Richmond Senate held an important debate on a proposal by [Albert G.] Brown to prohibit planters from planting cotton in the present year. The proposal was rejected eleven to eight. During the debate, some senators indicated they were already aware that cotton was not *king of the world* as they had believed before. . . .

Romero to MRE, 6 May 1862, in Romero, *Correspondencia* II, 164–66

The U.S. squadron commanded by Commodore [David C.] Farragut moved up the Mississippi River to Forts Jackson and St. Philip, the principal points defending New Orleans. . . . The squadron passed the forts and moved on to New Orleans. Rebel General [Mansfield] Lovell, commanding the southern forces in New Orleans, evacuated New Orleans. On 26 April, Commodore Farragut demanded the surrender of the city, which a battalion of marines immediately occupied. . . . Supposedly, Commodore Farragut ordered an expedition to Baton Rouge, capital of Louisiana, and that city and its arsenal fell to the federal forces. This government has hastened to establish communications with New Orleans and to open that port to foreign commerce. . . .[34]

The operations against Yorktown were moving slowly forward when the dissident forces abandoned it. . . . This greatly surprised the whole country, which had expected a desperate resistance to be made there. . . . The dissidents retired to Williamsburg, a few miles from Yorktown in the direction of Richmond, where they had previously built defense works. . . . Supposedly the retreat from Yorktown will contribute significantly toward demoralizing the southern forces.[35]

On 13 April, after a siege of several days, General Hunter's forces, forming the Army of the South, captured Fort Pulaski near Savannah on the Savannah River. . . . The garrison surrendered after a thirty-hour bombardment. . . . This victory gives the United States a very advantageous base for its operations against Savannah. . . .[36]

General Burnside has continued victorious in various battles with the rebels in North Carolina. Late last month, after eleven hours of bombardment, he captured Fort Macon. . . . General [Jesse L.] Reno, commanding one of the expedition's brigades, attacked the rebels in South Mills. He was repulsed. . . .

Various rumors have circulated regarding the rebel abandonment of Corinto. . . . The outcome of the battle of Pittsburg's Landing . . . still remains unclear. Both sides claim a victory. . . . The two armies occupy the positions they held before the battle. The southern army attacked the federals but could not throw them from their positions. . . . Therefore, the Confederates have seemingly suffered the reverse. . . . If the South does not retreat, as it has done elsewhere, a bloody battle will ensue, the outcome of which will significantly influence perspectives in this country.

General [Ormsby] Mitchel has sent several expeditions into Alabama's interior, which have obtained partial successes.

General McDowell, commander of the Department of the Rappahannock, has approached Fredericksburg, which the rebels have abandoned, even though it was considered one of the gateways to Richmond. The rebels burned the railroad bridges and committed the maximum damage possible to the railroad before evacuating.

The federal forces in New Mexico obtained several advantages over the dissidents who have already abandoned Santa Fe. . . .

The South's multiple reverses should necessarily cause a decline in confidence and public spirit. Allegedly Davis has his baggage ready to leave Richmond. The Confederate Congress adjourned in the hour of danger. Its members left Richmond precipitously, which the southern press ridiculed. . . .

The U.S. Congress has continued to attack slavery everywhere it can within the limits of its constitutional powers. One example is the Senate's approval of the treaty with England to abolish the slave trade. . . . Moreover, the Senate approved the foreign relations committee report that favored the United States recognizing and sending diplomatic agents to the Republics of Liberia and Haiti. In addition, Senator Sumner presented a bill to prohibit the slave trade among the slave states, whether by water or by land.

The House Committee on Territories reported favorably on Arnold's bill . . . "to declare liberty national and slavery divisive in the United States." The committee proposed only one amendment, which called the bill a "law to assure liberty to all persons under the exclusive jurisdiction of the United States."

The House approved a resolution of censure against Simon Cameron, ex-secretary of war, for having employed irresponsible people, who were not those designated by law, for the purchase of war materials. The House rejected a similar resolution against the current Secretary of the Navy Welles. During the last few days, the House has debated the bill to construct a Pacific railroad.

. . . The [Senate] Finance Committee still has not reported on the direct taxation bill already approved by the House. Apparently, the Senate will make substantial modifications. When this matter is resolved, Congress will consider revising the existing tariff. . . .[37]

While secretary of war, Cameron ordered Pierce Butler, a resident of Philadelphia, sent to prison. Butler has filed suit in Philadelphia accusing Cameron of illegal proceedings in violation of his civil liberties. The court ordered Cameron's arrest. Cameron's lawyer referred the matter to Seward, who in turn referred the matter to the president's decision. The president accepted full responsibility for the orders issued by Cameron. . . .

Romero to MRE, 13 May 1862, in Romero, *Correspondencia* II, 182–84

. . . .The occupation of Yorktown was followed by the defeat of the Confederate army at Williamsburg. . . . After a very weak resistance, the Confederate forces were expelled from that city. The federal forces have occupied it.

. . . General McClellan has continued to advance toward Richmond. Most recently he was twenty-two miles from that city. Richmond will probably fall into his hands soon, since so many withdrawals must have demoralized the dissident forces. They will hardly fight against a victorious army. . . .

The rebels have suffered other, perhaps irreparable, losses in the abandonment of Norfolk and the destruction of the armored steamer *Merrimac*. Norfolk is strategically an important point. Moreover, its greatest advantage is the location of the largest and best-equipped Union naval yard there. In addition, the *Merrimac's* ability to cause damage almost equals that of all the dissident armies. . . . The rebels revealed that the Union victories had made them very weak and have suggested their inability to offer effective resistance for much longer.[38]

The occupation of New Orleans is a more important event than southern papers have portrayed. . . . Such an important victory has given the U.S. government complete control of the Mississippi River. . . .

. . . The situation near Corinto has not changed in the slightest. General Halleck's forces are two miles from General Beauregard's. Forces from Texas and Arkansas have reinforced Beauregard. . . .

Before the evacuation of Norfolk, the U.S. fleet at Hampton Roads was preparing to attack Sewall's Point. The president and the secretaries of war and treasury had gone to witness the attack. They still remain there. The dissidents evacuated Sewall's Point just before Norfolk.

After capturing Island Number 10, Commodore Foote's Upper Mississippi River fleet moved against Fort Pillow, the next fortified rebel point. . . .

. . . After several sessions of debate, the House approved a bill to construct a Pacific railroad at government expense. The Senate sent that

bill to a special committee, which reported favorably with a few modifications.[39]

Yesterday the House debated the bill to a declaration that slavery ought
not exist in the territories. In these terms it passed eighty-five to fifty.

The Senate Finance Committee reported on the bill for direct taxation
approved by the House. The committee was divided, presenting two
reports. Both reports very drastically reduce the taxes imposed in the
House-proposed bill.

Senator Wilson proposed a bill to place the Negroes of the District of
Columbia on the same footing as whites with respect to judicial matters.

The same senator presented a bill to reduce the number of brigadier
and major generals in the U.S. army to thirty and two hundred respectively.

Fourteen Democratic representatives have signed a statement favoring
the reorganization of that party to respect the Constitution as it is and to
reestablish the Union as it was. . . .

On 11 May, fifty conservative members of both houses met to seek
agreement upon the steps to be taken to oppose abolitionism. . . .

A few days ago [James W.] Grimes proposed organizing Negro battalions to garrison the forts and coasts of the South during the unhealthy
season, which might wreak havoc on the unacclimatized white soldiers.
There was no more talk of this until recently, when Secretary of the Navy
Welles authorized commanders of vessels to employ Negroes in all areas
of the vessel that required his services, but especially as rowers in the
boats of the vessels. Thus, this government demonstrates an increasingly
more liberal spirit each day with respect to the unfortunate Negroes.
Nevertheless, it is still very far from arriving at a civilized and humane
position. . . .[40]

Romero to MRE, 27 May 1862, in Romero, *Correspondencia* II, 203–5

. . . [Recent federal] reverses on land and sea could produce significant consequences by giving Europe a pretext to recognize the South or
to intervene in this country's affairs.

Five Union ships, including the armored vessels *Galena* and *Monitor*,
which was considered invincible because of its victory over the *Merrimac*,
were ordered to move up the James River toward Richmond. . . . [Later]
the ships had to retreat. . . .

Thus, the federal naval forces' first setback has animated the rebels,
who had been depressed by their multitude of reverses. This incident has
been described here as very unimportant. . . .

. . . Banks had advanced with twenty thousand men from Harper's Ferry to Winchester. Recently, twelve thousand of his men were taken to reinforce General McDowell. The rebel General [Thomas J.] Jackson, with fourteen thousand men, attacked and defeated the remaining Union forces. . . . He forced Banks to retreat . . . to Williamsport, Maryland. Upon receiving news of Banks's defeat, this government sent him reinforcements and ordered General McDowell to cut off Jackson's retreat with part of his corps. . . .

The news of Banks's defeat awakened great excitement in Baltimore,. where southern partisans are very numerous, to the point where some feared the defeat might lead Jackson's forces to occupy Washington. The U.S. government is actively gathering troops. To this end, the president published an order taking possession of all the country's railroads.

General McClellan has continued to advance slowly on Richmond. Most recently his headquarters were located twelve miles from Richmond, and his advance parties were about seven miles away. . . .

On 9 May at Hilton Head, General Hunter, commander of the Department of the South, granted freedom to the slaves in his department, consisting of Georgia, Florida, and South Carolina. He declared circumstances placed those states in a state of siege, adding that a state of siege and slavery were incompatible in a free country. As soon as the president received notice of this decision, he nullified it. He had not delegated any power to the generals in matters relative to slavery, the president explained, but has reserved such power to use as he might believe suitable. . . .[41]

Lincoln's decision displeased some states, principally Massachusetts. That state's governor . . . claimed his state would not contribute additional forces if the president revoked General Hunter's order.

On 14 May, the Virginia legislature, fearing that the Confederate government would abandon Richmond, approved some resolutions in favor of defending that city to the bitter end. The legislature named a committee to communicate the resolutions to President Davis. He had never dreamed of evacuating Richmond, Davis replied, continuing that even if Richmond should be lost by the fortune of war, the Confederate army could successfully sustain the war in Virginia for the next twenty years.

The southern forces evacuated Pensacola, which Union forces occupied. Before evacuating, the rebels burned the Warrington naval yard and the other public property located in Pensacola. The loss of Pensacola considerably decreased the number of fortified points that the South occupies on its sea coasts.[42]

This government has requested twenty thousand more volunteers from the states to cover the losses in the army. The Senate introduced a bill to authorize the president to raise that force. . . .

The Senate is debating the bill on direct taxation. The House discussed and approved a bill for the confiscation of the property of rebels. A majority of only four votes defeated an article granting freedom to the slaves of dissidents.

Both houses have approved and the president has signed an agrarian law [Homestead Act] distributing unoccupied federal lands to citizens who wish to occupy and cultivate them. Proposed years ago, this project had always encountered opposition from Congress or from the president. . . . Another law recently signed . . . creates and organizes a Bureau of Agriculture. . . .[43]

Romero to MRE, 3 June 1862, in Romero *Correspondencia* II, 225

. . . The southern forces that had been fortified in Corinto under rebel General Beauregard evacuated that position. . . . The Union partisans claim that the rebels have disbanded and were demoralized even before abandoning Corinto. This government's enemies contend that the rebel forces moved to Richmond to fight General McClellan, who is now in front of that city. After achieving this, they will return to engage General Halleck, destroying his army with superior numbers. Halleck occupied Corinto as soon as Beauregard abandoned it. General Pope of the federal army of the west occupied Brownsville on the Corinto to Mobile railroad. . . . The rebel army must take this railroad to come to Richmond. . . .

General Curtis occupied Little Rock, the capital of Arkansas. Federal forces have occupied the cities of Natchez, Mississippi [*sic*—only one listed], on the river of the same name. . . .

Romero to MRE, 24 June 1862, in Romero, *Correspondencia* II, 262–65

The federal army near Richmond . . . holds the terrain that it has conquered with difficulty. On 31 May, one federal corps crossed the Chicahominy. . . . The rebels . . . attacked the advanced corps while isolated from the main body of the union army. . . . The federals . . . were driven from their positions and obliged to give ground. . . . The battle was renewed with new fury the next day. Considerably reinforced, the federals were more successful this time. . . . General [Joseph] Johnston, commander of the Confederate army, was wounded on the second day. General [Robert E.] Lee replaced him.[44]

After the battle, General McClellan advanced his forces, constructing several bridges to permit large numbers of troops to cross the Chicahominy simultaneously. As far as possible, he located his army in healthy places in the swamps below his camp. He suffers very sizeable losses from illness, perhaps the equivalent of one regiment per week. He has received some reinforcements. . . .

. . . Rebel General Beauregard has evacuated Corinto [Mississippi]. . . . For more than fifteen days not a single word has been published with respect to Beauregard or to Union General Halleck pursuing him. . . .

After rebel General [Thomas "Stonewall"] Jackson had compelled General Banks to retreat to Williamsport, General Frémont then threw Jackson out of all the points that he had occupied. . . . Apparently Jackson's expedition sought to threaten Washington to see if General McClellan would detach some forces to defend it. This objective failed. . . .

On the seventh, the federal squadron on the Mississippi River victoriously engaged the Confederate ships defending Memphis. . . . As a consequence of this victory, Memphis surrendered without resistance to the federal forces, in whose peaceful possession it currently remains. The United States already controls all the important strategic and fortified points on the Mississippi River, with the exception of Vicksburg, which serves the dissidents as a line of communication with the southern states to the east [sic—west] of the Mississippi. If Vicksburg were lost, communication with Texas, Arkansas, and Louisiana would be cut, hence the Richmond government should defend Vicksburg to the last extremity.[45]

The U.S. naval forces have begun to attack Charleston. The southern papers claim they intend to do the same with Mobile.

On the ninth, the secretary of war ordered the organization at Annapolis of an instruction encampment composed of fifty thousand men of the three branches to serve as the army reserve. At the same time, this reserve will offer [Washington] protection from any attack on the part of the South. Although still not organized, the camp was placed under the command of General Wood [sic—John E. Wool]. Wool will command Baltimore, while General Dix, who commands Washington, was given command of Fort Monroe.

. . . Congress approved and the president signed a bill that authorized the government to recognize the independence of the republics of Haiti and Liberia. The president has already named agents to represent the United States in these republics.[46]

Recently the U.S. House approved a bill that emancipated the slaves belonging to the president, vice-president, representatives, and senators, state governors, judges, and other people employed in the Confederate States, or who take part in the insurrection. In addition, this bill freed any slaves from the insurrectionary states that fall under the federal army's control. The president is authorized to enter into negotiations to acquire the right, by treaty or other means, to send all legally freed Negroes who voluntarily agree to go to Central or South America or to islands in the Gulf of Mexico. A bill was presented in the House to revise the tariff, raising some duties in order to increase the government's revenue.[47]

The Senate also approved and the president signed the bill which declared that slavery was divisive and could not exist in the territories. After discussing the bill on direct taxation, the Senate approved the House bill with many modifications.

The Senate just approved the House bill, which authorized the construction of the Pacific railroad. Thus, a matter initiated eleven years ago was concluded. At that time it was considered an unrealizable utopian dream. Now the government will disperse millions of dollars for this project, when war expenditures are immense and much greater than its income. Responding to the House resolution censuring the conduct of ex-Secretary of War Cameron, the president sent a message stating that he and the whole cabinet had approved the secretary's conduct, and therefore, if something was wrong in Cameron's conduct, he and the other cabinet officers were prepared to receive that part of the censure that corresponds to them.

In the last few days two important notes have come to light, one from the secretary of the treasury to the House Finance Committee and the other from the secretary of the navy to the Senate Naval Affairs Committee. The former note explained that the government has exhausted the resources supplied by Congress. . . . It concluded by asking for $150 million in new treasury notes. The second letter recommended the introduction of suitable reforms in the U.S. naval yards so that they could facilitate the construction of iron ships, or at least ships armored with iron, thus preventing the European powers from achieving any advantage over the United States in this important area.

The United States and England finally approved and ratified their treaty to abolish the slave trade. . . . The president sent this treaty to Congress, so that body might adopt the legislation made necessary by the provisions of that pact.[48]

On 18 June, with permission from his government, Lord Lyons, British minister in Washington, sailed from New York for Liverpool. . . . The voyage of Lord Lyons in the present circumstances has caused various comments. In my judgment it signified no more than that the present state of U.S.-British affairs does not require the presence of its minister in Washington. Supposedly the French minister also considers returning to Europe soon.

The Danish chargé proposed to this government to carry freed Negroes to the Danish island of Santa Cruz. The president lacked authority to dispose of such persons, Seward replied, but he would submit the matter to Congress for its resolution. . . . Apparently the Sultan's government has prohibited the entrance of Confederate ships into Turkish ports, ordering them to be treated as pirates. That decision has greatly satisfied the U.S. government. The State Department intercepted a dispatch from [Pierre] Rost, Confederate agent in Madrid, to the Richmond government, informing it of the improbability that the European powers would recognize the South. Rost proposed withdrawing the Confederate legations from Europe. . . . The Paris newspapers have published Seward's note to the U.S. consul in that city, [stating] . . . that the government does not intend to expand or increase the army, and since all the enlistment rolls are already full, in the future the offers of those who would like to serve cannot be accepted. . . .

Romero to MRE, 15 July 1862, in Romero, *Correspondencia* II, 301–4

. . . The rebel forces have defeated the large Army of the Potomac . . . obliging it to withdraw from twenty miles of terrain that it previously held.[49]

All these disasters [to the U.S. forces] apparently are owed to a chain of errors and stupid intrigues by ambitious persons. When General McClellan departed Washington, he wanted command of all the forces gathered there [in Virginia]. He adopted the James River route instead of Fredericksburg for the move on Richmond. Since the Army of the Potomac would be in a position where it could not protect Washington, McClellan's choice of route created the need for a considerable force to protect Washington in case of a rebel attack. If General McClellan would have advanced via Fredericksburg, his army would have protected Washington and threatened Richmond. The first error, then, was to divide the Army of the Potomac, making General McClellan march by the James River, while conserving an army corps under General McDowell in Fredericksburg, General McClellan marched very slowly toward Richmond. . . . If he would have pursued the Confederates after either Williamsburg or Fair Oaks, he might have taken Richmond. . . . [Instead] he gave the South time to unite a force superior to his at Richmond. Detaining himself for several months in the swamps and unhealthy lands along the Chicahominy River, he allowed from one-third to one-half of his army to become sick or incapacitated. His line [of communications] was, moreover, very extensive. As his effective force diminished markedly, he found himself weak at various points.

Meanwhile, after gathering all possible units for defense, the rebel army prepared to take the offensive. As soon as General [Stonewall] Jackson, who had been in West Virginia, was incorporated into the Confederate army, he attacked the union right wing. . . . The attack lasted one week with the greatest carnage and continual southern success. The Army of the Potomac . . . withdrew to a point called Harrison's Landing on the James River twenty-three miles from Richmond. The cannons of the federal squadron protected it there. The southern forces still wanted to expel General McClellan from their country and destroy the remains of his army. However, the fire from the federal naval squadron caused the Confederate army to retire with very heavy losses after eight days of continuous victory.

Reportedly General McClellan's withdrawal was only a strategic move, for no other purpose than to change a dangerous base of operations for an advantageous one. However, the evidence clearly and unavoidably reveals that the Union army has suffered a defeat that will be very difficult to repair. . . . The merit of General McClellan and his army consists in having executed a well-ordered retreat under the constant pursuit and fire of the Confederate army and in being salvaged [from a precarious situation] without being entirely demoralized. . . .

For the North, this battle produced the near destruction of the Army of the Potomac and the near impossibility of taking Richmond for the present. For the South, the victory could possibly produce French and British recognition of its independence and perhaps European intervention in the affairs of this continent.

The federal government has reinforced General McClellan. The president went to the encampment recently to observe for himself the state of things. According to rumor, Lincoln encountered the troops in a satisfactory state. Apparently McClellan still expected to take Richmond. At least he wrote in this sense to his soldiers. . . .

. . . Some attribute the blame for what has occurred to General McClellan. Others heatedly defend McClellan and blame the secretary of war and even the president. Several newspapers have asked the secretary of war to resign, accusing him of enmity toward General McClellan and therefore of not promptly forwarding the requested reinforcements. The Senate has requested the correspondence between General McClellan and the War Department. From the correspondence, they expect to learn who is responsible for what has occurred. Nevertheless, the president does not appear ready to remove either General McClellan or Stanton. . . . Military operations in other theaters . . . have also been unfavorable to this government. Federal troops attacked the South Carolina forces on James Island near Charleston. The U.S. forces were repelled and withdrew to Port Royal, apparently abandoning for now the project of taking Charleston.

The [federal] squadrons of the upper and lower Mississippi joined at Vicksburg, which they bombarded for three days . . . [without doing] much damage. . . . The Union command has considered, then, attacking it by land. For this purpose they are digging a canal to change the course of the Mississippi and thus to leave Vicksburg surrounded on all sides by land. If these labors are concluded successfully, they will represent an extraordinary work. . . .[50]

General Pope was named commander of the federal army in western Virginia. This appointment disgusted General Frémont, who asked to be relieved from command of his division. Pope issued an enthusiastic proclamation to his subordinates.

Civil war has burst out anew in central Tennessee. Confederate Colonel [Nathan B.] Forrest attacked and captured Murfreesboro and marched on Nashville, capital of Tennessee. The federal troops in Arkansas are in a bad situation. . . .[51]

At the end of last month, governors of eighteen northern states petitioned the president, requesting him to raise three hundred thousand more volunteers to replace the losses in the federal army. The president agreed to this request. Through the secretary of war, he designated the new quotas for each state. In some areas the citizens are reluctant to enlist, which made it necessary to offer premiums and rewards to those drafted. In the Senate some members remarked about the popular coolness [toward volunteering], assigning the lack of public confidence in the government to the government's vacillating conduct during the war. These senators have seized this opportunity to request radical changes in the conduct of the government. For this purpose [Preston] King of New York presented a bill in the Senate that authorizes the president to use the services of Negroes in any capacity he might deem proper. . . . The House has discussed the same question. Some have argued that, while insurgent property in slaves is respected and protected, there is no hope to end the Civil War. It is necessary, these people maintain, to inaugurate a new era in which Negroes should work not only as laborers, but should be organized as soldiers into regiments.[52]

Yesterday the president sent a message to both houses proposing the method of indemnification to be conceded to those states deciding to abolish slavery in conformity with Congress' recent plan. . . .

Congress has approved a revision of the present tariff, increasing the importation duties on some articles. They approved a law to confiscate the property of people taking part in the southern insurrection. . . .

A quite boisterous affair occurred in the Senate. The committee named by the government to examine War Department contracts found one in favor of Schubarth to manufacture fifty thousand rifles. Schubarth obtained the contract through the influence of Rhode Island Senator [James F.] Simmons, who, in turn, received a 5 percent commission on the contract. No statutory law prohibited this type of business; therefore, no penalty applied to those interested in the contract. Nevertheless, the Senate immediately passed a bill to punish such fraud. A senator immediately presented a resolution to expel Simmons from the Senate for the above-mentioned reason. The resolution remained pending for various days without anyone moving to discuss it. Finally, it was sent to the judiciary committee. This action is the equivalent of rejecting it because of the approaching end of the session. Allegedly some senators, who had made similar contracts, opted for this procedure out of fear that they might be discovered during the debate and suffer the same penalty.[53]

The Senate was occupied with the admission of West Virginia. . . . West Virginia's constitution recognizes slavery, which has impeded its admission until now. Congress seems determined not to admit any more slave states.

A little while ago, the so-called conservatives organized a public meeting in New York. Their program calls for the constitution as it is and the Union as it was. The speeches at that meeting almost justified the rebels' conduct, attributing all the blame for secession on the abolitionists and radical Republicans. In response, these latter groups have called a meeting in New York for this evening . . . that will have a more popular character. At this meeting the ideas of defending the government and of prosecuting the war against the South to the utmost will be expressed.

General Butler, commander of the Department of the Gulf, has had some difficulties with the European consuls in New Orleans. The Netherlands consul wished to protect some money from a New Orleans bank with his nation's flag. General Butler ordered the money seized despite the Netherlands consul's protest, which the other European consuls in New Orleans joined. Upon receiving news of these events and because the Netherlands minister made representations, this government dispatched the noted lawyer Reverdy Johnson to New Orleans to conduct an investigation into this affair. . . .[54]

Romero to MRE, 5 August 1862, in Romero, *Correspondencia* II, 324–26

. . . In the days preceding its adjournment, Congress debated almost exclusively the bill to confiscate rebel property. . . . Both houses finally approved the confiscation bill with Lincoln's modifications, and the executive signed and promulgated it. . . .

Congress also approved and the president promulgated a law . . . that authorized the government to use Negroes in any capacity considered useful toward suppressing the southern insurrection. Thus, they can already organize Negro regiments. In fact, a proscribed Pole is raising one in Washington.

On the evening of the day Congress closed its session, the president called the representatives from the border states together to propose a project he had devised to implement the gradual emancipation of the slaves in those states. The majority of these representatives opposed the project, and only a very insignificant minority acquiesced. . . .

. . . Since the Army of the Potomac's defeat near Richmond, the federal forces have been entirely on the defensive. . . . General Mc-Clellan will accomplish a lot if he can maintain his position on the James River while this government organizes a new army. Supposedly the rebel government is concentrating all the forces available in Richmond to dislodge General McClellan from the peninsula between the York and James Rivers. Afterwards, allegedly the Confederate army will fall on Washington with much larger forces than could oppose it. They have constructed two armored steamers in Richmond with the intention of attacking the U.S. squadron defending General McClellan's position.

While the South, intoxicated by its recent triumphs, acts so menacing and so active in its preparations to return to a commanding position, the North experiences an apathy and an inexplicable disinterest. More than a month ago, the president ordered the draft of three hundred thousand volunteers. Even though every state has offered premiums, considered exorbitant here, to those who enlist, the number of enlistments remains insignificant. . . . The governors already intend to use the lottery. If things continue in their current form, this government will need a conscription law just as the Richmond government did some time ago. [55]

Part of General Burnside's corps and a fleet of vessels armed with mortars, which had been in the Mississippi River under Captain [David D.] Porter, have reinforced General McClellan.

. . . Kentucky and Tennessee have remained at the mercy of wandering rebel guerrillas.

The bombardment of Vicksburg continues without any apparent effect. . . . The president, persuaded that neither he nor the secretary of war could effectively direct the federal army's operations and that many of its defeats are due to bad direction, decided to confer command of military operations to General Halleck. . . . Halleck, who previously commanded the Army of the West, established his headquarters in Washington. Recently he went to the James River to inspect General McClellan's army.

Despite the numerical and financial superiority that the North enjoys over the South, the astute observer is really struck by the North's continuing inability to subjugate the South. Far from being subjugated, the

South is in as advantageous a position now as ever. Doubtless, in the contest agitating this country, the North would possess all the advantages if its inhabitants were unified, but that is not so. At heart many northerners wish the South to triumph. The rest are largely divided on the questions of slavery and other matters. Division in the north has reached the point where, warring among themselves, they have forgotten to make war on the common enemy. Moreover, many people sustain the Union cause, not out of any patriotic or humanistic sentiment, but only and exclusively in the spirit of speculation. This divisiveness does not exist to such an extent in the South.

This government's financial situation is no less foreboding than the military situation. Congress authorized expenditures of $800 million for the coming year. U.S. bonds sell at a discount of 15 percent, and the exchange rate over Europe is from 28 to 30 percent. The direct tax law becomes effective this coming 1 September. Doubtless, the tax law will increase discontent. Since the heavy taxes which the law imposes are perhaps superior to the ability of those states to pay, that law could later even induce the western states to leave the American Union. [56]

General Butler's order to the foreign residents in his Military Department to take an oath of loyalty to the federal government furnished one ground for the dispute between General Butler and the European consuls in New Orleans. The president has already resolved this problem, deciding that although foreigners were not required to take the oath, they still must abide by the laws of the country while residing here.

A little while ago the newspapers claimed Seward would resign from the State Department because he disagreed with the new policy that the recent confiscation laws forced this government to pursue. . . . It seems certain now that Seward will continue at the head of U.S. foreign relations.

A recent law increased the [highest] ranks in the navy. Until now the highest ranking officers were captains. Congress has just created the ranks of rear admiral and commodore, the former corresponding to major general and the latter to brigadier general. . . . [57]

Romero to MRE, 27 August 1862, in Romero, *Correspondencia* II, 359–62

. . . An important battle is under way between the main bodies of the belligerent armies. . . . Currently it is only known that the battle took place. Such circumstances suggest that the battle might have been unfavorable to this government, which otherwise would hasten to publish its reports. . . .

On 9 August a battle took place in central Virginia at Cedar Mountain, south of Culpeper. Rebel General Jackson crossed the Rapidan River and attacked General Banks's corps. . . . The next day the rebels withdrew. . . . The engagement was indecisive. As often happens, both sides claimed victory. Nevertheless, more likely it was a reconnaissance of the southern forces or a diversionary movement to attract Yankee attention and to allow an attack in another place.[58]

. . . The federal naval forces have raised their siege of Vicksburg. They alleged that without the cooperation of land forces they could not possibly take the city. Having united to defend Vicksburg, the rebels, under General [John C.] Breckinridge, immediately and unsuccessfully attacked Baton Rouge, capital of Louisiana. . . . [In this campaign] the destruction of the *Arkansas*, which had caused so much damage to the federal squadron and which was so feared for its previous prowess, produced a rejoicing in the North as great as had the news of the *Merrimac's* destruction. Captain Porter, who was given credit for the destruction, was immediately promoted to commodore. . . .

Several regiments, organized under the president's July order to raise three hundred thousand volunteers, have already arrived in Washington. Moreover, reportedly some states have already filled their quotas. The governor of Rhode Island, where there are Negro citizens, ordered the organization of a colored regiment, which this government will presumably not accept. General Lane is raising a Negro regiment in Kansas. The order to draft three hundred thousand men to serve in the army for nine months or for the duration of the war . . . was issued without effecting the previous call for three hundred thousand volunteers. Thus, if both are filled, the federal army will receive a reinforcement of six hundred thousand men. . . .

So many American citizens, alarmed by the draft, hastened to depart the country that the government prohibited people encompassed within the draft law from leaving for foreign areas. . . .[59]

Upon receiving command of the Department of Virginia, General Pope proposed that his command live off the country. He also established severe regulations of secessionists and their property. The Richmond government requested that the U.S. government annul General Pope's orders, threatening reprisals in case Pope's regulations would be left in force. . . . General Halleck, commander of the U.S. forces, returned the latest communication from Confederate General Lee because it was drafted in terms disrespectful of the federal government. Halleck's action was apparently only an evasion to avoid responding to the principal point, since the earlier communications, conceived in the same terms, were not returned. Nevertheless, General Pope soon revised his orders, and the secretary of war issued orders greatly moderating the rigor of the war. . . .[60]

. . . Davis's message to the Confederate Congress alluded to the savage character taken by the Civil War, attributing responsibility to the U.S. government. Noting the provisions to increase the U.S. Army, Davis declared it necessary to modify the Confederate conscription law. He suggested requiring all Confederate citizens between the ages of twenty-five and forty-five to lend military service, instead of between the ages from twenty-five to thirty-five, as the law now reads.[61]

In the first session of the Confederate Congress, various bills were presented to confiscate the property of unionists. The approval and implementation of these bills would imprint a less humane character on the war than it currently has.

Lincoln has been developing his ideas to colonize the Negroes in some part of Central America. A short while ago, he called together a committee representing the Negroes of the District [of Columbia]. . . . He explained his plan to them in detail. He immediately appointed Kansas Senator [Samuel C.] Pomeroy to carry one hundred Negro families to the territory of Chiriqui on the border between New Granada and Costa Rica. Those two countries disputed this land's ownership.[62]

Recently, a New York newspaperman (Horace Greeley), whose paper is the organ of the radical faction, wrote to the president complaining of the policy pursued with respect to slavery. The president's . . . reply was very notable because it contained his program relative to slavery. He considered slavery subordinate to saving the Union. The president said that if he believed abolishing slavery would save the Union, he would not hesitate to abolish it, but if he believed he would achieve the same result by maintaining slavery, he would maintain it. . . .[63]

Romero to MRE, 12 September 1862, in Romero, *Correspondencia* II, 378–80

. . . At the end of last month, the war was in the slave states. The federal army held almost one half of Virginia, all of Kentucky, and a large part of Tennessee. Now the federal army has been thrown from Virginia, Kentucky, and Tennessee. Simultaneously the Confederates have invaded Maryland and threatened to invade or transfer the war to the free states of Ohio and Pennsylvania. The Confederate army is capable of cutting Washington's communications with the North and even of advantageously attacking this capital. . . .

The president and General Halleck, commander of the army, decided to withdraw the Army of the Potomac from its position at Harrison's Landing on the James River. Then, when united with General Pope's army, . . . they could immediately undertake operations against Richmond. Perhaps Lincoln and Halleck [merely] wished to withdraw General McClellan's forces from a position exposed to great dangers from the current season's unhealthiness and the location's proximity to Richmond. To distract Confederate attention so that the Confederate army would not molest General McClellan during his withdrawal, it was decided to have General Pope advance on Richmond by the road from Gordonsville. As soon as the federal army in northern Virginia crossed the Rappahannock, Confederate General Jackson advanced to fight it. The contending forces fought at Cedar Mountain on 9 August. . . .

At the same time the South learned that General McClellan had abandoned the James River. Judging that such a movement meant reinforcing General Pope in his march on Richmond via Gordonsville, the main body of the Confederate army under General Lee moved to reinforce Jackson, who had retreated after Cedar Mountain. Meanwhile, McClellan and the Army of the Potomac arrived at Alexandria. Most of the army was sent to aid General Pope. . . . Pope attacked Jackson at the same spot where the battle of Bull Run, so fatal for the northern cause, had taken place on 21 July 1861. . . . Pope claimed he would have completely destroyed Jackson's forces if General Fitz John Porter's corps would have cooperated as expected in the attack. On 30 August, General Lee and the main body of the Confederate army joined Jackson, and another bloody battle took place. Fate settled this battle decidedly in favor of the Confederates, who remained in possession of the battlefield. General Pope withdrew to Centerville, from where the government ordered him to retreat to Washington to defend the city. In addition to being very demoralized and subdued by the fatigue of the previous days, Pope's forces were also without munitions and food. Thus, this capital was in imminent danger of being captured. Such major disasters prompted the president to remove General Pope from command of the army, reappointing McClellan, who had not taken part in the previous battles. Allegedly, McClellan had opposed this campaign plan from the beginning.[64]

The U.S. Army withdrew then from Virginia, falling back to the fortifications constructed a year ago for the defense of Washington. . . . Thus, the Confederates remain in possession of all of Virginia, with the exception of Norfolk, Fortress Monroe, and the Potomac River bank opposite Washington. The U.S. generals reciprocally blame each other for the major disaster. General Pope attributed the defeat directly to General Porter and indirectly to General McClellan. The government is disposed to submit Generals Porter and [Charles] Griffin to a court martial, so they might respond to General Pope's charges. However, since General McClellan claims to need the services of both on the battlefield, the investigation of the facts was deferred until the end of the war. For their part, the accused generals and several others attributed the disasters to General Pope's ineptitude. . . .

Supposedly, after such an important victory the Confederate forces would attack this capital although, presumably, they would do so from the Maryland side, where the fortifications are not so strong.

The Confederate forces, commanded by General Jackson, crossed the Potomac and entered into Maryland at a ford a few leagues distant from this capital. . . . Instead of advancing on Baltimore or Washington, Jackson's force has moved toward Pennsylvania. Certainly it intends to attack Harrisburg, the capital of that state.[65]

In the slave state of Maryland, the Confederates have many partisans who surely will join them, reinforcing their army with several thousand men. Only armed force has kept Maryland loyal to the Washington government. Not unexpectedly, therefore, the dissidents have encountered all kinds of aid in Maryland.

Because of these events, the Union government finds itself in a worse situation than when the South started hostilities in April of last year. Richmond is entirely secure now and Washington is threatened.

. . . The Confederate forces under General [E. Kirby] Smith defeated General [William] Nelson in Kentucky. Taking advantage of this victory, Smith marched precipitously on Frankfort, Kentucky's capital. He occupied that city along with Lexington without resistance. The liberal [federal?] forces withdrew to Louisville on the Ohio River. These movements left the Confederates in possession of the whole state. Not satisfied, they were preparing to cross the Ohio River and attack Cincinnati, one of the richest and most populous cities of the west. Today's telegraph reports claim the Confederates were already near Cincinnati. Ohio's governor was making major preparations to defend that city, which was declared in a state of siege a few days ago.[66]

In Tennessee the liberal [federal] forces had to abandon many positions. Supposedly, even Nashville, the capital of Tennessee, must be abandoned soon. . . . The federal army has also abandoned Baton Rouge, capital of Louisiana, which the Confederates occupied. Thus, in less than fifteen days, this government has lost almost all the conquered terrain and almost all the advantages obtained in a year's campaign that cost rivers of blood and gold.

General McClellan's army left Washington to observe the Confederate movements and to attack them, if offered a favorable opportunity. Although he has the complete confidence of the army, he lacks that of the people, whose expectations have been disappointed. He still has not obtained a single victory.

Such an unnatural state of things cannot continue for long. The northern states begin to tire of a contest that has required so many sacrifices without returning the smallest advantage until now. The people want the president to change the government policy, the cabinet, and the commanding general of the army.

The government apparently lacks the will to make any of these changes. Currently the same factors continue that produced disastrous results in the past, and they have increased rather than decreased. Naturally, one can expect as disastrous military operations in the future as in the past.

Because of the most recent events, the price of gold, the barometer to measure the confidence that the commercial element of the country has in the success of this government's cause, has climbed to 20 percent. A little while ago it stood at 13 percent.[67]

The Central American ministers have protested against this government's projects to transport Negro colonists to those countries without their consent. The government has assured the Central American diplomats that it later rejected this plan of colonization. . . .

Romero to MRE, 9 October 1862, in Romero, *Correspondencia* II, 531–34

This government's situation has improved little [recently]. . . . On 22 September, the president granted liberty to the slaves in those rebel states that still are in rebellion on January of next year.[68]

The emancipation of the slaves in the dissident states has been one of the most heated questions during the present Civil War. The abolitionists and the radical Republicans have presented emancipation as the most effective means of ending the rebellion. The Democrats and moderate Republicans have considered it a step to make any reconciliation between the North and South impossible. Emancipation would give the dissidents new energy to continue the contest, they contend, without producing any compensating advantage because of the impossibility of making it effective. But they have neither debated nor evaluated the measure, if you wish, in terms of its intrinsic justice. In this country, few people occupy themselves with abstract questions.

A few days before the president's Emancipation Proclamation, he met with a committee of Chicago citizens, who came to speak in favor of emancipation. The president, in replying to some observations and without rejecting the measure, claimed he might be excused from decreeing emancipation because of the impossibility of executing it. His proclamation granting liberty to the southern slaves, he told the Chicagoans, would be the same as the Papal Bull against the comet. Nevertheless, he soon published the decree giving the step the character entirely of a military measure demanded by the necessities of war.

On . . . (17 July 1862), Congress legislated the confiscation of the property of citizens rebelling against the Union government. Because of that law, on July 22 the president proclaimed a period of sixty days for the dissidents to return to obedience to the government. . . . If they did not do so, he threatened them with the corresponding consequences. . . .

The Richmond government could not hide its alarm with that measure. Upon receiving knowledge of the Emancipation Proclamation, various resolutions were offered in the [Confederate] Senate and House proposing total war on the United States. Another proposed not to treat prisoners taken after 1 January as prisoners of war, but as criminals, subject to the death penalty. One resolution even proposed giving a twenty-dollar premium to slaves for each head of a U.S. citizen that they turned in.[69]

. . . The Virginia legislature already passed a law that exempted from criminal prosecution persons killing those who attempted to implement the president's 22 September proclamation.

On 24 September, Lincoln suspended the right of *habeas corpus* during the present insurrection. All insurgents, their accomplices and auxiliaries, he announced, should be judged militarily.

Apparently the president's energetic measures have encountered considerable opposition with the majority of the cabinet. Supposedly, Secretary of the Treasury Chase has favored the measures and Secretary of State Seward has opposed them. Publicly, both views have been generally well received.

A short while ago, proposals were presented to the Richmond congress to send some commissioners to Washington to propose a peace treaty. The resolution passed to the foreign relations committee, which divided in its report. The majority favored the resolution. From the beginning, nevertheless, the Confederate legislators agreed that peace must be discussed under the assumption that the seceded states already formed an independent nation and not because they even remotely considered returning to the Union. In spite of this, some in the North considered this conduct as a proof of the southern desire to reestablish the Union. These northerners even supposed that negotiations were already under way to permit the South to have a general congress and a totally independent government for internal matters, including slavery. The South would join with the North only in foreign relations matters. Needless to say, this project and in general all projects of compromise are presently rejected as vehemently in the North as in the South. The North wants the South to return to the Union unconditionally. The South, already considering itself independent, will make no arrangement that does not recognize its independence.

On September 24, the governors from twelve northern states met in Altona, Pennsylvania, to discuss current public affairs. Many feared the governors would take a hostile position toward the government because of its recent policy. It was presumed that they would request General McClellan's removal from command of the Army of the Potomac. This, nevertheless, was not so. The governors recognized the president's authority, praised his conduct, and especially the Emancipation Proclamation. They offered to continue their recent support. They only requested him to organize a large number of volunteers, in addition to those already levied, so that he would have a sufficient force and the people would receive a military education. . . . [70]

. . . General McClellan with a sizeable force attacked the rebel force at South Mountain on 11 September. General Lee continued his march toward Sharpsburg after this battle. . . . The Confederate army camped in Sharpsburg and awaited the federals, who arrived on the sixteenth. . . . The following day one of the war's hardest fought battles [Antietam] took place, lasting fourteen hours. . . . The next day the battle was not renewed. . . . On the nineteenth, the Confederates withdrew in perfect order, saving all their trains and recrossing the Potomac River to camp on the Virginia bank. Although both sides claimed victory, any victory clearly belonged to this government. Union forces took and conserved some enemy positions, obligating them to withdraw. Nevertheless, the victory was incomplete. . . . Certainly both armies were significantly crippled and rendered incapable of renewing the fight. . . . [71]

Since then, the two armies have remained near each other, but without renewing the fighting. For the federal government the battle of Antietam expelled the Confederates from Maryland and prevented the war from leaving Virginia. This alone represented a significant accomplishment although those expecting to see the invading army destroyed are not satisfied. In turn, the rebels claim they only intended to distract the attention of the enemy in order to permit the capture of Harper's Ferry with its immense stores of war supplies and its garrison of twelve thousand men. Having obtained that goal, nothing else remained to be done in Maryland.

After the battle of Antietam, the president visited the Army of the Potomac. Assuredly, he expressed himself very satisfied with its condition. . . . The chief recent federal victory occurred at Corinto, where Union General Rosecrans reported defeating the dissidents . . . [and] pursuing the Confederates until they were entirely dispersed. Nevertheless, this victory could not have been more than partial. . . .

Romero to MRE, 5 November 1862, in Romero,
Correspondencia II, 569–72

The House elections for the Thirty-eighth Congress were held in four of
the principal states. . . . Generally, it was blindly believed that the
Republican party would win the elections. The Republican party did not
participate in the contest under its true name, but rather concealed as the
Union party. It used the Union name to attract all those favoring the
vigorous continuation of the war until the Union is reestablished. Thus,
although two of the four states mentioned, Ohio and Pennsylvania, are
known Republican states, to everyone's great surprise, the Democratic
party won the elections. A faction of the Democratic party now sympathizes entirely with the southern insurgents. This faction claims the
South was correct in revolting and denounces this government's war as
unconstitutional and unjust.[72]

As soon as the Republicans recovered a bit from the surprise, with
some reason, they argued that the triumph of the Democrats was due to
the large numbers of citizens from those states who could not vote
because they were absent from their respective states serving in the army.
If these soldiers would have voted, the election would have turned out
very differently.

These election results have very greatly alarmed the government and
the Republican party. Since then, they have been very actively occupied
with the labor required to win yesterday's elections in the majority of the
northern and northeastern states. Elections are decided in New York,
which has the largest population and therefore the largest number of
representatives, when the elections in the other states have been indecisive. Both parties have worked most persistently in New York. The
election is lent great importance because in addition to federal legislators,
governors and other state officials were also elected. The Republicans
presented a very radical Republican as a candidate. He favors the most
active and energetic prosecution of the war until the South is conquered,
desolating the South if necessary. The Democratic candidate was very
opposed to the administration's policy and most favorably disposed toward
the South. These elections will decide, then, which policy this government will pursue toward the southern insurrection. . . .

The Army of the Potomac . . . has crossed the river and is in Virginia
now. Apparently events have sustained the rumor that the federal army
would not undertake any movement until after the elections. Although
the rumor does not seem well founded to me, the president also allegedly
awaited the election returns before making some changes in his cabinet
and in the command of the federal army.

If the Army of the Potomac has been inactive for the whole month, the Confederate army has not been. It has made some very successful, if small scale, raids to capture munitions. General [James E.B.] Stuart made the principal raid into Pennsylvania with a division of cavalry. . . .[73]

. . . Apparently from letters intercepted from General Beauregard, the Confederate strategy [in the west] was to attack the federal forces of Generals Buell and Grant, destroying them and occupying Louisville and Cincinnati. Thus, the Confederates would obtain possession of all of Tennessee and Kentucky and part of Ohio. At the same time, the Army of the Potomac [sic—Army of Northern Virginia] would invade Maryland and move on to Baltimore, Washington, and as far as Philadelphia. The plan's failure was attributed to the inaptitude of Confederate General Bragg, who was charged with executing that plan. Although some forces advanced far in the direction indicated, almost arriving at Louisville and Cincinnati, others suffered a reverse in Corinto, . . . [which] completely disconcerted them, forcing their retreat. If the Confederates were very disgusted with Bragg's conduct, removing him from command because he did not obtain all the expected advantages, this government was dissatisfied with General Buell's conduct. He permitted the secessionists to withdraw with very light losses when he could have completely destroyed them at Perryville. This alleged failure at Perryville produced such a public clamor against Buell that this government [replaced] him [with] . . . General Rosecrans, the hero of the battle of Corinto. . . .[74]

Reports of the depredations that the Confederate steamer *Alabama* has committed on the U.S. merchant marine on the high seas has produced great alarm and exasperation in the North. . . . It is also known that the Richmond government has other armored steamers under construction in England. When finished, these steamers will be engaged in destroying northern commerce. Supposedly the English government refused to impede the construction of those steamers, alleging a lack of evidence to determine if the vessels were being prepared for the Confederates. The New York Chamber of Commerce adopted some resolutions on this matter and forwarded them to the British parliament. It also requested this government to redouble its efforts to prevent an increase in the number of privateers capturing northern vessels. . . .[75]

U.S. cruisers have pursued some blockade runners even into the maritime jurisdiction of neutral nations. This has produced strong complaints from the English and Spanish governments. In reply, this government promised to give these governments appropriate satisfaction. . . . It has reiterated its orders to respect maritime jurisdiction of foreign nations in the strictest manner. The U.S. government and people seem to have very little concern for the danger of foreign intervention. Although

[William] Gladstone, a member of the British cabinet, proclaimed that Jefferson Davis has made a nation in the South, this remark alarmed only a few. This alarm disappeared completely upon learning that the British secretary of war had said that the South still is not a nation, and, when it would be, England would recognize it.[76]

The change in the French cabinet is also considered favorable to the federal cause. Supposedly the departure of [Duke Victor F.] Persigny, an intimate friend of Slidell, removed one of the South's most ardent supporters in the Tuileries cabinet.

The Richmond Congress . . . revised the conscription law to include those over thirty-six and under sixty who previously were exempted from forced military service.. . . .

Romero to MRE, 14 November 1862, in Romero, *Correspondencia* II, 585–86

On 8 November, General Ambrose Burnside was named to replace General McClellan in command of the Army of the Potomac. This decision has greatly surprised the whole country. It has greatly disgusted the Democratic party to which McClellan belongs. His dismissal seems related to his disobedience of this government's orders. . . . Three weeks ago the government had instructed General McClellan to attack the enemy. He did not obey this order. Apparently they have promptly sent whatever materials he requested to arm and supply his army. Meanwhile, the southern army has withdrawn from its positions near Winchester. It will not be possible to attack it now without penetrating deep into Virginia with a rigorous winter approaching that has already begun. The extremist faction of the Democratic party attributed McClellan's removal to Lincoln's spite after seeing his party had lost the elections. These Democrats have even gone so far as to speak of that general for the presidency. [John] Van Buren is the spokesman for the Democratic faction that just triumphed in the New York city elections. In a speech recently he stated his ideas for the program of this party. He wants this government to conclude an armistice with the South to permit the insurgent states to hold congressional elections. When gathered, this Congress ought to convoke a constitutional convention to concede the guarantees the South desires on slavery. The same convention, Van Buren continued, ought to decide if Lincoln should or should not continue as president. Since the decision ought to indicate Lincoln should not continue, Van Buren would suggest General McClellan to succeed Lincoln. Although this program appears absurd because neither this government nor the Richmond administration would adopt it, nevertheless, it does indicate the tendencies of the party that just triumphed in the elections and the difficulties that this government might expect.[77]

As a new U.S. Congress will not be installed until December 1863, the administration still has one year to develop its policy without great hindrances. Taking advantage of this time, they apparently intend to defeat the South during that period. Removing General McClellan is the preliminary step. His excessive caution and his extraordinary slow movements, whether from temperament or for political reasons, have presently rendered this country's forces ineffective for subjugating the South. And he probably would have continued in the same fashion if he had remained in command of the army.

The Republican party, and principally the abolitionist faction, has rejoiced greatly at General McClellan's removal. . . .

Romero to MRE, 11 December 1862, in Romero, *Correspondencia* II, 666–68

. . . Congress appears resolved to concede whatever faculties the government needs to prosecute actively military operations and to develop the emancipation measures that it has adopted. Congress hopes to diminish the difficulties that await the government when the next Congress convenes with the Democratic party in a majority. In the Senate a bill was initiated to approve the president's 22 September proclamation abolishing slavery in the insurgent states. The House has authorized the president to suspend *habeas corpus*. Recently the House has discussed the bill previously approved by the Senate, admitting West Virginia as a new state. The measure is evidently unconstitutional. However, yesterday the House adopted it as a revolutionary measure occasioned more by the necessity of war than for any other reason.

There is vague talk of an arrangement between the North and South. . . . Although currently almost impossible, noteworthy among the indispensable conditions allegedly demanded by the South, if it is to return to the Union, was the conquest of Mexico and its division into slave states.

. . . General McClellan's removal has not activated military operations along the Potomac in any way. When General Ambrose Burnside assumed command, it was presumed that a general battle would occur before much time passed. Apparently, Burnside was ordered to march on Richmond by the Fredericksburg road. One of his corps appeared before Fredericksburg demanding its surrender. The demand was refused. . . . He still has neither crossed the river nor attacked the city. . . . Supposedly, the move on Fredericksburg was only intended to deceive the Confederates, attracting their attention there in order to march on Richmond by another route. Since nothing like this [move on Richmond] has occurred recently, the story seems only an invention, destined to hide the ill success of the federal movement. The approaching winter, which will certainly be very rigorous, makes it unlikely that the march on Richmond will take place during that season.

General Banks's expedition, composed of twenty thousand to thirty thousand men, left New York this past week by water. . . .

Another expedition composed of two armored steamers and various transports also recently from New York. . . . One reliable person with access to official sources just assured me that General Banks's expedition was headed for New Orleans, and the other, under General [William H.] Emory's command, was destined for Texas.

. . . The rebels captured an entire Union brigade in Tennessee. In Arkansas the federals just won a victory. . . .

With very few exceptions, the press and the general public really believe or appear to believe that the French mediation proposal was a friendly measure toward the United States. Their odium toward England blinds them so inordinately that they judge Great Britain's refusal to enter the mediation project as hostile toward the United States. They believe France wanted the Union reestablished because they considered it England's natural rival. Thus, the Americans believe that France proposed mediation in an attempt to help the Union. Hence, some argued that England refused to enter the plan because more than anything it wanted this country divided. Aware of the [French] emperor's intentions, England feared that France would obtain its objectives if the mediation were successful. Moreover, if the sections of this country were left alone, England was certain, division was inevitable. Russia is presumed to have great sympathy for this country. Supposedly Russia refused to enter into the mediation arrangement because of its benevolent sentiment toward this country. . . .[78]

Romero to MRE, 18 December 1862, in Romero, *Correspondencia* II, 727

. . . The grand Army of the Potomac . . . crossed the Rappahannock on 11 and 12 December. It encountered little resistance from the Confederates and occupied Fredericksburg, which the southern forces had evacuated without difficulty. The Confederates retired to a strong position, previously selected for its defensible nature. The position was very well fortified.[79]

On 13 December, General Burnside [unsuccessfully] attacked the Confederate positions. . . .

Persuaded of the futility of renewing the attack on the Confederate position, fearing the enemy would cut off his path of retreat and destroy his army, and already demoralized by his repulse, General Burnside decided to withdraw. . . .

When news of the repulse of the thirteenth arrived here, it was feared that the Confederates, if conscious of the magnitude of their triumph, would harass and perhaps destroy the federal army. That would have been easy because a large intervening river cut off General Burnside's retreat. Then, upon learning Burnside's army was already on the northern side of the river, public opinion unanimously proclaimed his miraculous escape from total destruction.

Although saved, nevertheless, the army remains so demoralized that other military movements would be impossible to undertake immediately. Almost certainly then, it will be brought to this capital to spend the winter. . . .

Allegedly the president will confer the command of the army on General McClellan again. . . .

. . . This government will recuperate with difficulty from this terrible blow. Many here believe that it will be impossible to raise and organize another army and that this battle could be considered as the consummation of southern independence.

Before such an extraordinary event, all others have lost their importance. The effects of the Fredericksburg disaster will make themselves felt soon. . . . These forthcoming changes can be no less than radical. . . .

1863

Introduction to 1863

On 1 January 1863, Lincoln issued the Emancipation Proclamation, which undermined foreign interference in the Civil War because it placed the Union on the antislavery side although it did not prevent Napoleon III from suggesting mediation in early 1863. Napoleon's mediation proposal may have been as concerned with his venture in Mexico as it was with the course of the Civil War. The double victory in the summer of 1863 at Vicksburg and Gettysburg permitted Charles Adams, U.S. minister in England, to pressure the British government into halting the sale of vessels for commerce raiding to the Confederate government.

In 1863, the U.S. government faced major financial and manpower problems. It turned to conscription to obtain replacements to fill the depleted ranks of the army. The call for seven hundred thousand men in mid 1863 and early 1864 revealed that 15 percent of the names drawn failed to even report for the draft. All males from twenty to forty-five were required to enter the draft, but if they were selected, they could seek a substitute or purchase commutation of service for $300—about 100 percent to 150 percent of the annual salary of an unskilled or semiskilled wage earner. The U.S. government advanced economic and financial stability with the passage of the National Bank Act, which, combined with an 1865 act, created a uniform currency for the country. The bill facilitated the use of currency to finance part of the cost of the war.

The year 1863 proved a turning point for both the Civil War and for Romero's role in the United States. The persistent and increasingly effective blockade of the South, the Union victories at Gettysburg and Vicksburg, and the restructuring of the Union military command are often viewed as the turning point in the Civil War. Romero resigned in early 1863. He expressed frustration because he was receiving neither his pay check nor adequate expense money to conduct a campaign to influence and shape U.S. policy that had even a remote chance of success. After a short stay in Mexico, President Juárez and Secretary of Foreign Affairs Sebastián Lerdo de Tejada persuaded Romero to return to the United States with a promotion from chargé to minister and with assurances that funds would be available for his salary and for legitimate legation expenses to conduct a lobbying campaign to maximize Mexican effectiveness within the U.S. political system. During the brief period of Romero's resignation, the Mexican liberals had correctly perceived that French Emperor Napoleon III would send Archduke Maximilian to govern Mexico. Thus, upon his return, Romero struggled urgently to harness U.S. power and good will to the Mexican liberal side. Romero's absence during the summer and part of the fall of 1863 meant that the reseñas scarcely mentioned the battles of Gettysburg, Vicksburg, or Chickamauga. He returned in time to describe the battle of Chattanooga in the fall of 1863. In late 1863, Romero discovered California Congressman James McDougall was a determined ally. McDougall labored long and hard against the Franco-Maximilian intervention in Mexico.

Political Reviews—1863

Romero to MRE, 10 January 1863, in Romero, *Correspondencia* III, 125–27

. . . At the end of December, Confederate General Bragg moved toward Nashville, the capital of Tennessee, held by Union General Rosecrans with a considerable army. . . . The armies met on 31 December [1862] near Murfreesboro. . . . Desisting in his plan to take Nashville, General Bragg retired from the battlefield. . . . Although the battle was indecisive, the final result undeniably favored the federal government. . . .[1]

At the same time as the battle of Murfreesboro, another battle took place at Vicksburg. The outcome at Vicksburg was decidedly adverse to the U.S. government. Vicksburg is the key to the Mississippi for the Confederates. If Vicksburg is lost, the Confederacy will be cut into two, and the whole river will fall under federal control. The Confederates retain two quite strong points on the Mississippi, Vicksburg and Port Hudson. . . . The Confederates have gathered a very large army at Vicksburg. They have extended and reinforced their fortifications and propose to defend that city at all costs. This government does not contemplate another attempt to take Vicksburg at this time.

The Union forces suffered an even more terrible disaster in Galveston, where five vessels protected its small garrison. . . . The federal fleet had to surrender after being boarded by the attackers. . . .[2]

General [Nathaniel] Banks's expedition arrived at New Orleans where he relieved General Butler from command of the Department of the South. Soon after arriving in New Orleans, Banks moved up the river to Baton Rouge, capital of Louisiana. . . . His principal objective appears to have been to recover the Mississippi. Since General Butler's removal was supposedly done at the French government's request and to please the emperor, the North has responded very poorly to the removal.[3]

The Army of the Potomac has remained inactive at Falmouth [Virginia]. Its condition is not very satisfactory. Its senior generals are jealous and divided. The soldiers are greatly dissatisfied because of the absolutely careless payment of their wages. Generally the soldiers' pay is six months in arrears.

General [John G.] Foster, commanding the Military Department of North Carolina, successfully entered into that state. He partially destroyed one of the principal southern railroads. . . .

On 1 January, the president issued a proclamation, declaring the slaves in the rebel states free. . . . The president pretends to give liberty to the slaves who are beyond his jurisdiction while at the same time preserving in slavery all those who, being within his power, he could make free. Some slave states are endeavoring to abolish slavery peacefully. Currently Missouri appears the state most seriously disposed to adopt this reform. The partisans of emancipation have won the Missouri elections. . . . In my opinion, slavery will not survive the war. This country's internal situation is quite bad. A clamor is being raised everywhere against the government's ineptitude. While the current cabinet continues, it is widely believed everything will get worse. Elections have been held for senator in various states, and the opposition party has won almost all.

The financial situation is no more pleasing. Because of the most recent military disasters, the general dissatisfaction, the enormous sums of paper money that this government has expended, which everyone begins to believe will be irredeemable, the treasury notes, which sold at a 32 percent discount until recently, have now declined to one-half face value. Congress has just authorized the government to issue $100 million in treasury notes to cover the back pay of the army. It is currently adopting the measures necessary to reestablish the government's credit and to save the country from bankruptcy. The public debt is already more than $1 billion. . . .

Davis issued a proclamation on 23 December, declaring General Butler an outlaw. Davis personally went west to activate military operations. He remained for several days. . . .

Romero to MRE, 13 January 1863, in Romero, *Correspondencia* III, 153–54

The Army of the Potomac has moved again to attack the Confederate forces commanded by General Lee. Lee's army is allegedly very weak after detaching forces to serve in the west. . . . Ostensibly, the detached

federal force was detained because rain made the roads very difficult to
move the artillery and heavy trains on. The real reason, however,
involved dissention among the generals who commanded that army. The
dissention delayed the movement and made the projected surprise impossible. This frustrated movement led to the removal of General Burnside,
who commanded the army, and two of his three corps commanders.
General [Joseph] Hooker succeeded General Burnside. Because of his
activity and decisiveness, Hooker is not expected to remain inactive.[4]

The military court of inquiry, which heard the case of General Fitz
John Porter, accused of disobeying the orders of his superior, condemned
him to dismissal from the service and prohibited him from holding any
federal government position of trust in the future. The president confirmed the sentence. This is the first case during this war to sustain the
responsibility of a superior officer. Nevertheless, the Democratic party to
which General Porter belongs attributes the sentence to political motives.
Thus, a new issue poisons the factions in the North, which struggle more
furiously among themselves than with the southern insurgents.[5]

The newspapers are certain that Union General [John] McClernand,
who achieved a major success at Arkansas Post, has arrived at Vicksburg,
where the attack is going to be renewed. . . .

The Confederate vessel *Alabama* engaged and sank the U.S. steamer
Hatteras off the coast of Galveston. Like the *Oreto* or *Florida*, the
Alabama has continued to commit wholesale depredations against the
U.S. merchant marine.

Supposedly General Butler will return to New Orleans and General
Banks will go to Texas. Surely, since General Butler's removal did not
produce the desired effect, which was the removal of the French minister
in this capital, this government has decided to return Butler to the post
from which it had relieved him in an apparent effort to please the French
emperor.

. . . The House has been discussing a bill to organize 150 Negro
regiments. This bill has encountered the most violent opposition from
the Democratic ranks in Congress. A finance bill has already passed that
does not seem to satisfy the wishes of those who understand the gravity of
the present situation. . . .

. . . Each day the opinion becomes more widespread that southern
independence is a reality and that it is impossible to conquer the South.
The northern faction that sympathizes with the men and ideas of the
South continues to win elections everywhere, making it very strong. The
factional discord that divides the North becomes more bitter every day.
These factions profess a greater hatred for each other than the South
professes for the North. Since the debt increases and the U.S. government's credit falls in accelerated fashion, the financial situation is quite

bad, with the outlook worse for the future. Many do not so much wonder whether the North will be able to subjugate the South or not, but rather, when the next Congress is installed, or a new president elected, another civil war will erupt or not in the North.[6]

This country's decadence is so great that a considerable faction has already formed that favors French intervention in this country's internal affairs in order to terminate the present difficulties. If this should occur, the United States would even lose its own sense of dignity. After this, it cannot seem strange that some people have joyfully received the emperor's remarks dedicated to the United States at the opening of the *corps législatif.*

Romero to MRE, 19 February 1863, in Romero, *Correspondencia* III, 222–23

. . . The House approved the bill . . . regarding the organization of 150 Negro regiments for service. . . . The friends of the measure have assurances the Senate will approve the bill.

Senator [Charles] Sumner presented a bill obligating all Negroes to military service, whether they had been rescued or were fugitives from the insurgent states. The Senate rejected the bill.

Both houses approved the bill giving Missouri financial aid to abolish slavery within its jurisdiction. They granted Missouri $20 million if the abolition is immediate and $10 million if it is gradual. Supposedly, Kentucky will soon solicit similar assistance for the same purpose. Strangely, while slave state representatives and senators favor this measure, those from the free states have violently opposed it. A senator from Illinois and another from Indiana went so far as to claim that their states will refuse to pay federal taxes to pay for Missouri's slaves as a bribe to keep that state in the Union. . . .[7]

Congress is discussing and surely will soon approve the budget that the secretary of the treasury submitted. . . .

The House rejected a bill to construct a canal from the Great Lakes to New York, to enlarge those canals already existing, and to make them sufficiently large to allow passage of legislative war vessels. The debate was among the most heated in the present session. A marked antagonism was noted between congressmen from the eastern and western states. The westerners use a style that can scarcely be differentiated from that of the slave holders in Congress on the eve of seceding from the Union.

The legislatures from Illinois and New Jersey have approved resolutions that denounce the conduct of the Lincoln government in more severe terms than those used toward the secession leaders. In the wearisome ballad of the southern sympathizers, the Illinois and New Jersey legislatures say that the present war, which ought to be limited to reestablishing the Union, has degenerated into a war to abolish slavery.[8]

Some states have proposed calling a national convention in Louisville to agree upon the necessary reforms of the constitution. These reforms would grant the slave states additional guarantees of slavery, thus paving the way for their return to the Union. Naturally, this movement encountered opposition from the Republicans. However, several legislatures have already approved this proposal, which certainly will unite a considerable number of representatives. . . .

The report by President Davis's secretary of the treasury covers a period of ten months and ten days in the past year. Expenditures during this period amounted to $375,244,413, that is, a rate of $8,338,764 per week. Revenues consisted of $17,332,079 in contributions and $434,351,242 in diverse revenues, a total of $457,855,704 [sic—totals $451,683,319], which sum not only was sufficient to cover the expenses but, in addition, to pay $68,166,894 of the public debt, leaving a balance of $14,000,000. . . .[9]

Romero to MRE, 28 February 1863, in Romero, *Correspondencia* III, 259–60

. . . Both houses have approved a bill establishing conscription, which is considered a precautionary measure against a foreign war. The U.S. Senate approved a bill authorizing the president to issue letters of marque. . . . The lack of news from Vicksburg and the west suggest that if any reports exist, they are not favorable to Lincoln's government. The Army of the Potomac has remained inactive since General Hooker assumed command. Currently no signs indicate that it will undertake operations soon.

The demonstrations of Democrats against this government have continued to increase. The Democratic convention, gathered in Hartford to make a nomination for Connecticut's governorship, passed [critical] resolutions that left way behind those of the Illinois and Indiana legislatures. . . . Another Democratic convention was going to meet in Frankfort, Kentucky, for the same purpose as that of Hartford. However, the Union commanding general in Kentucky, receiving notice of the meeting's objective, labeled it collaboration with the traitors and ordered it dissolved by force. Some believed this incident would produce a great sensation, but it passed entirely unnoticed. The Washington government's financial situation has continued to deteriorate daily. Its treasury notes have devaluated to 74 percent over gold in the last days. Thus, the purchase of a $100 in gold requires $174 in treasury notes. This alone makes quite clear how far this government's credit has fallen. . . .

Romero to MRE, 6 March 1863, in Romero, *Correspondencia* III, 267–68

. . . The Thirty-seventh Congress approved and the president has already signed a so-called indemnity law in which the executive is conceded wide-ranging power, beginning with the suspension of the right of *habeas corpus*. Decided Democratic opposition prolonged the debate. . . . The House approved and thereby enacted the law authorizing the president to issue letters of marque. Among the other interesting measures that Congress adopted in the final hour was a law organizing the Idaho territory. . . . This Congress authorized expenditures, totalling $2,277,000,000, in this form:

In the special session of July 1861	$ 264,000,000
In the first regular session	913,000,000
In the second session	1,100,000,000
Total	$2,277,000,000

Congress has adopted all the financial measures proposed by the secretary of the treasury. A large part of the authorized expenses are destined for the U.S. Navy in the form of purchases, construction, and repair [of ships].

. . . Naval operations have continued unfavorable for the U.S. government. . . . The steam rams *Queen of the West* and *Indianola*, captured by the Confederates, . . . were converted into destructive instruments against this government. . . .

Romero to MRE, 19 March 1863, in Romero, *Correspondencia* III, 320–22

On 14 March, the Senate closed the special session. . . . Some of the promotions to brigadier and major general were disapproved.

Military operations have continued in absolute paralyzation. Two naval actions have occurred, one near Savannah and the other on the Yazoo River. Federal armored steamers unsuccessfully attacked Fort McAllister, . . . which forms part of the defense near Savannah. . . . The operations in the Yazoo River and in the Mississippi are still not well understood. Almost daily the telegraph announces that an attack upon Vicksburg is about to commence and that the Confederates are about to evacuate that place. Neither event occurs. The second rumor is all but impossible.

General Halleck, commander of the U.S. Army, sent instructions to General Rosecrans, commanding the Military Department of the Tennessee, regarding the treatment that ought to be given to citizens of that state and regarding the occupation of their property. Those instructions contain quite rigorous provisions that will contribute toward the return of hostilities to the inhabitants of Tennessee. Just arriving from there, a trustworthy source informed me that the citizens decidedly and uniformly favored secession. The federal authorities, he added, rule that part of the state that has submitted to them with an iron hand. General Rosecrans's army of ninety thousand is quite demoralized, he continued, and the Confederates have gathered a superior force near the federal camps in a concerted plan to destroy the federal army completely and assuredly. . . .

[Ernest] Roumain, chargé d'affaires of the Republic of Haiti, has arrived in Washington and been received by this government. Those acquainted with the very profoundly deep-rooted prejudices in this country against colored people, who are considered to form the link between man and beasts, will find no difficulty in understanding the impression produced in this city by the reception of the colored person as minister from a foreign country. . . .[10]

Since Cameron has resigned as U.S. minister in St. Petersburg, the president has again nominated Cassius M. Clay for this post. Clay had preceded Cameron, but returned to serve in the Union army. Disagreeing with the president's policy, however, he did not enter active service. . . .[11]

Romero to MRE, 8 April 1863, in Romero, *Correspondencia* III, 387–88

General Banks's forces and the squadron of Admiral Farragut departed New Orleans this past mid-March to attack Port Hudson, the principal Confederate fortified point in the lower Mississippi. Port Hudson gives the Confederates control over the river between that city and Vicksburg. . . . Banks did not attack Port Hudson, however, but retired to New Orleans. Two federal ships have managed . . . to cut the water communications between Vicksburg and Port Hudson. However, this advantage is more than offset by the danger they run by being in enemy terrain, full of [hostile] batteries, and by the difficulties they will have in obtaining provisions and munitions. . . .

Commodore Porter's squadron in the upper Mississippi has attempted to attack Vicksburg in different forms. Until now, however, all its efforts have been unavailing. . . . The earlier confidence about capturing the place has declined greatly. A short time ago, it was announced that the Confederates had invaded Kentucky again. General Burnside will command the defense of that state. . . .

. . . Failure would destroy the already gravely weakened confidence of the northern people in this government's ability to subjugate the insurgents.

All these events have again caused a rise in the gold price, the premium of which fell to 40 percent a month ago. Today gold is again priced at a 50 or 60 percent premium.

The Union army lost one of its best commanders. General [Edwin] Sumner died recently in Syracuse of pulmonary congestion.

The Senate approved a list of nominations to the rank of general at its last special session. From a total of 170, 48 are major generals and 122 are brigadier generals.

General McClellan's official preliminary report of the operations of the Army of the Potomac . . . attributes the failure of his military operations to the government for not attending to his suggestions and to the lack of support he desired and which was necessary for his plans to succeed.

. . . [The Congressional] Committee on the Conduct of the War attributed all the Army of the Potomac's setbacks and even those in the west solely and exclusively to General McClellan. In truth, the report appears more an accusation against the general than anything else. With only Republican members signing, the congressional report serves as a pretext for the Democrats to declare the report was nothing more than a Republican party stratagem to discredit General McClellan, thereby preventing his rise to the presidency in the next election. . . . In my opinion, both sides have exaggerated in pursuit of certain political objectives. The politicians have spoken of the coming presidential election for the first time. [12]

Apparently a reaction favorable to the Republican party has begun in the northern states. This party won the elections held early this month for governor and for state and federal legislatures in Rhode Island and Connecticut. The comparatively minor importance of these states would not allow these triumphs to compensate for the Republican losses in more important and more populous states. . . . [13]

Late last month, a riot of workers from several railroad companies occurred in New York. The treasury notes that currently form the exchange media of this country have fallen into discredit. This has caused a considerable price increase in all articles, even the basic necessities of life. The workers earn a [paper] dollar a day. This sufficed to satisfy their needs when [paper] money had its nominal value. After falling to its current level, however, the workers' wage is no longer sufficient. Thus, the strikers are demanding their wages be increased twenty-five cents a day. At the same time, they have taken up arms to prevent other workers who were disposed to accept a lesser daily wage from occupying their jobs. The railroad companies had to accept these demands, which to a certain point were just. Everything has been settled peaceably.[14]

John Kasson, commissioned to represent the United States in an International Postal Congress, which will meet in Paris to create uniform rates, has departed for Europe. This Congress is meeting because the U.S. postmaster general suggested it to friendly countries, which, I suppose, includes the Mexican Republic. . . .[15]

Romero to MRE, 14 April 1863, in Romero, *Correspondencia* III, 407–8

The military operations against Charleston . . . have already begun . . . under very bad auspices for this government. . . .

Thus, the certainty of a federal capture of Charleston is dissipating. . .

In North Carolina, the Confederates under General [Daniel H.] Hill besieged the federal forces located in the city of "Little Washington." U.S. General [John G.] Foster has reportedly surrendered. . . .

The federal forces have evacuated Jacksonville, Florida. . . . On 10 April, federal General [Gordon] Granger repelled Confederate General [Earl] Van Dorn, as Van Dorn attempted to capture Franklin, Tennessee. . . . The Confederates surprised and captured a federal brigade in Williamsburg. The immediate consequence of these Union disasters has been a rise in the gold price. Its value climbed yesterday to a 58 percent premium.

. . . Popular meetings have occurred almost daily in New York and other important cities. The Democrats met on 7 April in New York's Cooper Institute. They approved resolutions and made speeches . . . that very bitterly censured the government's policy. Some Democratic factions do not approve these resolutions and speeches. The central committee of the Democratic party, which is considered the defender of party dogma, has disapproved these resolutions and speeches.

General McClellan attended a meeting at the Music Academy of New York to raise funds to aid the Irish who are dying of hunger for lack of work. Acclaimed there as president, he was obliged to make a speech. He avoided saying anything regarding politics, limiting himself to speaking about the Irish in terms that will not please the British government. . . .

On 11 April, the second anniversary of the bombardment of Fort Sumter, Postmaster General Blair made a very important speech at a large popular gathering in a New York square. Coming from a cabinet member, it would appear an authorized interpretation of this government's policy. . . . I recommend that you read it in its entirety. . . . Very notable, even Blair's good judgment was overcome by the predominating passion in this country to consider Great Britain as the United States' major enemy. Therefore, he did not say a single word against France. Perhaps he sacrificed his good judgment to please his audience. In the cabinet Blair has always favored a determined policy toward Europe and opposed Seward's policy of conciliation and submission. However, there is no reason to believe that Blair's views prevail in the cabinet anymore now than previously. [16]

In a dinner given in New York in his honor, Indiana Governor [Oliver P.] Morton, one of the Republicans most decidedly in favor of continuing the war against the South, announced . . . that if the U.S. government does not recover the Mississippi and open it to navigation, the midwestern states will separate from the Union and either join the southern states or form a separate confederation. In the latter case, the Pacific coast states would follow the example of the midwestern states without delay. Governor Morton's speech . . . on the eleventh repeated and amplified his prediction, if one can so label a description that all apparently believe to be the natural course of events, but which no one has currently dared to mention in public. If some misconception exists in Morton's opinion, it is only with respect to the number of likely confederations from the northern states. Supposedly there could not be less than five, because the six northeastern states . . . would combine to form another separate nation. [17]

Armed resistance to the president's orders, advised by the leaders of the Democratic party, has begun in Reading, Pennsylvania. The U.S. government ordered the arrest of some citizens accused of conspiring against the existing order. The local population opposed the arrests, which they called arbitrary because they were made administratively. Some of those arrested made statements that suggest a conspiracy was being organized to separate the western states from the Union. Thus, Morton had scarcely indicated his fears when events revealed how well founded the fears were. . . . [18]

Romero to MRE, 12 November 1863, in Romero,
Correspondencia III, 554–55

Upon returning to this country [Romero had returned to Mexico for six months], I encountered public affairs in the same condition . . . in which I had left them this past May. . . .

[While Romero was absent in Mexico], the Confederate Army of

Northern Virginia again crossed the river under General Lee, invading Maryland for a second time. Then, General Meade, commanding the Army of the Potomac, fought the Confederates at Gettysburg. Although the outcome appeared indecisive, the Confederate forces retired, recrossing the river and remaining in Virginia. Since then nothing serious has occurred between the two armies contending on the Potomac. . . .

. . . The Army of the Cumberland, . . . under General Rosecrans, attacked Confederate General Bragg's forces at a point near Chattanooga, called Chickamauga, but was unable to dislodge Bragg from his position. Therefore, the battle was a defeat for the federal forces. This government apparently evaluated the battle in the same fashion, since shortly thereafter General Rosecrans was relieved of command. General [George] Thomas replaced him. The Army of the Cumberland was put under General Grant's orders. Grant now commands all the federal forces in the west. He has obtained the most important victories that this government has won this year, namely, the capture of Vicksburg and Port Hudson on the Mississippi River. These victories divided the Confederacy into two sections without communications between them and brought the Mississippi under federal control.[19]

Some time ago a second expedition departed to attack Charleston. Since on this occasion the expeditionary force is prepared to take the time necessary to capture that place, . . . if . . . the [expeditionary] force continues to attack with the perseverance revealed until now, everything suggests that important port will fall sooner or later.

There are also vague rumors of the departure of a land expedition from New Orleans to occupy Brownsville and the left bank of the Rio Grande. . . . The previous expedition that went by water suffered a misfortune in the Sabine Pass, forcing it to return to New Orleans. The most recent news from New Orleans announced the impending departure of a naval force to aid the new expedition. . . . The federal government has also obtained . . . important political advantages that have contributed in a major way to augmenting its prestige and to improving its situation. Republican candidates or candidates favoring the war have won the early October elections in Pennsylvania, Ohio, and in other principal parts of this Union. The elections held on 5 November in New York, Massachusetts, New Jersey, Maryland, Wisconsin, and elsewhere were no less favorable for candidates supporting the government than the earlier ones.[20]

These circumstances and the administration's possession of a majority in the Congress assured them that, at least for another year, their measures will not encounter [unmanageable] opposition in Congress. They can pursue military operations with the activity that circumstances and the government's desire require.

Since England apparently has already separated itself from France in the common action that both powers had been pursuing with respect to the United States, the external complications rising from the American question have recently taken a quite favorable turn. A short while ago Lord Russell declared in a speech, which, while not official, nevertheless expressed his government's opinion, that England would not intervene militarily in this country's internal affairs. Moreover, apparently a change very favorable to the Union government occurred recently when the British government ordered the detention of two armed steamers that were being constructed for the Confederate government in Liverpool.

As the British government had already allowed the construction of several other steamers without hindering their departure, the seizure of these two suggests British policy intends to be more friendly towards the Washington government in the future. . . .

Romero to MRE, 4 December 1863, *Correspondencia* III, 568–69

. . . A battle [has occurred] in the vicinity of Chattanooga between the forces of Union General Grant and of rebel General Bragg. The former dislodged the latter from several important positions in this battle. . . . At about the same time, General Meade moved the Army of the Potomac against Confederate General Lee. . . . After the two armies faced each other and fought some skirmishes, Meade retreated to his old position north of the Rapidan near Washington. He will allegedly make winter quarters there.

In Charleston operations continued without notable progress even against Fort Sumter. . . .

The Democratic candidate won the recent mayoral elections in New York City. . . .

Romero to MRE, 12 December 1863, in Romero, *Correspondencia* III, 571–72

The U.S. Congress convened on 7 December. On the same day they elected a speaker. A Republican won with 101 votes. A majority required only 88 votes. This vote confirms the view that the government can count upon a respectable majority in that body. The president's message . . . contained no reference to Mexican affairs. The message undoubtedly conformed with the policy that the cabinet apparently has adopted. This policy consisted in feigning ignorance about events in Mexico. The president's message called attention to the proposal for reestablishing governments in the states that wish to return to the Union (against the opinion of some who desire to reduce them to the condition of territories), to the almost general amnesty conceded to rebels who would take an oath of adherence to the federal government, and to the so-called 'Emancipation Proclamation,' which Lincoln had declared in effect as a temporary war measure until the Supreme Court should declare it unconstitutional. . . . .

The secretary of the navy's report suggests that at the beginning of this administration, the U.S. fleet consisted of only 78 vessels. In December, 1862, it already had 427 ships, which increased to 588 in the current year. The navy has adopted armor plating and artillery with a load and reach previously considered impossible. The current fire power of the navy is 5,777 cannon, without counting 700 cannon of a new invention, which will be included in the present month's figures.

The secretary of war reports that armory expenses alone [repair and modification of weapons] during the year amounted to more than $42 million dollars. Additionally, the government has purchased 1,577 cannon and 1,032,841 muskets and rifles.

Although the war has correctly absorbed the resources and attention of the government, the secretary of the interior's report mentions expending many thousands of dollars improving the capital [building and grounds] and introducing Potomac water to Washington. The postmaster general reported his department's revenue was $11,163,789.59 and that the expenses exceeded the revenue by $150,417. Thus, during the recent years, the size of the deficit has greatly diminished. Expenses and income are expected to balance out soon.

. . . The secretary of the treasury's report awoke great interest. Reportedly, the current U.S. debt has risen to a thousand one hundred million dollars, and if it continues in this manner until July of the coming year, it will climb to a thousand seven hundred million dollars. Nevertheless, even then it will not be half of England's debt, which is four thousand million dollars. Of course, the latter pays a much lower rate of interest. According to Chase, the interest on the U.S. debt will be $86 million in the coming year. If the war should last until 1865, the debt would then increase by one thousand five hundred million. The interest would still not reach the $140 million that England pays. Even in the most unfavorable situation, with its immense resources, this nation is expected to emerge triumphant from its commitments. . . .

1864

Introduction to 1864

The military campaign became more intense, expensive, and costly in human lives. Major General Grant was promoted to lieutenant general and given command of all U.S. forces. He made General William T. Sherman commander in the west. These two generals launched a dual assault upon the main Confederate armies. From the Wilderness campaign in May 1864 until the war in Virginia ended in April 1865, Grant's army always remained near Lee's army. After the Wilderness conflict, other major engagements were fought at Spottsylvania and Cold Harbor before the two armies entered siege warfare at Petersburg and Richmond beginning in June 1864. Grant refused to be panicked when the Confederates attempted to force a withdrawal of Grant's forces by initiating a campaign in the Shenandoah Valley that threatened Washington. After Grant selected several inept commanders, he appointed General Philip Sheridan to command Union forces in the valley. Sheridan soundly defeated the Confederate force in the valley, ending any threat to the North from that area. Meanwhile, Sherman confronted the Confederate army under the command of General Joseph E. Johnston and his successor General John Hood near Atlanta. After driving Hood from Atlanta, Sherman cut loose from his supply lines and headed for the Atlantic coast, leaving General George H. Thomas behind to handle Hood's army. Sherman reached the sea in December about the same time Thomas was shattering Hood's army near Nashville.

In 1864 Lincoln's government resorted to two large drafts to fill the army ranks for Grant's assault upon Lee's army and Richmond. There were clear signs of continued decline in popular support for, or understanding of, Union goals and the bloody war. Twenty-five percent of those whose names were drawn for the preinduction physical failed to appear. The U.S. government established the Office of Commissioner of Immigration in mid-1864 to induce foreigners to migrate to the United States with the promise of a reduced waiting-time for U.S. citizenship in return for military service.

The rapidly rising prices and slowly rising wages produced hardship among the employed. Workers responded with an increased tendency to organize national trade unions. To the six pre–Civil War national unions, the period from 1863 to 1873 saw the addition of twenty-six more, beginning with the locomotive engineers in 1863. Employers responded with employer associations, such as those formed in Michigan and New York City in 1864.

Since 1862, some Republican politicians, called radicals, had become increasingly disappointed because of their inability to align the Lincoln administration behind their program for freeing slaves and prosecuting the war more energetically and punitively. This radical Republican hostility toward President Lincoln and Secretary of State Seward was not restricted to their differences on domestic policy and the conduct of the war. They differed markedly on the proper foreign policy for the United States to follow in face of the French puppet Maximilian's empire in Mexico. This dispute between Lincoln's administration and many radicals came to a head when Maximilian formally accepted the Mexican throne under Napoleon's protection. Romero had labored hard with Representative Henry Winter Davis (Maryland), Senator James McDougall (California), and Representative John Kasson (Iowa) to produce a resolution condemning French action in Mexico. The Davis resolution stated U.S. refusal to recognize any monarchy created in the new world under foreign influence and upon the ruins of an American republic. While Romero preferred the Davis resolution, he developed a strategy of keeping various resolutions alive, while laboring diligently behind the scenes for the toughest one. If Romero's first choice failed, there were fall-back plans. Finally, the Davis resolution passed on 4 April 1864, by a vote of 104 to 0. Yet Senator Sumner prevented the resolution from passing in the Senate because he believed it unwise to challenge the French while in the midst of the Civil War.

By early 1864, Romero had become convinced that Lincoln and Seward would not provide effective assistance for Mexico. In response to the Lincoln administration's stance, Romero became interested in ousting Seward or unseating Lincoln. Toward this end an informal alliance of convenience bloomed between the radicals (and other opponents of the administration) and Romero. For example, Romero supplied resolutions or calls for information that friendly radicals introduced in Congress to embarrass the administration. Romero's sources kept him privy to the secret sessions of the Senate Foreign Relations Committee. He supplied information and critiqued speeches for opponents of the administration during the summer and fall of 1864.

After interviewing the various Republican and Democratic candidates for the presidency in 1864, Romero lent his confidential support to radical favorite General John C. Frémont's effort to win the nomination away from Lincoln. When Frémont's candidacy failed to capture the

Republican nomination, Romero tried to encourage the independent candidacy of Frémont. When this hope failed, Romero aided Senators Wade, McDougall, and Zachariah Chandler and Congressman Schuyler Colfax through subtle means to defeat the Lincoln-Seward team.

The 1864 presidential election turned on the military campaigns, but General McClellan, supposedly a Democratic proponent of ending the war, rejected that option in the late summer of 1864 because the Union forces were winning battles. Grant and Sherman refused to retreat even when they suffered temporary setbacks. Lincoln faced a great deal of opposition within his own party, which, however, weakened and then crumbled as Grant and Sherman fought on determinedly. The success of the Union armies contributed to Lincoln's victory in the fall of 1864. Lincoln, who had announced his reconstruction plan in December of 1863, encountered a radical alternative during the summer political campaign in the form of the [Senator Benjamin] Wade-[Representative Henry Winter] Davis bill.

The Mexican minister strove to end the Civil War in order to free the power of the Union to hang as a Democlean sword over the neck of Maximilian and Napoleon. In late 1864, Romero offered to undertake a trip to the Confederate capital in Richmond, alone or with the other Latin American diplomats in Washington, in search of a mediated end to the war. Seward expressed appreciation for the offer without requesting its implementation.

When Union military and political leaders anticipated victory in the winter of 1864–65, Romero kept pointing to the unpleasant possibility that the Franco-Maximilian forces would offer refuge to the defeated, fleeing rebels. This refuge might allow the Confederates to recover from their wounds and renew the attack alone or aided with French-Mexican forces in the future. While many rejected such a scenario as unlikely, the possibility of guerrilla or raiding activity from rebel forces based in Mexico could never be dismissed. General Grant repeatedly declared in 1865 that the Civil War would not be over until the French were expelled from Mexico.

Political Reviews—1864

Romero to MRE, 6 January 1864, in Romero, *Correspondencia* IV, 2–3

. . . War operations are completely suspended because of the winter. Nevertheless, the siege of Charleston continues. . . . General Grant still occupies Chattanooga and General Meade, the Valley of Virginia. Following their triumphs of last year, both engaged in labors of organization and discipline, no less than in the convenient stockpiling of supplies of all kinds. The opposing forces operating in Tennessee continued their strategic movements, which have led General [William W.] Averell to cut off General Longstreet from all communication with Virginia. As a consequence, supposedly Longstreet is completely isolated and will have to surrender.

. . . The difficulty of communication because of heavy snows and because many rivers are frozen has prevented a quorum [in Congress]. . . .

. . . The reports of the Confederate secretaries of the treasury and navy . . . call attention to the completely bankrupt condition that the secretary of the treasury revealed to Davis. As the only measure to escape bankruptcy and to confront the enormous budget of 1864, he proposed to negotiate a loan of $500 million. The interest on this sum should be paid in specie, since Confederate paper has fallen into complete discredit. Already the quantity emitted amounts to $800 million. The secretary of the treasury desired to retire $600 million of this sum through the indicated loan, leaving the rest in circulation. Even if the Confederate Congress would approve the proposal, it appears unlikely the Confederacy can realize the loan. Since Secretary Memminger called this the South's only hope, it is inconceivable how the rebel states can sustain themselves much longer. . . .[1]

Romero to MRE, 4 February 1864, in Romero *Correspondencia* IV, 24–25

. . . The rebels are making a major effort to organize a respectable army to begin campaigning this coming spring. Therefore, they are enforcing most vigorously the conscription law passed by the Confederate Congress. Assuredly, intending to present another army no less numerous and respectable on 1 February, the president decreed a draft of five hundred thousand men. Nevertheless, the forces raised in previous drafts should be subtracted from this number.

With less than a year before this coming November's presidential election, all parties are preparing to enter the ballot. A large part of the Republican party favors the reelection of Lincoln. He will certainly be one of the candidates at least.

The Democratic party has decided on General Grant, unquestionably the most distinguished commander of the present war and the one most favored by fortune. Therefore, they intend to make him a lieutenant general, increasing his influence and making his election easier. . . .

Romero to MRE, 25 February 1864, in Romero, *Correspondencia*
IV, 71

Already the various parties have initiated the labors to assure their
candidate's election to the presidency. . . . The Lincoln partisans initiated the election campaign by organizing popular mass meetings in favor
of Lincoln's reelection on the 22d of this month, Washington's birthday.
Then, many state legislatures passed resolutions approving Lincoln's
policy and recommending his reelection. Thus, it can be said that
Lincoln is the official candidate. The other parties do not want to be left
behind. . . . However, I have been assured that General Grant does not
want the nomination [of the Democratic party]. Therefore, that party will
probably turn to General McClellan. The Republican party is deeply
divided over its candidate. Thus, while one wing favors the renomination
of Lincoln, another wing favors the nomination of Chase. The pure
abolitionist fraction of that party, although it has not presently designated
a candidate, will probably decide on General Frémont. [2]
The publication of a manifesto by Chase's partisans, favoring his
candidacy and opposing Lincoln's election, surprised many. After the
manifesto's publication, harmony between the president and his secretary
of the treasury scarcely seemed possible. Certainly that publication has
only confirmed what many have known for a long time, namely, the
upcoming elections have caused a complete schism in the cabinet.
Seward, Blair, Welles, and Bates favor Lincoln's reelection while Chase
and Stanton favor Chase's election. The ill feelings among the cabinet
members extend to the extreme that some do not even greet each
other. . . .
Sailors are very scarce to man the war vessels recently constructed.
Since bounties to those who enlist in the army range up to $500, and,
since there are no bounties for those who enlist in the navy, naturally,
everyone has preferred to enlist in the army. Eighteen vessels are ready to
sail, but they completely lack crews. Congress is currently occupied in
remedying this problem. . . .

Romero to MRE, 10 March 1864, in Romero, *Correspondencia*
IV, 90–91

. . . Two federal incursions have entered Confederate territory, and
both have suffered ill fortune. General [Quincy A.] Gillmore undertook
[unsuccessfully] . . . to recover the state of Florida. . . . [3]
. . . The second [disappointing] campaign involved the cavalry of the
Army of the Potomac commanded by General Judson Kilpatrick. . . . [4]

The U.S. Congress remains in session without having done anything noteworthy recently, except to create the high army rank of lieutenant general. Once the rank was created, the government immediately conferred it upon General Grant, as already had been announced. This general has just been received with demonstrations of great appreciation in Washington. Supposedly, he will take supreme command of the U.S. Army, and General Henry Halleck, who has commanded it until now, will command the Army of the Potomac.

While the majority of state legislatures has declared to be in favor of Lincoln's candidacy in the coming election, two or three of them, including West Virginia, have had demonstrations favoring Chase, currently secretary of the treasury. . . .

The Confederate Congress . . . publicized the profound rancor that reigns in the South against the Lincoln administration and the Republican party. It also reaffirmed the determined resolution not to reunite with the United States on the previous basis and to defend the odious institution of slavery at all costs. Now Congress has repeated what Davis had already stated in the name of the Confederacy, namely, that they would prefer domination by any foreign power a thousand times more than to reunite with the North.

The society called the "Chamber of Commerce of the State of New York" has published an interesting work regarding navigation by steamship lines. It solicits subventions and favorable legislation from the state legislature for the establishment of several such lines using New York as the port of departure. Those lines considered necessary for Europe are principally a weekly to Liverpool, a bimonthly to Le Havre, and others to the Hanseatic cities, to Lisbon, to Cadiz, and to Genoa, touching at Barcelona and Marseille. For the Americas, the New York Chamber of Commerce would establish a bimonthly line to Punta Isabel at Brazos Santiago with a branch in New Orleans. The publication also called attention to the importance of establishing an active commerce with Mexico, expecting that a railroad would be constructed to Monterrey and then to Mazatlán. Other projected bimonthly lines would run to Rio de Janeiro, Pernambuco, and Bahía with a branch to Buenos Aires. When speaking of the South American nations, the chamber acknowledges its fear of European invasions and abuses. Mexico itself, the New York Chamber observed, at one time the enemy of the United States, confides in the United States' good faith, expecting this country to aid it with friendship and sympathy. . . .

Romero to MRE, 18 March 1864, in Romero, *Correspondencia*
IV, 108–9

With the next election already approaching and the election campaign
having opened, the different parties hasten to formulate and publish their
platforms as one of the surest means of winning supporters. So far, two of
the three published platforms have approved the principle of defending
and sustaining the Monroe Doctrine, which very notably reveals the
tendencies of public opinion in this country. These platform statements
amount to a formal commitment not to permit the French to establish
either monarchy or a colonial regime in Mexico, or even to intervene in
Mexican internal affairs. . . .[5]

. . . There are now three [Republican] candidates for the presidency:
Lincoln, the official candidate, sustained by the moderate Republicans
who sustain the current government; Chase, supported by the radical
Republicans, enemies of the government; and General Frémont, the
candidate of the abolitionists. If Lincoln is reelected, Seward will continue as secretary of state for another four years. Under Seward this
government's policy in regard to Mexico would not change in a single iota
from what it has been recently. Thus, we want the election of any other
candidate.

Senator Pomeroy, chairman of the committee that proposed Chase,
spoke in the Senate on 10 March in favor of Chase's candidacy. Pomeroy
suggested a platform to his fellow committee members, the third article of
which reads:

"We will sustain the Monroe Doctrine by means of which the des-
potism afflicting Old Europe should be prevented from extending itself to
the New World. With the doctrine we will liberate our country from
tyrannical usurpations, and with it we will guide this great American
contest for the development of popular institutions."

The program of General Frémont's supporters is no less explicit on this
point than the general himself was in a speech given before a large crowd
in Cooper's Institute, New York, on 29 February, to introduce the English
abolitionist, George Honpson. . . . Honpson denounced "the attempt of
a European power to establish an Austrian throne on the ruins of a
brother Republic, this attempt seeks to ridicule the public spirit of this
country and is eminently hostile to the establishment of its liberal
principles." This allusion produced the longest and most enthusiastic
applause from the auditorium.

The New Nation, a weekly newspaper that General Frémont's supporters have begun to publish in New York, has very acrimoniously censured
this government's foreign policy. . . .

Apparently the Democratic party will also split, having at least two candidates. Certainly one will be General McClellan, whose views in respect to Mexico are perhaps even more favorable to Mexico than General Frémont's. The so-called Tammany Hall faction of the Democratic party has already published its program. . . . Although it states nothing regarding Mexico, should that faction's candidate triumph, he would certainly follow a policy toward Mexico very distinct from the current government. Generally, the Democratic party has more audacity, better comprehension of foreign relations questions, and more attachment to the traditional policy of the United States than the Republican party. . . . My opinion about each candidate as things now stand [is as follows]. Lincoln evidently has the most advantageous position. If the army should obtain positive advantages over the Confederates before the election date, his reelection is certain. If the army does not obtain advantages and, even more likely, if it suffers some reverses, the election would fall to the Democratic party's candidate, provided that party is not divided. However, if the Democrats should be divided, the election would fall to Chase or any Republican candidate who is not a well-known abolitionist.

Although Chase has written a letter announcing his withdrawal from the contest because his home state [Ohio] legislature passed some resolutions favoring Lincoln's reelection, knowledgeable persons consider this a stratagem to obtain greater success. . . .

I know that Generals Frémont and McClellan each seek a favorable opportunity to express his views on Mexican affairs. I will arrange for them to have the opportunity. It is believed here, and not without foundation, that the Mexican question could decide the coming presidential election. During the Texas War, the Mexican question entirely decided the election for [James] Polk. Hence, supposedly the current Mexican question, which is more serious, ought to influence the election more markedly than in the prior case. . . .

Romero to MRE, 24 March 1864, in Romero, *Correspondencia* IV, 114–15

. . . General [William T.] Sherman's expedition has departed from Vicksburg, . . . headed for Selma, Alabama, to destroy the large deposits of munitions that the Confederates have there. Sherman moved very near to Selma but could not attack because General W[illiam] S[ooy] Smith's cavalry . . . could not meet Sherman in Meridan. . . . Nevertheless, General Sherman allegedly obtained great advantages by destroying various important railroads and valuable rebel properties before returning to Vicksburg. . . .[6]

. . . The president named Lieutenant General S. Grant to the command of the U.S. Army, removing Major General Halleck from this command at his own request. The order thanked Halleck for filling that difficult post with ability and zealousness. Major General Sherman was entrusted with command of the military division of the Mississippi, and Major General [James B.] McPherson was entrusted with command of the Army of the Tennessee.[7]

. . . Lincoln also decreed the enlistment of another two hundred thousand men. Congress had authorized this number in addition to the five hundred thousand men ordered to be raised by the coming 1 February. Voluntary enlistment must be completed by the coming 15 April. Thereafter a draft will fill the quotas.

Among congressional actions, the most important is the declaration that in those areas where slavery still exists, the fathers and sons of slaves who enter U.S. military service will become free by that very act. In addition, the nation assumes no commitment to indemnify the proprietors.

Supposedly Congress granted the president the important authority to sell a large quantity of reserve gold that should lower the price of gold and raise relative value of paper. Nevertheless, presently the measure has not influenced the market, and the price relationship between gold and paper remains the same as before this step.[8]

. . . The only new item is the very vague rumor that the friends of [John P.] Usher, currently secretary of the interior, have attempted to present him as a candidate. There is also a vague rumor that Major General Halleck would be proposed as a candidate for the Democratic nomination. . . .

Romero to MRE, 15 April 1864, in Romero, *Correspondencia* IV, 132–33

. . . Preparations on both sides indicate that the campaign will open soon. General Grant has been reorganizing the Army of the Potomac. He will assume immediate command when operations begin. The election campaign has also been paralyzed. Chase appears definitely to have withdrawn from the race. Everyone seems to agree to leave the preparatory labor for the election until the last hour, out of fear that the debate and different aspirations might divide the factions and thus easily allow the southern sympathizers to elect their candidate. . . . The Mexican question will obviously play a large role in the election. . . . The platform of the Rhode Island Democratic convention in its second article stated: "Be it resolved that the French invasion of Mexico is a violation of the Monroe Doctrine which a Democratic administration would never have tolerated."

Recently, Congress has very heatedly debated a resolution to expel two representatives who have favored recognizing southern independence. Although the majority of Congress voted for the expulsion resolution, it was not adopted because a two-thirds vote of the members present is required. Nevertheless, the House approved a vote of censure against these representatives. Almost all the Democratic representatives voted against expulsion, while many voted for censure. This has produced a new division among the Democratic legislators. They are now designated War Democrats and Peace Democrats.[9]

. . . The Senate has approved a constitutional amendment abolishing slavery in the United States. . . .

Romero to MRE, 29 April 1864, in Romero, *Correspondencia* IV, 166–67

. . . Fort Pillow in Tennessee has fallen. . . . The troops of Confederate General [Nathan B.] Forrest are charged with committing great cruelty there, butchering all the Negroes and their officers. Of somewhat greater importance, the federal fortifications at Plymouth, North Carolina, also surrendered after resisting Confederate attackers for three days. . . .[10]

Recently, rumor has General Banks suffering a significant defeat in Louisiana. . . .

Romero to MRE, 13 May 1864, in Romero, *Correspondencia* IV, 171–72

. . . The Union army campaign has commenced with considerable activity against the Confederate army under General Lee. After attaching various forces to the Army of the Potomac, which raised its strength to more than two hundred thousand men, General Grant prepared to march against the enemy at the same time that General Burnside with thirty thousand soldiers was to advance on Richmond via the James River. Moreover, General Sherman would move on the enemy in the west with an army of a similar size. After crossing two rivers, the Rappahannock and the Rapidan, the Army of the Potomac encountered the main body of Lee's troops near a place called the Wilderness on 7 May. A very bloody three-day battle followed. Afterwards Lee retreated toward Richmond. . . . Several generals were killed, among them Wardemorth [*sic*—James S. Wadsworth], a rich New York proprietor, who, carried away by his enthusiasm for the northern cause, had taken up arms, and John Sedgwick, a major general with a very important command. . . . On the ninth, the president's proclamation recommended that in the churches and elsewhere in the country thanks should be given to the All Powerful for the victories. He requested the people to ask for the triumph of the U.S. cause. . . .[11]

. . .There is considerable anxiousness to learn what is happening now and also the details of what has happened in the fighting at the Wilderness, since currently one can only ascertain vaguely that the Union troops have gained some considerable advantage over the enemy. Reportedly, General Butler has arrived at City Point on his march toward Richmond, without learning if he is about to encounter Confederate General Beauregard, who ought to be a short distance away. . . . The House is debating the so-called "Tariff Bill," a proposal to increase importation duties. . . . The third article of the platform of the New Jersey Germans contains the declaration to "repel in a determined manner the European efforts to intervene on Mexican soil." . . .

Romero to MRE, 26 May 1864, in Romero, *Correspondencia* IV, 190–91

Colonel [José Augustín] Arguelles was charged with fraudulently selling more than one hundred slaves from a cargo that the colonel had seized in the District of Colón [Cuba], where he was political chief. Arguelles having left the United States surreptitiously . . . , his wife appeared before the Grand Jury of New York. Upon ascertaining the facts, the secretary of state submitted the wife's letter and [another] document to the *Herald* and the other New York newspapers for publication. Nevertheless, the jury continued to try the U.S. marshal for having assaulted, illegally arrested, and violently kidnapped Arguelles. The accused [marshal] will probably not be punished, but it is feared that the trial might cast a shadow on the administration, even though it has used the trial as a pretext for condemning and persecuting the infamous slave trade. . . .[12]

The president has proclaimed that a citizen of this country serving as the consul for a foreign country in the United States is not excused from his obligation to serve in the army. He canceled the exequatur of the Belgian consul in St. Louis, Missouri. Finding himself in such a situation, the Belgian consul had refused to serve. . . . The armies of Generals Grant and Lee have not ceased to move and to·engage in skirmishes and armed contacts of varying size. . . .

. . . A New York newspaper [published] . . . General Lee's proclamation and several evaluations of the recent battles from a perspective contrary to those current in the North. All in all, General Grant has doubtless obtained some advantage. He has conducted the campaign both actively and prudently, while contending with the able strategy of a powerful adversary. . . .

The German radicals of Alton, Illinois, adopted . . . resolutions to sustain the Monroe Doctrine . . . at a meeting held to reach agreement regarding the presidential election.[13]

Romero to MRE, 2 June 1864, in Romero, *Correspondencia* IV, 205–6

. . . General Grant has had to change his campaign plan. Apparently he planned to advance by the road from the north in the direction of Richmond, obligating Lee to devote himself exclusively to defending that route. Meanwhile, well reinforced, General Butler would attack Richmond from the southwest [*sic*—southeast] where he probably could not be resisted. This project called for an effective contribution from General [Franz] Sigel, operating on the road to the east [*sic*—west], and from Butler, cutting the southern road leading into the Confederate capital. However, Butler has revealed little tactical expertise according to public opinion. He has placed himself on the defensive by fortifying his position instead of advancing on Richmond. Moreover, Sigel . . . suffered a defeat of some magnitude. Both Butler and Sigel failed to render the road assigned to them useless for the Confederates.[14]

This dual failure has caused General Grant suddenly to vary his plan of attack. Unable to fight Lee successfully in his formidable positions, Grant quite capably and boldly moved to the flank. By means of a rapid and well executed march, Grant moved much closer to Richmond by the south side. Supposedly he is going to unite with Butler's forces in order to attack Richmond en masse from that side. This move has revealed Grant's strategic ability to be at a level with that celebrated in the Confederate Lee. Most regrettably, Generals Butler and Sigel did not understand or were unable to fulfill their part in the combined operations. . . .

. . . The Democratic party will allegedly join the radical Republicans in order to defeat Lincoln's candidacy. As you know, the Democratic party will nominate General McClellan. The candidates of both factions [Democrats and radical Republicans?] have advocated the revindication of the Monroe Doctrine.

. . .The Confederate Senate received poorly some resolutions proposed by one of its members to procure an armistice, while striving for a settlement with the United States. This reveals the spirit of resistance and rancor that reigns in the South. . . .

Romero to MRE, 9 June 1864, in Romero, *Correspondencia* IV, 222–23

. . . General Grant has arrived at the right bank of the Chicahominy to the east of Richmond. . . . A successful attack could have ended with the occupation of Richmond. . . . In the end the Confederates conserved their positions. . . .[15]

General [William T.] Sherman was already near Merritla [*sic*—Marietta] in west Georgia. Confederate General [Joseph E.] Johnston has contained Sherman's advance at this point. Neither that army nor General Butler's has had any formal engagement during the last week.

. . . The radical Republican convention that met in Cleveland on 31 May named General Frémont as its presidential candidate and General [John] Cochrane for vice-president. . . . From the tenor of the letters in which both generals accept the nominations, from the manner with which Democratic papers have spoken of that convention, and from the fact that a Democrat has been nominated as vice-president, it seems beyond dispute that a formal agreement exists between the radical Republicans and the War Democrats to cooperate in support of the new candidates in order to prevent Lincoln's reelection.[16]

The day before yesterday, the convention of the administration's faction of the Republican party gathered in Baltimore. Yesterday it nominated Lincoln for reelection and Andrew Johnson of Tennessee for Vice-president. It was assumed that [Hannibal] Hamlin, the current vice-president and a member of the radical Republican faction, would be renominated, but it was not so. The convention preferred a War Democrat. The convention's platform contains an article that apparently approves the president's policy in Mexican affairs. This article declares that the American people will never view with indifference any European power's subversion by force or deception of any republican government on this continent, and they will view the efforts of European powers to establish monarchical government in America with suspicion and as menacing to the peace and independence of the United States.[17]

Allegedly the Baltimore convention requested, and Lincoln promised to change, the cabinet if he is reelected.

The convention of the Democratic party proper will meet in Chicago on 31 July. . . .

In his letter of acceptance, General Frémont abstained from any reference to that plank relative to the Monroe Doctrine in the platform of the convention that nominated him. For better reasons, Lincoln will do likewise. . . .

Romero to MRE, 16 June 1864, in Romero, *Correspondencia* IV, 232–33

After undertaking a risky march to attack Richmond from the southeast, . . . General Grant has crossed the Chicahominy and James rivers. His position is exactly to the south of, and a short distance from, the Confederate capital. He has completed the reunion with General Butler's forces. For ten days during these movements nothing official was published about the war. Apparently this was done so that the enemy would not become aware of General Grant's intentions. . . .

General Hunter, who succeeded in command of Sigel's army corps after the latter was removed because of the defeat he suffered, . . . has won a complete victory in west Virginia over Confederate [William E.] Jones. Jones died in the action and his forces have been completely shattered. . . . The House has approved the repeal of the famous fugitive slave law. . . .[18]

Romero to MRE, 23 June 1864, in Romero, *Correspondencia* IV, 238–39

. . . General Grant had moved south of Richmond. . . . From there, it would appear easier to attack the Confederate capital. Petersburg, lying to the south of Richmond, is very well fortified and prepared to resist a siege. That city was assaulted at once. After a bloody battle, even its second line of trenches was taken.[19]

. . . However, making an extraordinary effort, the Confederates had recovered their second line of fortifications, pushing the enemy back to the first. Now reportedly, Petersburg is going to be bombarded. . . .

. . . The truth about the military moves is difficult to discover. Frequently newspapers insert Confederate reports and news items that contradict the reports of the Union commanders. . . .

. . . General Hunter's repulse in Lynchburg . . . is described here as a simple reconnaissance.

The Senate approved the bill pending that addressed speculation in paper and gold. Then the president signed it, and so it has become law. This law purposes to place obstacles to the speculations of alternatively buying and selling paper money, which is continually done in this country and especially in New York. These actions give gold such a high price that paper loses its esteem as a consequence. In order to hinder this trade, done on a large scale and almost always on credit, the government has prohibited the sale of gold or paper except by cash in certain places and by certain people. This decree should produce the same results as one signed twelve months ago that authorized the government to sell its stored up gold to prevent the depreciation of the paper money. Nevertheless, it is feared that this new law might be as potent for this purpose as the previous law was. In spite of that earlier law, gold has continued to climb in price. Today, notwithstanding the recent passage of the new decree after being debated for three days, gold fluctuated in New York from 210 to 236, or in other terms, at a premium over paper of from 110 to 136 percent.

. . . An investigation by the House Committee on Public Expenditures with regard to the New York customs house has not proven the charge in which the customs house employees are accused of fraudulently dispatching merchandise for the Confederacy. Therefore, the report mentioned vessels that were dispatched for Matamoros, but the cargos of these vessels are consumed mainly in Texas despite being processed under the current regulations to avoid the cargos falling into the hands of the Confederates. . . .[20]

Romero to MRE, 30 June 1864, in Romero, *Correspondencia* IV, 246–47

General Grant's army suffered a considerable rebuff in front of Petersburg. . . . On 27 June General Sherman suffered another reverse while attacking north of Chattanooga[?] . . . .

On the other hand, General Hunter, for whom some anxiety was experienced, . . . has been victorious in all encounters. . . .

Upon receiving the Baltimore Convention's nomination for the presidency . . ., Lincoln stated his adherence to the convention platform. . . . However, he took particular care when alluding to the Monroe Doctrine plank to limit his agreement with it. He explained his position in terms that revealed his desire not to commit himself in any absolute form but to express his stand ambiguously in preparation for any eventuality. . . .

. . . The president has just accepted Chase's resignation from the office of secretary of the treasury, naming David Tod, ex-governor of Ohio, in his place. The reason for the resignation seems to have been that Congress did not agree with Chase's plan to augment internal taxes. . . .

. . . The Confederate Congress retains the same very firm resolution to sustain its cause although in language much more courteous than in previous cases. It also demonstrates great moderation and confidence in the justice of its cause. . . .

Romero to MRE, 7 July 1864, in Romero, *Correspondencia* IV, 253

Some of Grant's forces had suffered a rude defeat between Petersburg and Weldon while attempting to destroy the railroad between those two cities. . . . After this defeat, General Grant has limited himself to defending his position near Petersburg.

Meanwhile, Confederate General [Richard] Ewell, with an estimated twenty thousand to thirty thousand men, has marched against General Hunter. Hunter has been obliged to retreat. . . . Ewell's movement has greatly agitated the states of Maryland and Pennsylvania. The Pennsylvania governor has called up all those capable of bearing arms. . . .[21]

The president named Tod to replace Chase as secretary of the treasury. But failing to obtain Senate approval, Tod did not accept the nomination. . . . Some relate the Senate's disapproval of Tod to its wish for Lincoln to renovate his whole cabinet.

. . . The New York *Messager Franco-Américaine* . . . lays great weight on the fact that Lincoln has not assented to the Monroe Doctrine resolution except in a very ambiguous and cunning manner. . . . His reply has been interpreted as favorable to the French interests in Mexico. . . .

Romero to MRE, 14 July 1864, in Romero, *Correspondencia* IV, 260–61

At first view, the inattentive observer would assume this government's situation has never been as bad as at this moment. Washington is under siege by Confederate forces. Communications with the North are cut at various points. The resistance of the armies of Lee and Johnston has stopped the armies of Grant and Sherman. The Union currency is very much depreciated, and the local authority of New York is in open conflict with the federal government because of the proceedings adopted by the president in the case of José Augustín Arguelles. Nevertheless, for the careful observer and for the person who is aware of this country's affairs, despite the current obstacles, the present federal situation is more comfortable than it has been for a long time.

I learned several important details [of military affairs] from Wade, chairman of the committee on the conduct of the war, who has just returned from the headquarters of the Army of the Potomac. . . .

After fruitless efforts to route Lee's army and take Petersburg by force, General Grant has proposed to pursue both objectives by the well-tested means of starvation. To this end Grant has destroyed part of the railroads connecting Richmond with the South. There railroads bring the provisions necessary to sustain the Confederate army. Grant has fortified himself south of Petersburg. . . . General Lee assumed he could compel Grant to raise the siege if he sent a sizeable force to attack Washington. For this objective and to remove a part of the force that the scarceness of provisions made very difficult to maintain, Lee sent General Ewell's corps . . . under General [Jubal] Early, to invade Maryland and Pennsylvania and to attack Washington. [22]

Until now, General Early had fulfilled the purpose of this expedition. . . . He has crossed the Potomac above Harper's Ferry, destroyed a large part of the railroad that runs from Baltimore to the Ohio River, and invaded Maryland and Pennsylvania. . . . He has threatened Baltimore and Washington. . . . General Early has had to work upon many points that have obliged him to subdivide his forces very considerably. Thanks to this circumstance, he cannot attempt anything serious either against Washington or Baltimore, since both are well fortified and adequately garrisoned. Meanwhile, this government should have issued orders to bring sufficient forces from the North, not only to expel the Confederates from this side of the Potomac, but also to cut off their retreat and prevent their reuniting with General Lee. General Grant has been assured, I have learned, that Early's forces will not return to where they departed from. If this is so, Lee will remain considerably weakened and he will have more difficulty opening his communications to the South. Judging that the federal forces in Louisiana could not undertake any military operations during the present season, this government is returning all troops not needed to conserve the federal positions in that state and Texas to Washington. . . . General Grant also ordered nine thousand men from General Burnside's army corps to defend Washington. If necessary, Burnside could send more forces. . . .

General Butler has been relieved of the command of the forces in the Bermuda Hundred and ordered to return to Fort Monroe.

. . . Yesterday afternoon the Confederate forces threatening this city withdrew. . . . Reportedly, only an insignificant section of the railroad between this city and New York is destroyed. Communication with the North should be reopened before the week ends.

If the Confederate forces, which appear less numerous than was originally believed, manage to recross the Potomac and rejoin Lee's army, this government will appear ridiculous, not only in the eyes of the European nations, but even to the U.S. public. Then the president and his cabinet will lose much of their remaining prestige. . . .

Romero to MRE, 21 July 1864, in Romero, *Correspondencia* IV 271–72

. . . Forces were sent in pursuit of Early's forces, but either they did not want to or they could not reach the Confederate troops. Consequently the rebels recrossed the Potomac with their immense booty collected in Maryland. At this hour, they ought to have rejoined Lee's army. Supposedly Grant has sent his cavalry to impede that reuniting. Since General Grant had sent a part of his forces to Washington, his line remained a little weakened. Grant's weakness offered the Confederates the opportunity to repair the section of the Weldon railroad that had been destroyed. It is already in operation again. General [William T.] Sherman's army is already in front of Atlanta. . . .

Encouraged with their successful invasion of Maryland, the Confederates have sent similar invasion forces into Kentucky and Missouri.

On 18 July the president proclaimed that within fifty days a half-million men would be drafted to reinforce the army.

The Democratic representatives and senators have published a manifesto to the nation denouncing the imprudence of many of the laws passed in the last session of Congress by the Republican majority. They attributed all the evils of the situation to that party. This manifesto, written with passion and to undermine the Republican party in the coming presidential elections, also bitterly censured the administration's foreign policy. . . .

Romero to MRE, 30 July 1864, in Romero, *Correspondencia* IV, 280–82

. . . The Richmond government was not pleased with the frequent retreats of General [Joseph E.] Johnston, who commanded the Confederate army in Georgia. Relieving him of command, it confided command to General [John B.] Hood, previously a corps commander in Johnston's army. Hood initiated his new command by taking the offense against the federal army, which occupied a part of Atlanta. . . . The federal army suffered the near irreplaceable loss of General McPherson, one of its most experienced and valiant commanders. . . . Beyond doubt this action [at Atlanta] has not produced decisive results. . . . If the

Confederate army should abandon Atlanta, it is feared, with reason, that those rebel forces will move to reinforce Lee. Lee would then have sufficient force to send a respectable expedition to capture Washington or to assume the offensive against General Grant.[23]

The Army of the Potomac has repelled two attacks from Lee's forces in front of Petersburg. . . . The Confederates have defeated the federal forces in West Virginia. Supposedly General Averell, commanding the federal cavalry, has been killed or seriously wounded. General Hunter, the commander of the military department of West Virginia, has been replaced by one of his subordinates, General [Philip S.] Crook.

At the beginning of this month, several distinguished southerners arrived in Niagara and established themselves on the Canadian side. These people claimed that the Richmond government had sent them to open peace negotiations with the Union president. . . . Through the editor of the *New York Herald*, one of the most influential members of the Republican party, they solicited a safe conduct from the president to go to Washington and from there to Richmond. At first, it seems, the president offered them the desired safe conduct. However, when they did not reveal their plenipotentiary powers, nor offer any proposals, Lincoln feared to take a false step. Thus, when time came to send them the safe conduct, he sent them a document addressed "to whom it may concern." This safe conduct guaranteed the trip to Washington and the return to Richmond to the competently authorized commissioners of those people who command the army making war on the United States and who came to make peace proposals upon the basis of reestablishing the Union and abolishing slavery. Upon receiving these documents, the southern agents accused this government of bad faith, stating that this was not what they had been promised. Lincoln closed the door to any settlement, they asserted, because he fixed conditions that ought to have been the result of negotiation. The agents considered the terms ludicrous. From the terms in which they expressed themselves on that occasion, they doubtless were not duly authorized commissioners of the Richmond government, but rather distinguished southern individuals who came for their own reasons or at the unofficial suggestion of the Confederate authorities.[24]

The conduct of the southern agents has generated much conjecture. Some believe this incident is the prelude to an immediate peace. Others, and this opinion seems most probable, consider the proposal to meet with Lincoln as a stratagem to place Lincoln in a false position and impede his reelection. To the less attentive observer, the conduct of the southerners suggests that the South desires peace while Lincoln has placed all kind of obstacles before them. Those agents made clear that no hope for a settlement exists while Lincoln is president. They indicated that they could achieve an understanding with a Democratic president. They have made it appear to many that the election of the Democratic candidate would assure an immediate peace.

While the southern commissioners were negotiating with Greeley, a Union colonel, on his own or by presidential order, went to Richmond to confer with Davis. The colonel, upon returning to his camp, claimed that Davis said his program was to maintain southern independence or to continue fighting until the whole population inhabiting the rebel states was exterminated. Thus, there is not much hope for peace at present.

U.S. officials have uncovered a conspiracy, organized in Missouri, that sought to form a republic composed of the western states. Certainly no project of this type will succeed currently. If the war should be prolonged much longer and its evils become harshly felt, the people of this country might naturally expect a complete dissolution of the Union. . . .[25]

Romero to MRE, 6 August 1864, in Romero, *Correspondencia* IV, 286–87

. . . Persuaded that he could not take Petersburg by force, General Grant decided to undermine its principal fortification. After spending one month to construct the mine, he decided that the Ninth Army Corps would make the assault at the moment of the explosion [which would blow open a gap in the Confederate fortifications]. On the morning of 30 July, the mine was exploded. . . . The Confederates reformed their lines and later repelled the attack. . . . Since then General Grant has not undertaken any operations against Petersburg. The opposition newspapers considered the Petersburg disaster as the end of the campaign against Richmond, believing Lee will assume the offensive in the future.[26]

. . . Lee, judging himself very secure in Petersburg, sent a sizeable column to attack Washington, placing this government in grave difficulties. During the past week Confederate forces have invaded Pennsylvania. The first time, they burned Chambersburg and withdrew at once. Afterwards the rebels returned in more respectable numbers. They crossed the Potomac, occupied Hagerstown, and defeated General Averell, who attempted to contain their march. Pennsylvania has ordered the enlistment of thirty thousand men to repel the invasion. General Sherman's army has not renewed its military operations against Atlanta. . . . General [Edward M.] McCook, who was sent with an expedition to the interior of Georgia, engaged the Confederates but was soon . . . completely defeated.[27]

Senator Wade of Ohio and Representative Winter Davis of Maryland, both Republicans and friends of the administration, have published a manifesto attacking, with more severity than reason, Lincoln's conduct in refusing to sign a bill from Congress regarding the reconstruction of the rebel states. The charges against the president are so terrible and well founded that they will most probably contribute very powerfully toward preventing his reelection. Both influential men have been decided friends of Mexico. . . .[28]

Romero to MRE, 13 August 1864, in Romero, *Correspondencia* IV, 293–94

. . . Commodore Farragut's squadron . . . attacked the Confederate forts defending the entrance to Mobile Bay. . . . If . . . Mobile was as well defended as Charleston, it would not be difficult to repeat the same scenes at Mobile as at Charleston, namely, the federal squadron besieging the port for a year under the great likelihood that it would fall [eventually]. . . .[29]

The seriousness of Confederate preparations for an expedition to invade the northern states prompted General Grant to come to Washington briefly before returning to his camp.

The government has ordered an investigation into the causes that produced the disaster at Petersburg on 30 July.

General [Philip H.] Sheridan has been named chief of the Military Department of West Virginia and has occupied Washington. A battle is expected soon between Sheridan's forces and the Confederates under General Early. . . . The Confederates defeated and captured Union General [George] Stoneman, who had gone on an expedition to destroy railroads. . . . If this government should occupy Mobile, it could move army corps to that port to attack the Confederates from the rear.

Changes in Lincoln's cabinet have been rumored. . . . Supposedly Secretary of War Stanton's resignation has been offered and accepted. . . . On August 11 there was a huge meeting in favor of General McClellan in this city. Although the speakers who harangued the crowd were not very distinguished people, the event is considered of great importance because it displayed the popularity that General McClellan enjoys.

The Democratic party is prepared to name its presidential candidate in Chicago on the twenty-ninth of this month. Presumably, the nomination will fall to General Dix, General Grant, General McClellan, or [James] Guthrie of Kentucky. If Dix, a person of broad popular acceptance, or another person of merit should be nominated, that person would very probably be elected because Lincoln seems to be more discredited in the public mind each day. Already his reelection appears very remote. . . .

Romero to MRE, 20 August 1864, in Romero, *Correspondencia*
IV, 310–11

On 14 August General Grant moved the Second Army Corps, com-
manded by General [Winfield S.] Hancock, from its location in front of
Petersburg to the vicinity of Fort Darling . . . only eight miles from
Richmond. . . . For the movement to have produced some important
results, it should have been more rapid and it should have surprised or
captured some part of the Confederate lines. Today it was announced that
General Hancock has moved a part of his force in another direction.
However, again his efforts have not been crowned with major success.

General Sherman retains his position in front of Atlanta. Since Sherman could not effectively cut the line of communication from Atlanta to
Macon, which provides the Confederates with reinforcements and provisions, the Confederate forces are now attempting to cut Sherman's communications. Sherman, having moved a long way from his base of
operations, has to defend a very long line of communications. In effect,
Confederate General [Joseph] Wheeler appeared in front of Dayton
[Ohio] and requested the federal forces defending the city to surrender. . . . Reportedly, many reinforcements are moving from Chattanooga to the federal defenders. In that case, the Union forces will be
able to hold Dayton. In the contrary case, if the Confederates occupied
Dayton, they would completely cut General Sherman's line of communications.[30]

Considering himself very secure in Richmond and Petersburg, General Lee apparently has sent a considerable part of his forces to reinforce
the Confederate general in Atlanta and to aid General Early in the
Shenandoah Valley. The strengthening of Early has compelled General
Sheridan to return to Winchester. . . .

. . . From Mobile [we learn that] . . . in addition to Fort Gaines, which
surrendered to Commodore Farragut, the Confederates evacuated Fort
Powell, which the federal forces immediately occupied. The federal
forces were repulsed at Fort Morgan. . . .

A great desire for peace is becoming evident in this country. The
Confederate commissioners in Niagara are constantly visited by the most
influential Democrats. . . . A convention of those Democrats who favor
peace at all costs met in Syracuse. . . .

The Confederate raider *Tallahassee* appeared a few miles from this port
[New York] a few days ago. The *Tallahassee* has been wrecking havoc
among U.S. ships in its vicinity. Already over a hundred vessels have
been destroyed. Apparently no steam war vessel here was ready to harass
the Confederate raider. Today, the papers announce that the *Tallahassee*
has withdrawn to the Canadian coast. . . .[31]

Romero to MRE, 27 August 1864, in Romero, *Correspondencia*
IV, 316–17

General Grant's movement of General Hancock's Second Army Corps
last week . . . was only intended to distract Confederate attention in order
to permit another more important movement . . . against a part of the
Weldon Railroad. This railroad is one of three lines that link Richmond
with the rebel states. . . . When the Confederates tried to dislodge [the
Union forces], they could not.[32]
   . . . Since one cannot believe that the Confederates are resigned to
leaving closed one of the principal sources from which they draw the
materials they need to continue the campaign, presumably they have left
[Union] General [Gouverneur K.] Warren in possession of the railroad
while they undertake other movements to obligate that general to abandon his present position.
   . . . Supposedly, General Lee is transferring the theater of the war to
the Shenandoah Valley and will only leave behind the force necessary to
defend the fortifications of Richmond and Petersburg.
   Nevertheless, nothing has occurred yet between the contending armies
of Generals Sheridan and Early to indicate that this major shift of troops
has been instituted. . . .
   . . . Confederate General Wheeler, who . . . was attacking Dayton,
Ohio, in order to cut Sherman's line of communication, was repulsed by
federal forces arriving from Chattanooga. Thus, General Sherman's line
of communication remains intact. . . .[33]
   Confederate General Forrest surprised the garrison at Memphis, an
important Tennessee city. After occupying Memphis for several hours, he
was driven out. . . .

Romero to MRE, 1 September 1864, in Romero,
Correspondencia IV, 328–29

   . . . Unable to dislodge General Warren from his position on the
Weldon railroad, the Confederate forces fell upon General Hancock's
army corps, [which was] protecting another part of that railroad. . . . The
fact that the U.S. forces retained control of the Weldon Railroad is
sufficient reason to consider the battle's outcome favorable to federal
arms. Still, this victory was certainly far from decisive. . . . General
Early still remains in the Shenandoah Valley with a considerable
force. . . . Desiring to cut Sherman's communications with Chattanooga, Confederate Generals Wheeler, [John H.] Morgan, and Forrest
were preparing separate excursions.

Fort Morgan, which defends the entrance to Mobile Bay and which had remained under Confederate control after Commodore Farragut's victories, finally surrendered to the federal forces. Now the federal capture of Mobile is made much easier.

On 29 August the Democratic party convention met in Chicago to nominate candidates for president and vice-president in the coming November elections. On the thirtieth, that party's political platform was presented and approved. . . . The platform contains no plank relative to Mexico or to the Monroe Doctrine when everything suggested that this party would be most explicit on this point. As soon as I can see some of the delegates from the convention, I will inquire about what led to that omission. . . . Perhaps the convention believed it more convenient to say nothing about that affair in order not to excite fears and to retain greater liberty for future action. Yesterday the convention nominated General McClellan as its candidate for president on the first ballot with 202 votes against 23 for [Horatio] Seymour. Ohio Congressman George H. Pendleton was nominated for vice-president. Then the convention adjourned, after agreeing to reconvene if convoked by the executive committee. The Republican press has received the nomination of these candidates with great displeasure. The Republican press assumes that General McClellan's triumph in the November elections would be the equivalent of the triumph of the rebels with whom it considers him in contact. In the area of commerce the situation has improved considerably, since the price of gold fell close to 20 percent in two days. . . .[34]

Romero to MRE, 30 September 1864, in Romero, *Correspondencia* IV, 357–59

Not believing it desirable to assault the Atlanta fortifications, General Sherman sent part of his army to cut the Macon railroad, which connects Atlanta with the South. . . . Considering his positions in Atlanta untenable, General Hood evacuated the city. Sherman's army soon occupied the city. Sherman agreed upon a truce because he believed it desirable to rest his forces in Atlanta. . . . The truce terminated a few days ago. . . . Alarmed at the Atlanta disaster, Davis visited Hood's army.

General Sheridan, commanding the federal army in the Shenandoah Valley, has attacked [and defeated] Confederate General Early three times. . . . If General Sheridan continues his triumphal march uninterrupted [and] takes Lynchburg, he will cut another railroad connecting Richmond with the South. Thus, Sheridan will make General Lee abandon Richmond or fight the federal army to recover the railroads.[35]

Maintaining his army in front of Petersburg, General Grant has continued to occupy the Weldon railroad. General Lee has not made an effort to recover that railroad. . . . Supposedly Lee is preparing a major attack upon Grant, but it has not occurred until now. On the contrary, Grant might well seize the initiative. . . . It is vaguely reported that the Confederates are prepared to evacuate the capital. Supposedly, they have already sent out the archives and other valuable objects.

Great changes have occurred in the presidential campaign. . . . All the developments were favorable to the administration. General Frémont, deciding that he has no likelihood of being elected president, has withdrawn from the race. His supporters will probably vote for Lincoln. When General McClellan accepted the Democratic nomination, he repudiated the platform of the Chicago convention. He was supposed to ask for peace at any cost. [McClellan's repudiation of the Chicago peace plank] has placed him in a false position with his own supporters and very considerably diminished his likelihood of election.

The [political] question has been reduced to one between those who favor the continuation of war until the reestablishment of the Union and those who favor peace at any price. The former will vote for Lincoln and the latter for General McClellan. The number of the former has risen very noticeably since the federal military situation has improved so much with the victories of Sherman and Sheridan. Currently the end of the war seems both certain and near. Twelve months ago, when the situation appeared bad for this government, Lincoln's reelection was considered impossible. Today his reelection is believed certain. The Republicans who were most energetically opposed to Lincoln, like Wade and Winter Davis, and even Chase, have just reconciled themselves with him. They are working for his reelection. Well-informed people believe that the federal army will undertake some daring movements a few days before the elections to assure victory completely. If these [preelection] movements are successful, they could only produce the desired result.

On 23 September Postmaster General Montgomery Blair resigned from the cabinet. Blair was one of our best friends in Lincoln's cabinet and my personal friend. Thus, I have felt his resignation quite deeply. He has been replaced by William Dennison, the ex-governor of Ohio, who should begin exercising his office today. . . .[36]

Romero to MRE, 14 November 1864, in Romero, *Correspondencia* IV, 411–14

Lincoln was reelected on 8 November without any of the feared disturbances. General McClellan only obtained a majority in three of the twenty-five states that voted in the election. All the rest gave large majorities to Lincoln. Thus, the people of the United States expressed their determination actively to pursue the war against the South. The election has made this clear to all partisans of the South. The consequences of this election are impossible to foresee. In the opinion of many statesmen of this country, however, the election ought to contribute effectively toward terminating the present Civil War, as much because it will give more force and material to this government, as because it will discourage the rebels. Obviously the least the rebels can hope for is another four years of war against the colossal power of this government, the devastation of their homes, and the destruction of their country. [37]

The Republican party also elected many members to the next Congress where the administration will have a two-thirds majority. According to recent announcements, the Republicans will proceed to abolish slavery without delay, repealing the constitutional articles that sanction it. Both sections of the divided nation already know that slavery must end in the present contest. The governors of several leading southern states, gathered in a convention, made various recommendations to the Confederate Congress. One of the most important was to decree the organization of a Negro army. Knowing the opinion of southern men regarding the Negro race, this suggestion alone suffices to make clear the extremity to which the Confederate States have arrived.

In an address . . . to the Confederate Congress on 7 November, Jefferson Davis discussed the convenience of arming the Negroes. Although he seemed decidedly opposed to that idea, he was apparently unwilling to oppose openly the chief concern of his fellow politicians. He recommended experimentally arming forty thousand Negroes who could be organized into an army corps if necessary. On the very day of the Confederate Congress' installation, a Tennessee representative offered a resolution that the Confederate States should not lend any aid to the establishment of a monarchy in Mexico. . . . [38]

Military operations have not progressed much since my last review. On 27 October as General Grant left City Point for the front of the Army of the Potomac, he told me that soon a great battle would occur to extend the federal lines to the southwest of Petersburg up to the South Side railroad. On the same day, General Butler's army would move to attract the enemy's attention in front of Richmond and to prevent reinforcements being sent to Petersburg. . . .

. . . As a consequence of these operations, the federal army could only extend its lines for two miles. Since then, neither of the contending armies has undertaken anything serious.

General Sherman has left Atlanta in pursuit of General Hood, who was north of that city threatening and cutting Sherman's communication line with his base of operations. The papers claim that Sherman's campaign plan is to march from Atlanta toward Charleston or Savannah and to seize one or both cities with the aid of U.S. naval forces. Thus, Sherman would establish his line of communication by water. This plan is quite daring because General Sherman would have to penetrate deeply into enemy country with a large army. If successful, it will very considerably improve the Union military position [and] . . . be a great blow to the South. The Confederate government sent General Beauregard to take command of Hood's army and the Army of Tennessee, retaining Hood, however, in his present position. . . .[39]

Romero to MRE, 12 December 1864, in Romero, *Correspondencia* IV, 465–66

. . . The president's annual message very decidedly expressed his determination not to make peace with the South, except on the conditions of rejoining the Union and the definite abolition of slavery. Lincoln also judged it to be completely useless to open conferences with the Confederate authorities. He assumed force was the only means of reducing them.

Lincoln's declaration, combined with the secretary of the treasury's not very flattering report on the federal public treasury, made gold rise 20 percent. . . .

There was a change in Lincoln's cabinet. . . . Attorney General Edward Bates resigned in order to retire to private life. After accepting Bates's resignation, the president nominated James S. Speed of Kentucky to succeed Bates. Speed's nomination is awaiting Senate confirmation. The president named Chase to fill the high office of Chief Justice of the Supreme Court, vacant since [Roger Taney's] recent death. . . .

. . . General Sherman . . . left the Army of the Cumberland under General [George] Thomas to pursue the Confederate Army of Tennessee under General Hood. With the rest of the army, Sherman left Atlanta on 14 November for the Atlantic coast. He divided his force into several columns that operated in different directions. . . . Everything indicates that Sherman's only objective is to gain a base of operations on the coast. Through his movements he proposed to threaten several places in order to keep the southern forces divided and to prevent their concentration.[40]

. . . The Confederate newspapers admit that Sherman will arrive at his [unknown] destination without difficulty. Some observers believe this march across the rebel states and the change of base of operations will produce decisive results favorable to this government. However, I believe everything will depend on the military operations that General Sherman might later undertake from his new base.

While Sherman was marching from Atlanta east, General Hood was advancing with his army to the northwest. General Thomas's army has retreated before the enemy columns toward Nashville, the capital of Tennessee. Nevertheless, the contending forces battled in Franklin, a few miles from Nashville. . . . Most likely Hood triumphed, since he continued to march toward Nashville, where Thomas had retreated to. Allegedly General Hood now intends to bypass Nashville, invade Kentucky, and unite with the forces of Confederate General Breckinridge. Everything suggests that since General Sherman's march to the Atlantic, the federal forces have been outnumbered in the west, and therefore, the Confederates should be able to obtain great advantages in that region.

At Hilton Head in South Carolina, U.S. General Foster moved to destroy one of the southern railroads and to unite with General Sherman. Confederate General [Williams J.] Hardee attacked and defeated Foster, thus frustrating this important combination. . . .

The United States now has a problem with Brazil that has caused considerable discussion in Europe. The Confederate steamer *Florida* was in the Brazilian port of Bahia when a U.S. naval vessel entered that port, captured the Confederate ship, and brought it to this country. . . . A proposal exists in Europe for the maritime powers to protest to the United States against this violation of maritime right. . . .[41]

Romero to MRE, 31 December 1865, in Romero, *Correspondencia* IV, 509–10

. . . General Sherman and his army arrived at Savannah without having suffered any misfortune during a long and difficult march. On the contrary, Sherman caused great damage to the enemy, destroying railroads and devastating several towns. . . . Confederate General Hardee, defending Savannah, . . . evacuated all of his forces without difficulty. Reportedly he moved toward Charleston, which is believed to be the target of General Sherman's army.[42]

Recently General Thomas attacked and defeated General Hood, who was besieging Nashville. . . . Hood not only had to raise the siege, but was obliged to retreat very hurriedly to Georgia in order to save the remains of his army. . . . General Grant sent an expedition to attack Wilmington, North Carolina, from the land side. The expedition was frustrated and the troops that took part have returned. At once another more formal expedition was organized against the same port. . . . However, General Butler judged that the Fort Fisher, defending the entrance to Wilmington, could not be taken by assault but only by formal siege operations, which he was not prepared to undertake. Hence he decided to reembark his forces, thereby postponing the attack on Wilmington until another occasion. . . .[43]

The president has ordered the conscription of three hundred thousand more volunteers.

This government has ordered the suspension from service and trial of the commander who seized the steamer *Florida* in the Brazilian port of Bahía. This apparently will settle the question. . . .

1865

Introduction to 1865

The U.S. economy was in disarray as a result of the war. While the income tax grew to supply 20 percent of the required federal revenues by the end of the war, and manufacturing and sales taxes generated another 23 percent of federal revenue needs, loans and issues of paper currency covered the bulk of the war expenses. The U.S. public debt in August 1865 stood at $2.8 billion. The southern economy was in shambles. The northern workers had seldom struck during the war although the New York City strikes in 1863 were a major exception. Yet real wages had declined between 1860 and 1865 by 33 percent. In order to recover their lost economic position, workers tried to organize a national union in late 1865, but the effort failed. In 1865, consumer cooperatives became a popular device in an effort to organize resistance to the burden of a disordered economy. This economic burden fell heavily upon common people.

In early 1865, Sherman began his march through the Carolinas while Grant continued to attack the railroads supplying Petersburg and Richmond in order to force Lee to stretch his defense to protect these supply routes. In February 1865, a conference at Hampton's Road, Virginia, briefly raised some hope for an end to the war. The Confederate leadership, however, insisted unrealistically upon a prior recognition of its independence, which Lincoln unhesitantly rejected. Although Romero's offer to travel to Richmond to initiate negotiations to terminate the war was not acted upon, Montgomery Blair obtained permission for his father, Francis P. Blair, Sr., former kitchen cabinet member and editor during Andrew Jackson's administration, to visit his old friend Confederate President Jefferson Davis. The senior Blair hoped to persuade Davis to end the war in order that there might be a joint military campaign to throw Maximilian and Napoleon out of Mexico. This plan offered the Confederacy a face-saving manner to terminate the war while upholding the Monroe Doctrine. Romero was privy to the early discussions of the project. He authorized the senior Blair to offer Davis command of one of two corps, which would enter Mexico under General

Grant's overall command. One corps would consist of former Confederate troops, the other of former Union soldiers.

Lincoln was inaugurated for a second term in March. Richmond and Petersburg fell several weeks later. Lee surrendered one week after evacuating Richmond, and Lincoln did not survive Lee's surrender by a week. A southern Democrat, Andrew Johnson, chosen at the Union party (Republicans joined by some War Democrats and old Union party people) convention in 1864 to serve as Lincoln's running mate as an act of unity, became president of a Republican administration in which the radical faction played a major role. The remaining Confederate forces surrendered within seven weeks of Lee's surrender. The human costs of the war were more than six hundred thousand dead and at least four hundred thousand wounded.

Anticipating the plight of the freed slaves, Congress passed the Freedman's Bureau Bill in March 1865. By December, twenty-seven states had ratified the Thirteenth Amendment, which abolished slavery. Since the political and social consequences of the war were unclear and radical Republican suspicions of President Johnson surfaced rather early, Congress formed the Joint Committee of Fifteen in December to oversee reconstruction.

A few days after Lincoln's assassination, Romero met with President Johnson, believed to be a staunch advocate of applying the Monroe Doctrine to the French intervention in Mexico. Directing General Grant to act upon his own authority to aid the Mexican Liberals, Johnson wanted arms made available to the Liberals. It was not clear that the State Department would pursue Johnson's good intentions in Mexico.

The radicals distrusted Seward's intentions. They altered the diplomatic appropriations bill to prevent the recognition of Maximilian's regime. The legislation only permitted funds for a minister to the Republic of Mexico. Romero continued his lobbying and political contacts with a wide variety of opponents of a soft policy toward the empire in Mexico. Congressmen John Conness (California), Thaddeus Stevens (Pennsylvania), Elihu Washburne (Illinois), Samuel S. Cox (Ohio), Nathaniel Banks (Massachusetts), Speaker Schuyler Colfax (Indiana), Senators Zachariah Chandler (Michigan), Benjamin Wade (Ohio), and James McDougall (California), General John Logan, New York businessman James Beekman, New York politician Thurlow Weed, and editor of the New York *Herald*, James Gordon Bennett, were among the targets of Romero's incessant lobbying activity in 1865. Romero also maintained his contacts with past and current cabinet members Montgomery Blair, Postmaster General William Dennison, and Attorney General James Speed. Finally, Romero retained contacts in the State Department that alerted him on foreign relations activity.

In 1865, Romero established links with a major new force, General Grant. Grant and Romero discovered their shared views in April and May 1865. They formed an alliance that worked effectively over the next several years and a friendship that remained close until Grant's death in 1885. Grant agreed with Romero's view that the Civil War and the liberal struggle against the Franco-Austrian invasion were parts of one general contest. Grant worked with Romero to create a force of former U.S. and Confederate soldiers to help drive out the French. Grant and Romero selected a commander from a small list of candidates consisting of Generals William T. Sherman, Phillip S. Sheridan, John M. Schofield, and Frank P. Blair, Jr. After Sherman revealed a lack of interest and Sheridan was judged of greater service in command of the Union forces along the Mexican-Texas border, from where he could funnel supplies, advice, and recruits to the Mexican liberal forces, Schofield was tapped for the mission. Johnson, Grant, Schofield, and Romero worked out the terms of Schofield's contract and the size of his force. They were then outmaneuvered when Seward persuaded Schofield to accept a diplomatic mission to France to extract a promise from Napoleon to depart from Mexico. Seward was aware that Napoleon was not likely to allow Schofield to talk with him privately. Despite Romero's reservations, Schofield went to Paris and never commanded the forces on the border. Other generals—Lewis Wallace, Frank P. Blair, and Joseph E. Johnston—were supposed to prepare the operation pending Schofield's return. Eventually, Wallace and others moved some volunteers to the frontier, and apparently several hundred, perhaps several thousand, individual volunteers did join Juárez's forces. However, the massive, organized bodies of troops, envisioned by Romero and Grant, did not join the Mexican liberals. Still, U.S. arms, funds, and recruits became more accessible to Juárez's army, indicating a level of success for Romero.

Political Reviews—1865

Romero to MRE, 24 January 1865, in Romero, *Correspondencia* V, 34–35

. . . General Sherman has sent some of his forces from Savannah. . . . It is believed, nevertheless, that Sherman's goal now would be to attack Charleston. Confederate General Hood managed to cross the Tennessee River without large losses. . . .

After the repulsion of General Butler's expedition, which was to attack Fort Fisher in the entrance of the port of Wilmington . . ., General Grant sent another expedition under General [Alfred H.] Terry, [who]

. . . captured the fort on 15 January. The news of this victory produced very great jubilation in the North because it was totally unexpected and also because the other expedition, believed more formidable, had just returned humiliated.[1]

The fall of Fort Fisher will contribute largely toward the fall of Wilmington. . . . The impact of the fall of Fort Fisher in New York can be properly appreciated by noting that it produced a drop of more than 20 percent in the price of gold.

General Butler, commander of the first expedition, was removed from command of the Army of the James and ordered to return home to await orders.

. . . For several days Congress considered the bill to revise the constitutional article recognizing slavery. Congress still has not decided the issue. Congress has approved votes of thanks to Generals Sherman and Terry and to Admirals Farragut and Porter.

. . . Informal peace negotiations have opened between the North and South. Early this month, Francis P. Blair, [Sr.], and Montgomery Blair, both personal friends of the president, traveled to General Grant's camp for the purpose of passing from there to Richmond. . . . Francis P. Blair decided to go to Richmond alone. After remaining several days in Richmond to confer with the Confederate authorities, he returned directly to Washington. Certainly he communicated the results of his mission to the president. Blair undertook a second trip to Richmond in a government steamer on 20 January. . . . The second trip has persuaded many of the apparently not unfounded expectations that Blair's activity could produce peace. In my judgment, the war in this country has reached a crisis period that will lead either to peace or to the prolongation of the war for some time. A few days ago, a newspaper considered to be an organ of Jefferson Davis said that the South preferred to be a European colony rather than submit to the North. This idea found very little support in the Confederacy. Now, the ablest periodical in Richmond, the *Richmond Examiner*, just wrote that the least humiliating thing that could happen would be to return to the Union.[2]

The Confederate Congress has created the rank of commanding general of the Confederate armies. This position has been given to General Lee. . . .[3]

Romero to MRE, 8 February 1865, in Romero, *Correspondencia* V, 58–59.

. . . Upon returning from his second trip to Richmond, Blair maintained that his mission had not produced any conclusive result. This was the popular belief for some days. Then, nevertheless, a semiofficial report of that journey was published. Apparently the South desires to make peace, even to return to the Union, but, given the jealousy and rivalry existing among the public men of Richmond, no one wanted to assume the responsibility of accepting that alternative. Everyone fears that [negotiating for peace] would serve as a pretext for his enemies to attack him. Shortly after [Blair returned from the second mission], a commission from the South, composed of three of its most distinguished people, the vice-president, a senator from Virginia, and the assistant secretary of war, had reportedly presented themselves at the federal lines. They solicited permission to come to Washington. Secretary of State Seward went immediately to Fort Monroe to confer with those emissaries. Soon the president departed for the same place with the same purpose. It was unavoidable not to believe that peace might result from the conferences being held at Fort Monroe. . . . On 4 February the president and Secretary Seward returned to Washington with the news that the conference had ended without agreement. The southern commissioners insisted upon recognition of their independence as an indispensable condition for peace. The president explained that his government would not accept peace except upon the submission of the South to the Union. So everything ended. . . .[4]

. . . Although the first attempts toward this goal [of peace] have not had the desired outcome, many believe other, more successful efforts will soon follow. Additional peace talks will be more likely if the Union armies meanwhile obtain decisive victories over the South.

. . . In the last session of the current U.S. Congress, the Senate approved a constitutional amendment to abolish slavery by the two-thirds vote that is necessary in these cases. However, two-thirds of the House did not approve it. In the current session this matter was reconsidered. At the end of last month the necessary vote approved the amendment. Since then the state legislatures have been ratifying it. If three-fourths of the state legislatures approve the amendment, it becomes a constitutional amendment. If one excludes the southern states, certainly enough legislatures that recognize this government will vote to approve the amendment. With this objective, it has been proposed in the Senate not to count the votes of the seceded states in the computation of votes for the presidency. . . .[5]

Romero to MRE, 23 February 1865, in Romero, *Correspondencia* V, 81

. . . The strategic movements of General Sherman have produced the submission of a large part of South Carolina, including its two principal cities. After leaving Savannah, Sherman . . . feigned an attack on Charleston and Augusta while the main body of his army moved on Columbia. The Confederates abandoned Columbia, which General Sherman immediately occupied. Once the Union army possessed Columbia, Charleston was cut off. The Confederates also evacuated it.[6]

. . . In order to cooperate with the Army of the Potomac in the final attack on Richmond, General Sherman supposedly will move into North Carolina after conquering South Carolina. Allegedly, General Beauregard has also been concentrating his forces and has ordered the major part of Hood's army to oppose the federal advance. . . .

. . . General Sherman's complete victory over the main body of Beauregard's army would mean the fall of Richmond, ending the context. . . .

A few days ago the Army of the Potomac also executed a move with the intention of extending its line in the direction of the southern railroad. . . .

Romero to MRE, 28 February 1865, in Romero, *Correspondencia* V, 98–99

. . . Wilmington fell into Union hands, giving this government an important military position that will serve very advantageously as a base of operations for General Sherman's army when it enters North Carolina.[7]

Fort Anderson [on Cape Fear River in North Carolina], as well as Wilmington, was occupied with very little resistance. These [Confederate] losses and the abandonment of Charleston reveal very clearly that General Lee plans to concentrate all his forces and to fight the federal army in detail. From this point of view, the federal victories are not as great as they would have been if the Confederate forces would have been destroyed in Charleston and Wilmington.

Following this system of concentration, the Confederate army will allegedly abandon Richmond and withdraw to Lynchburg.

As is natural in moments of adversity, great despondency and alarm reign in Richmond. The Confederate government and General Lee have urgently requested Congress to order the organization of Negro regiments as the only measure that could save the insurrection. The Confederate House approved the appropriate bill, but a Senate majority rejected it. This proposal to raise Negro troops has profoundly divided the Gulf states and the border states. The latter accuse the former of risking the fate of the Confederacy in order not to lose a few slaves. Probably the law of necessity will compel the Confederate Congress to adopt this measure.[8]

. . . The U.S. Congress has been occupied in approving a revenue bill for the coming year and a bill authorizing the government to negotiate a three-hundred-million-dollar loan to provide the necessities of war. Both houses have already approved this bill. . . .

Romero to MRE, 9 March 1865, in Romero, *Correspondencia* V, 113–14

. . . The president has been inaugurated for a second term. . . .[9] . . . Union General [Quincy A.] Gillmore took Fort White and immediately occupied Georgetown in South Carolina. . . .

On 6 March New York experienced a great festival to celebrate the recent victories of the U.S. Army. I call your attention to the first article of the program, which . . . several of the most distinguished citizens of New York City approved on 22 February.

> 1. Be it resolved that the war to suppress the rebellion, now rapidly nearing its inevitable end, involves essentially the principles of self government, human liberty, and christian civilization; that the people of the United States have ample grounds to congratulate themselves in the realization that, while they have successfully sustained their elected government and the life of the nation, they have, at the same time, defended and vindicated the inviolable doctrine that this continent is perfectly dedicated to the cause of free institutions and republican government. . . .

Romero to MRE, 16 March 1865, in Romero, *Correspondencia* V, 124–26

. . . On 9 March General Sherman was apparently local in Laurel Hill, North Carolina, and all was well until then. On 12 March General Schofield also communicated . . . that he had defeated Confederate General Bragg's forces. . . .

Confederate General [Wade] Hampton also claimed to have defeated General Kilpatrick's cavalry in South Carolina.

It is already almost certain that General Sherman will arrive without serious opposition at a point from which he could operate against Richmond in combination with the forces near that city.

General Sheridan's victory in western Virginia . . . is much more important than first appeared. . . . Sheridan apparently defeated Early at Waynesboro at the beginning of the month. . . . The Union army destroyed a large part of the Lynchburg railroad and the James canal, both very important communications routes for Richmond. It also destroyed a large amount of Confederate property. Richmond cannot resist [if it receives] many blows like this.

A combined expedition has left New Orleans to attack Mobile, now the only important port that remains in Confederate power. . . .

Richmond has remained the theater of great political agitation. The Virginia legislature, wishing to resolve the question of Negro enlistment, authorized the governor to organize the necessary number of regiments from Negroes. Moreover, the governor ordered the Virginia senators in the Confederate Congress to vote in favor of the bill permitting the enlistment of Negroes in the Confederate army. Because of this, Senator Hunter, who has voted against that measure, changed his vote. Thus the bill was approved. This bill authorizes the arming of one-fourth of the Negroes between the ages of sixteen and forty who live in the Confederate States. According to the census, there ought to be some three hundred thousand. Before changing his vote, Hunter expressed his opinion on the matter. His speech should have left his political comrades very unsatisfied since he argued quite clearly that the adoption of this measure meant the moral, political, and practical ruin of the Confederacy. . . .

Secretary of the Treasury [William P.] Fessenden resigned from the cabinet on 4 March, in order to return to the Senate as senator from Maine. The president first named Senator [Edwin D.] Morgan of New York as secretary of the treasury. After Morgan refused the nomination, the president immediately offered it to Hugh McCulloch, the chief of one of the sections of that same department. Secretary of the Interior Usher also resigned his post, effective as of 15 May. The president nominated [James] Harlan, senator from Iowa, as secretary of the interior. . . .[10]

Romero to MRE, 30 March 1865, in Romero, *Correspondencia* V, 180–82

. . . Another few weeks like the past weeks will produce the end of the southern Confederacy.

. . . Judging from recent events, General Lee's goal has been apparently to prevent the armies of Sherman, Schofield, and Terry from combining at the point toward which all were moving. . . . Following Lee's plan, the forces of Johnston and his subordinates have engaged Sherman and Schofield several times. . . . The Confederate forces claimed victories in all these encounters. . . . However, in my judgment, the fact that the federal forces could continue advancing until they all united proves that these encounters were either relatively unimportant skirmishes or that they had outcomes favorable to the federal forces.[11]

On 21 March General Schofield communicated that on that afternoon he had occupied Goldsborough [North Carolina] without resistance and that the armies of Sherman and Terry were in the vicinity. The three armies joined on the 22d. . . .

The extreme weakness of the Confederate forces was revealed when they could not prevent those three armies from uniting. If they could not fight the enemy forces in detail [when divided], everything would suggest much less capability of doing so now with the three armies united. The Confederacy remains, then, at the mercy of those armies.

Nevertheless, the disasters for the Confederate cause do not end here. Probably believing that the Army of the Potomac was debilitated after detaching considerable forces under Schofield and Terry, General Lee assaulted the federal fortifications in front of Petersburg on the morning of the twenty-fifth. By surprising the Union forces, the assault was crowned with success [at first]. . . . Then the federal forces managed to dislodge the Confederates.

The South's situation is represented as little less than desperate. Their army is greatly reduced and very demoralized; the daily desertions are scandalous. Even worse, the army apparently considers the cause lost.

The South's political situation is no more flattering. On 13 March Jefferson Davis leveled various charges against the Confederate Congress for not having adopted several measures that he considered indispensable for the salvation of the South and for having approved others too late to produce good results. He requested broad authority over various materials, men, and money. This document has painted the South's situation in the darkest colors when Davis ought to be more interested in obscuring its weakness. Supposedly Richmond has never been more seriously menaced than now, nor the situation as critical as now.

The Richmond Congress prolonged its sessions several days to examine the matters mentioned in Davis's message. It conceded him some of the authority he requested and denied him other. A committee . . . report replied to Davis with charges similar to those he leveled at Congress. The congressional committee declared Davis vacillating, unsteady, weak, and inept. It also stated that Congress had named General Lee commanding general of the Confederate army in order to remove the direction of military operations from Davis's hands. All the disasters suffered recently by Confederate arms were attributed to Davis. Arriving at these extremes [mutual recriminations of the Confederate executive and legislative branches], the Confederacy is apparently on the verge of complete dissolution.

. . . Davis mentioned that in an interview with Lincoln at Fort Monroe, Davis's commissioners suggested a method for U.S. negotiation with the South without recognizing the Confederate government nor the governments established in the insurgent states. Generals from both armies would mediate in the form of a military convention. Lincoln rejected that idea then. Later he implied he would take the proposal under consideration again. Then he said it was unacceptable. In a meeting between Confederate General [James] Longstreet and General [Edward O. C.] Ord, commander of the federal Army of the James, at the request of the latter, Ord suggested that a satisfactory arrangement to the present difficulties could be arranged by means of a military convention. If General Lee desired to discuss this with General Grant, Ord said, Lee's wish would not be refused provided he has authorization to negotiate. As a consequence of this, General Lee wrote General Grant on 2 March, proposing a conference for the indicated reason. Lee stated that he had the necessary powers. General Grant responded on March 4, denying his authority to enter into that conference. Grant claimed that he was only authorized to conclude a purely military convention. He was certain that General Ord could only have mentioned such a convention to General Longstreet. . . . Lincoln went to City Point over a week ago and still remains there. His trip was allegedly motivated by personal and not public reasons, for a change of climate and to recover from a recent illness. Now, nevertheless, the president has reportedly conferred with Generals Grant, Sherman, Meade, Ord, and Sheridan in Hampton Roads, on board the steamer *Ocean City* yesterday. . . .

Romero to MRE, 6 April 1865, in Romero, *Correspondencia* V, 195–96

. . . The news is contained in two words: "Richmond captured," an event of very significant consequences. The news has justly produced the greatest rejoicing in this country, which was even more ardent because it was unexpected.[12]

This past 29 March, the army under General Grant's immediate orders commenced military operations. General Sheridan marched with his forces from City Point to Dinwiddie Court House in the direction of the railroad on the southern side. . . . Sheridan fought a hard battle there in which the federal forces triumphed completely. At the same time, leaving the forces absolutely necessary to defend his fortifications, Grant fell upon the enemy line with all the remaining troops. He broke it at various points and captured several of the rebels' principal defense works. After these losses no other alternative remained to General Lee except to withdraw from Petersburg and Richmond. This he did on the morning of 3 April. The federal forces occupied both cities at once.

. . . Lee withdrew toward Lynchburg heading for the Danville railroad. Wishing to cut off Lee's retreat, Grant pursued Lee's army. . . .

The abandonment of Richmond could be considered as the decisive day of this war. In effect, after having lost that city and the large, rich region that it dominates, the Confederate cause cannot possibly be sustained much longer. This is true even though Lee has withdrawn in good order, saving the major part of his army. The most decided southern partisans already admit that the contest could be prolonged for several days out of total desperation and in order for the leaders to obtain advantageous terms. In effect, the victorious armies of Grant and Sherman will not delay long in destroying and dispersing the demoralized remnants of the forces of Lee and Johnston. As of now, the Civil War can virtually be considered terminated. . . .

The president still has not returned from City Point. Seward had a rather serious accident yesterday. While entering his coach, the horses bolted. Seward jumped from the coach, but fractured an arm near the shoulder and suffered some lesions in the face and head from the fall. . . .

Romero to MRE, 15 April 1865, in Romero, *Correspondencia* V, 216–17

. . . Lee's army has surrendered.[13]

. . . General Lee probably intended to make General Johnston advance toward Danville to unite both forces. In turn, General Grant marched from Petersburg to the junction of the Richmond-Danville and the Petersburg-Lynchburg railroads. Grant arrived at this point first. At that moment I would consider Lee's army totally lost. On 5 April General Sheridan advanced with his cavalry and two corps of the Army of the Potomac to Burke Station where a battle took place that ended in a complete defeat for Confederate arms. . . . After that engagement General Grant wrote General Lee on 7 April, proposing that Lee should surrender since he was in a desperate situation. Lee sought a general arrangement that would produce the complete reestablishment of peace. Grant refused because he lacked proper authority. After several exchanges on 9 April, Lee agreed to surrender his whole army upon the condition that all of its officers and soldiers would take an oath not to take up arms against the U.S. government again. They would also turn over their arms and war material, except for their horses, swords, and pistols. . . .

Lee's surrender is so important and significant that it could be considered the end of the war without exaggeration. . . .

. . . It is expected that Johnston's army will surrender to General Sherman. Johnston's army will certainly not be able to resist the mortal blow of Lee's surrender. If this [psychological] blow should be resisted,

Johnston's army will not be able to resist the combined armies of Grant and Sherman. They combine a force five times Johnston's strength. To make Johnston's situation even more critical, recently General Stoneman, commanding the cavalry of Thomas's army, has reportedly cut the only railroad by which Johnston could retreat.

The attack on Mobile has already commenced. . . . Mobile might fall to the federal forces even before learning the news of Lee's surrender.

The remaining organized forces in the rebel states will either follow Lee's example or be easily conquered and dispersed by the federal forces.

Once the war is concluded, the work of pacification and reconstruction will quickly follow. In my judgment it will be less difficult than believed now. Some steps have already been taken along that road. While the president was in Richmond, he made proposals relative to returning that state to the Union to members of the Virginia legislature who had remained in that city. The triumph of federal arms will considerably augment the number of Union partisans in the South who will hasten to establish provisional governments in order to renew relations between those states and the federal government.

These important events had scarcely passed before this government began to take some measures in respect to the European nations, which clearly revealed that as the situation here improves, the current foreign policy will change. The first of these measures was a presidential proclamation . . . declaring almost all southern ports closed. . . . The U.S. Congress had authorized the government to close these ports at the beginning of the war. Closing the ports undoubtedly would have been a simpler and less costly means of impeding their commerce than the blockade. However, the European nations informed the Union government that they would not tolerate the closure, which they considered did not accord with international law. The federal government decided upon the blockade to avoid complications. . . . Certainly the European nations will not seek a fight on those grounds. . . . Another presidential decree . . . declared that any nation not conceding U.S. war vessels the same rights conceded to third-party vessels will receive similar treatment from the United States. Since some European nations proclaimed neutrality in the U.S. Civil War, they have not permitted Union war vessels to do what they denied to the Confederate privateers. . . .[14]

The president returned from Richmond this past Sunday. The day before yesterday, while welcoming a popular meeting, Lincoln made a speech in which he limited himself to defending his reconstruction plan.

Seward continues quite indisposed because of his accident. Besides the fracture of the arm . . . they have found another fracture in the upper jaw.

Davis has apparently established his residence in Charlotte, North

Carolina, a place not very far from General Johnston's headquarters. Some believe Davis will head to Texas in order to pass into the Mexican Republic. This does not seem very probable to me.[15]

Today the report was published of the capture of Selma, Alabama. . . . The reports have also announced the surrender of Lynchburg, a strategic point of much importance in Virginia. In addition, the capture of Montgomery is announced. . . .

Romero to MRE, 20 April 1865, in Romero, *Correspondencia* V, 249–50

. . . Suddenly a change of administration has occurred from which Mexico will supposedly be among those able to draw the most advantage. Power has been transferred from the Republican party, to which Lincoln belonged, to the Democratic party, to which the current president Andrew Johnson belongs. Certainly Johnson was only chosen vice-president a few months ago to conciliate the Democrats. No one imagined the vice-president would become the president of the United States.[16]

. . . [Previously I reported] details of Lincoln's assassination, of the attempted assassination of Seward and his son, and of the inauguration of the new president. Now . . . Lincoln's remains lie in the Capitol. The corpse will be transferred to Baltimore tomorrow and then subsequently to the other principal cities of this country before arriving at Springfield, Illinois, where the body will rest permanently.

The new president even conserved the same cabinet as Lincoln. In some speeches he stated the need to punish severely the instigators of the southern insurrection. . . .

On the evening of the day on which Lincoln was assassinated, there had been a cabinet meeting that Grant attended. The cabinet, assuming the war concluded, decided to suspend the enlistment of volunteers and the draft, to cease purchasing provisions and war supplies, to reduce the number of generals and officers, and to remove the existing restrictions about conducting trade with the southern states. I have been assured this would all be carried out within a short time.

. . . Allegedly Sherman received a proposal from Johnston to surrender under the same terms offered to General Lee. General Grant, to whom General Sherman submitted this matter, supposedly replied he would only recognize unconditional surrender. Other military groups remaining in Virginia have offered to surrender upon the same terms as Lee.[17]

The forces of General [Edward R. S.] Canby had already taken Mobile. . . .[18]

Jefferson Davis was in Danville on 5 April. On that date and before General Lee's surrender, he proclaimed that the evacuation of Richmond did not signify anything. Perhaps later events have made him change his mind.

Some members of the Virginia legislature, who had remained in Richmond after the federal forces occupied that city, issued a circular to their colleagues and to other distinguished Virginians to meet in Richmond to discuss how to reestablish their relations with the federal government. This was done with the agreement and authorization of General [Godfrey] Weitzel, commander of the federal forces in Richmond. When the [U.S.] government became aware of that step, it disapproved, removed General Weitzel from command of Richmond, and ordered some of the people who had signed that circular to leave Richmond. . . .[19]

Romero to MRE, 27 April 1865, in Romero, *Correspondencia* V, 267–68

. . . Johnston surrendered in effect on April 18, with all the Confederate forces. However, General Sherman conceded him such conditions that . . . it really appeared doubtful who had surrendered to whom, Johnston to Sherman, or Sherman to Johnston.

In the capitulation . . . the existing Confederate state governments are recognized, the U.S. congressional confiscation laws are abrogated, and in principle, the obligation to pay the Confederate debt and the legal existence of slavery are recognized. As is easy to suppose, with the current president and in the present state of things, the U.S. government could not approve such terms. . . . A cabinet meeting formally disapproved the capitulation and informed General Sherman that he only had authority to conclude a strictly military settlement. Moreover, he ought not to attempt to discuss nor confer on political questions of any type. General Grant, who had moved his headquarters to Washington, immediately journeyed to North Carolina to direct the military operations against Johnston in person. Last night a telegram received here reported that when Grant arrived in Raleigh, he immediately notified Johnston that the armistice between the armies was terminated while the Union government decided upon a suitable course with respect to the capitulation.[20]

General Breckinridge, Davis's secretary of war, attended the conferences between Sherman and Johnston to arrange the capitulation. Davis was in the vicinity and approved the conditions. If the terms had been accepted, they would have ended the war in one blow, since the terms encompass all the Confederate forces still making war against this government.

On 20 April General [James H.] Wilson, commanding a cavalry division of Sherman's army, captured Macon, the very well fortified capital of Georgia. Since that capture was made during the armistice, this government ordered the evacuation of Macon and the release of all the prisoners taken there.

In an official report directed to General Dix, the federal secretary of war claimed that General Sherman's order to General Stoneman to retire from Salisbury and join him left Davis and his friends free to retreat to Mexico and Europe. Davis's escape seemed to be confirmed later. . . .

Many of the officers who surrendered with General Lee have supposedly expressed a desire to go to Mexico to fight against Maximilian. This government has not placed any difficulties to their departure for foreign parts. . . .[21]

Lincoln's body is now in Albany after having passed through Baltimore, Hamsburg, [sic—Harrisburg?], Philadelphia, and New York, where it received funeral honors. . . .[22]

President Johnson has continued to receive various commissioners for different states, societies, and organizations. In replying to the many speeches directed at him, he has invariably contended that treason is a very great crime and ought to be punished in exemplary fashion and that he has always desired to serve the people and to be a faithful interpreter of its will and aspirations. He has defended and will defend the rights of the people against the privileged classes, and with respect to the course his administration will follow, he added, he has nothing new to say. Resting entirely upon his antecedents and his past life, he will not back down a bit. . . .

During the last two weeks no news arrived from Mexico. Public opinion has been so preoccupied with Lincoln's assassination that, even had there been reports of great interest, they would have gone totally unnoticed. . . .

Romero to MRE, 4 May 1865, in Romero, *Correspondencia* V, 292–93

. . . April witnessed the end of the U.S. Civil War. This government disapproved the first surrender that General Sherman concluded with the Confederate army of General Johnston. . . . General Johnston had stated, General Grant told me, that he would not imitate General Lee, pretending that he did not surrender out of necessity and that he could resist still longer. On 26 April, then, General Johnston with all the forces in North and South Carolina and Georgia surrendered to General Sherman upon the same conditions conceded to General Lee's army. . . .

After this only two Confederate armies remain. They will surrender soon also or be conquered. The principal army belongs to General Kirby Smith, commander of the Confederate forces west of the Mississippi River. The other is that of General [Richard] Taylor in Alabama and Florida. Supposedly, both are negotiating to surrender. . . .

Very confident the war has already terminated, General Grant has ordered two of the armies under General Sherman's command, the Army of the Tennessee, commanded by General [Oliver O.] Howard, and the Army of Georgia, commanded by General Slown [sic—Henry W. Slocum], to come to Washington. Only the Army of North Carolina, commanded by General Schofield, will remain in that state.

For his part, the secretary of war has ordered an immediate reduction in the expenses of the army insofar as possible reducing its size, suspending the purchase of provisions and war material, canceling the leases of steamers that have been serving as army transports, and adopting various other measures of similar purpose.

Today Lincoln's body should have been buried at Springfield, the capital of Illinois. His assassin, John Wilkes Booth, was discovered on 26 April and killed during the arrest. . . .

Seward has almost recovered. . . . Presumably soon he could assume his duties in the State Department.

. . . The president claims to have uncovered evidence that Jefferson Davis and his emissaries in Canada planned and ordered the assassination of Lincoln and the attempted assassination of Seward. Johnson has offered a reward of $100,000 for the arrest of Davis and $25,000 to those who capture each of his accomplices within the borders of the United States. . . .

Romero to MRE, 25 May 1865, in Romero, *Correspondencia* V, 333–34

This government already considers the Civil War east to the Mississippi terminated. Therefore, it has declared that, beginning in the coming month, anyone caught armed in that region will be treated as a bandit and not as a soldier. Thus, the Civil War has remained confined to Texas and the part of Arkansas and Louisiana that form the military department west of the Mississippi commanded by Confederate General Kirby Smith. For several days it was believed that this general would follow the example of Lee and Johnston without loss of time. However, soon one of his proclamations arrived . . . announcing his resolve to continue the war in his department despite the disasters that the Confederate cause has suffered. Kirby Smith indicated he soon will receive aid from the nations sympathetic to the Confederacy. To the proclamation has been added General [John B.] Magruder's speech delivered at the same time in Houston. Texas will fight in defense of the Confederacy, Magruder claimed, and it will soon receive the effective aid of its neighbor.

This has given an entirely distinct aspect to the situation in the trans-Mississippi. Now it is not only believed that the insurgents will offer resistance but also that they will soon receive aid from Napoleon, either directly or through the intermediary of his agent Maximilian. Therefore this government is resolved to send sizeable forces to Texas under General Sheridan. . . .

Davis was captured . . . in Georgia. He was conducted from there to Fort Monroe where he is currently held. . . . Apparently, they have still not decided if he will be tried civilly or militarily, nor even whether he will be accused of treason or of complicity in the assassination of Lincoln. Meanwhile, the trial of Booth's accomplices continues its legal course. Apparently it was decided not to implicate Davis in this trial.

On 23 and 24 May, there was a grand review in Washington of the armies of Generals Meade and Sherman, which were camped in the vicinity. On 23 May there was a review of General Sherman's cavalry forces and of four army corps from the Army of the Potomac. The following day the Armies of the Tennessee and Georgia passed in review. One hundred and forty thousand men passed in review on the two days. Already another seventy-five thousand men have begun to gather. They will pass in review later. This force has no special duty and could be used in any emergency. This very imposing spectacle seems directed more toward influencing the European nations than any other purpose.

On 22 May a presidential proclamation declared pirates all vessels that make war on the United States after 1 July. . . .

The movement of citizens from this country who wish to emigrate to Mexico has quieted down very considerably. . . . A telegraphic report stated:

"San Francisco. May 22, 1865.—The bark Broutes, ready to depart for Arizona with four hundred emigrants for Mexico and carrying 260 boxes of firearms on board, has been detained by customs officials who requested instructions from Washington by telegraph. It is believed that the emigrants, the majority composed of Americans, were going to Mexico to aid Juárez."

I have deemed it desirable not to take any step in this matter until I receive the details. . . .

Romero to MRE, 12 June 1865, in Romero, *Correspondencia* V, 350

Texas's promise of resistance disappeared as soon as the news of General Johnston's surrender arrived there. Much earlier General Sheridan was known to be marching toward that state with a considerable force. Confederate General Kirby Smith surrendered to General Canby upon the same terms conceded to the armies of Lee and Johnston. Inspite of this, the movement of troops to Texas has not been suspended. . . . Soon, close to thirty-five thousand men will be united along the Rio Bravo, probably under General Sherman's command.

This past 29 May, the U.S. president issued two proclamations. In the first, he specified the conditions for conceding amnesty to southern citizens. In the second, he ordered the reorganization of North Carolina's government. . . .

Various telegraphic reports from San Francisco . . . indicate that some citizens wishing to emigrate to Mexico attempted to seize a Peruvian steamer in that port. They intended to make war on French commerce in the Pacific. These citizens were arrested. Apparently General [Plácido] Vega has had some role in that affair. Two weeks ago, he telegraphed me to request the Peruvian minister in Washington to place the steamer under his orders. . . .

Romero to MRE, 15 June 1865, in Romero, *Correspondencia* V, 385–86

The president of the United States issued two proclamations. . . . The first opened the coastal trade with the ports of former rebel states that had been opened for foreign commerce. . . . The first proclamation also declared that having organized a government, Tennessee would be readmitted into the Union. The second proclamation organized a provisional government for Mississippi, naming William L. Sharkey governor. . . .

On 12 June Seward finally resumed his post in the State Department. During the incapacitation of his son, Seward's nephew Clarence A. Seward, a New York lawyer, fulfilled the function of assistant secretary of state.

. . . Yesterday's *World* stated that Seward will leave the cabinet by this coming July because he made promises to the French government about Mexico that Johnson does not propose to comply with. Nevertheless, this seems very unlikely to me.

. . . General Grant departed more than a week ago to attend a meeting in New York on 7 June and to visit the great western fair of Chicago. He has received enthusiastic and spontaneous popular ovations along the whole way. It is not recalled if this has ever been done in this country for any other citizen.

They continue to discharge those troops who enlisted for a fixed time that is about to expire. However, those drafted for the duration of the war, as most were, still have not been discharged. As I understand it, there is also no disposition to discharge them very soon.

Currently, the principal question in this country is whether or not the insurgent states will have to concede the right of suffrage to the Negroes. On one hand, doubtless this measure ought to be adopted because of its convenience for the North in preventing southern discontents from achieving a preponderant influence [in the South]. However, on the other hand, this measure conflicts so much with the racial prejudices of this people that they will scarcely decide in favor of it. . . .

Romero to MRE, 30 June 1865, in Romero, *Correspondencia* V, 433–34

On 17 June the president issued two proclamations . . . [that] provided for the organization of provisional governments in Georgia and Texas, naming James Johnson as military governor of the department of the former and Andrew J. Hamilton of the latter. Hamilton filled that same post for a few days during Lincoln's administration. . . .

On 21 June the president also proclaimed the organization of a provisional government for Alabama and named Lewis E. Parsons governor. Thus, only South Carolina and Florida of the rebel states remain to be organized.

. . . Official reports have already been received of the occupation of Galveston and Brownsville and the surrender of all the Confederate forces in Texas. . . .

. . . The Treasury Department's instructions, issued on 27 June, regulate commerce in those places recently held by the insurgents and which the president has opened to commerce. We ought to be aware of these instructions because they affect commerce with Brownsville.

. . . The trial of the defendants and accomplices in the assassination of Lincoln and the attempted assassination of Seward ended yesterday. The court martial immediately pronounced the sentences, which were sent to the secretary of war for submission to the president. . . .

A great divergence of opinions continues regarding what is called here the question of reconstruction or reorganization and its principal subordinate point, the question of conceding the suffrage to freedmen. Some contended that the North will have no security until affairs in the South are placed in the hands of the freedmen. Others believe that each state must decide this question for itself, according to its necessities and wishes. However, almost all agree that the suffrage ought to be conceded to the freedmen with more or less restrictions. This will probably be done in the end. The president's reserve had not permitted anyone at present to discover what his policy will be on this point. . . .

Romero to MRE, 7 July 1865, in Romero, *Correspondencia* V, 454–55

On 30 June the president proclaimed the organization of a provisional government for South Carolina, naming [Benjamin F.] Perry as provisional governor.

The court martial that tried the criminals and accomplices in the assassination of Lincoln and the unsuccessful assassination attempt on Seward condemned four of the accused to death and three to life imprisonment. The eighth received six years in prison. The president approved those sentences the day before yesterday. Today they will be carried out on the persons sentenced to death.

The president's illness was more serious than believed. . . . Although he is almost entirely recovered, . . . by direction of his doctor, he still does not receive visitors.

Four July passed tranquilly in Washington. The only commemoration here was a celebration by the colored people. The dinner prepared at Saratoga was very unsuccessful. None of the more noted generals invited cared to attend. In the toasts and speeches made there, no one spoke a single word about Mexico or the Monroe Doctrine. On the other hand, in a speech in Chicago, Henry Winter Davis spoke almost exclusively about our affairs. . . .

In a recent speech, General Sherman again recommended that the United States not occupy itself with foreign questions that could produce another war but rather with its internal development and prosperity. He claimed the United States needs peace above all things. . . .

Romero to MRE, 27 July 1865, in Romero, *Correspondencia* V, 512–13

On 13 July the president proclaimed the organization of a provisional government for Florida, naming William Maroin governor. Thus, the so-called reconstruction question has been settled.[23]

The Spanish government decided to turn the Confederate steamer

Stonewall over to the United States. The *Stonewall* had sought refuge in Havana but this government had claimed that vessel. . . .[24]

The secretary of war has created a new military [regional organization] of the United States. Using five major generals from the regular army, he has established five military departments: the one for the Atlantic will be commanded by General Meade, another for the Gulf will be commanded by General Sheridan, another for the Pacific will be commanded by General Halleck, another for Mississippi will be commanded by General Sherman, and the last for Tennessee will be commanded by General [George] Thomas. Each department contains several military subdivisions, commanded by the principal generals of this country. General Schofield commands North Carolina. . . .

A short while ago a convention composed of businessmen from the United States and Canada met in Detroit to reach agreement upon the measures necessary to protect commerce between Canada and the United States. At this meeting the U.S. consul general in Canada either proposed the annexation of these provinces to the United States or explained that such would be the inevitable consequence of recent events. This remark caused much discontent among the Canadian delegates. The Canadian provinces have viewed it with even more disgust. . . .[25]

Romero to MRE, 31 August 1865, in Romero, *Correspondencia* V, 592

. . . Since the war ended, important public concerns have been restricted more to domestic affairs, . . . [especially] to reorganizing the former rebel states. The most notable question refers to suffrage for colored people. Apparently, black suffrage will remain undecided until Congress resolves the issue with respect to federal elections. This congressional decision will serve then as an example for the states with respect to their particular elections.

In regard to the implementation of the amnesty law, the president continues to grant individual pardons to persons not encompassed in its general provisions. A few days ago the newspaper reported that Thomas Corwin, ex-minister to Mexico, had taken Johnson unawares. For contemptible considerations, he worked to obtain a pardon that the newspaper reporter judged the president could only have conceded if deceived.[26]

. . . A military tribunal is trying Henry Wirtz, captain in the Confederate army and commandant of Andersonville Prison. The federal prisoners in Andersonville allegedly received very bad treatment, some even dying from hunger and want of shelter. . . .[27]

Johnson has issued a proclamation canceling all prohibitions against trade with the southern states in contraband of war.

One of the most notable documents that has come to light these days is the speech given in Clarksville [Tennessee] by Montgomery Blair. . . . After Blair's terrible attack upon Seward and Stanton in his other speech on the Monroe Doctrine, he returns with the same energy to attack Seward for his domestic policy. Now, just as before, the accusations leveled against Seward are of enormous weight. They are based on facts that Blair could observe and thoroughly appreciate as Seward's cabinet colleague. . . .

Romero to MRE, 23 September 1865, in Romero, *Correspondencia* V, 658–59

The provisional governors in the southern states appointed by the president have been busy organizing conventions to draft new constitutions and to reestablish relations between those states and the federal government. The conventions of Alabama and South Carolina are now convened and have commenced their work. The former began by abolishing slavery in the state, by declaring null and void all the acts while the state was separated from the Union, by ordering that the debt contracted during that time not be paid, and by ordering that Negroes ought to be conceded the right to appear as witnesses in court. The South Carolinian convention commenced by recognizing the validity of the acts of the Confederate administrations and by annulling the states' secession act. In spite of this, it has had to abolish slavery in the state.[28]

This manner of reconstructing, with the same people who a short time ago served the Confederate government and without conceding suffrage to the Negroes, is going to produce the greatest division in the North. The radical faction of the Republican party views this system of reconstruction with the greatest disgust. It leaves power in the hands of the Democrats and allows the recent rebels to reorganize the states. The radical plan would deny political rights to all who aided the Confederate government and could concede suffrage to the Negroes. The conservative faction of the Republican party, nevertheless, appears to approve the president's plan for reconstruction. Currently it can be said that the reconstruction question is in embryo. Furthermore, it will not develop until Congress convenes. If the executive does not obtain a legislative majority on this question, the House will not admit the representatives from the reconstructed states. Then the executive plan will be defeated. Certainly Congress will devote primary attention to this question. It will occupy the major part of Congress' time, even to Mexico's detriment, since time will scarcely remain for debate on the Mexican question.

The conventions of the Democratic and Republican parties of New York have already met. The parties approved platforms and nominated candidates. . . . Both parties adopted almost identical platforms, expressing their confidence in the president and choosing candidates for the secondary posts of the state from among the most distinguished generals of the recent Civil War. The conservative faction predominated in the Republican convention. The outcome of the elections in the coming October will influence considerably the policy that the president will follow.

. . . In some official correspondence, Seward explained to [Charles Francis] Adams, U.S. minister to London, that the U.S. government does not consider itself obliged to pay a single cent of the Confederate cotton loan contracted in London . . . whether the British government does or does not support the holders of those bonds. Seward's notes . . . have, I believe, established a precedent that we ought not to lose sight of when we are expected to recognize the loans that Maximilian negotiated in Europe. [29]

The Irish masonic society, called the "Fenian Brotherhood," strives to make Ireland independent. The Fenians, whose leaders have recently caused so much alarm in England, held a large meeting in New York last night. . . . [30]

Romero to MRE, 12 October 1865, in Romero, *Correspondencia* V, 689–90

. . . Closing their sessions after having reestablished their relations with the federal government, the Alabama and South Carolina conventions have fixed a day for the election of governors, legislators, and other functionaries. Mississippi has already held these elections. [Former Confederate] General [Benjamin G.] Humphreys was elected governor. [31]

The North Carolina convention is now meeting. Already it has nullified its act of secession, which was therefore never valid. Therefore, it has also declared that the state debt contracted to make war on the federal government suffers from the same defect. It set 2 November as the election day for governor and legislators. [32]

The day before yesterday elections were held in Pennsylvania, Ohio, Iowa, and New Jersey. According to the current reports, the Republican party won in three states. However, in Ohio a relative plurality favored the Democrats in comparison with the number of votes that they obtained in the last elections.

Next month's New York elections are without dispute the most influential in the country for the coming Congress. [33]

At a Democratic party meeting in Albany on 5 October, the distinguished orator John Van Buren, son of ex-President Martin Van Buren, made an important speech. The speech, [which focused] largely on the Monroe Doctrine and Seward, seemed important enough to merit translation here:

> . . . Do you know that Seward is committed against the Monroe Doctrine? When drafting their platform, the Republicans had to avoid the declaration which the Democratic party made in their New York Convention not to permit any foreign government to plant monarchical institutions on this continent without the U.S. government and people resisting. (Applause.) This clear and firm declaration had to be erased. Speaking of President Johnson's administration, you will observe that the Republicans simply say regarding the foreign policy under their care: 'Resolved, that we have complete confidence in President Johnson's conduct of relations with foreign nations, in his prompt action against them in all just demands, assuring reparations for national insults and prejudices, and in the maintenance of our government's fixed policy to prevent the intervention of foreign powers in the institutions of this continent.'

> Maximilian's occupation of Mexico is represented as hostile to our tranquility and menacing to our institutions. Yet, what are the Republicans going to do in this respect with Seward [in charge of foreign affairs]? Absolutely nothing. Without doubt you are familiar with the fact that when the two [sic—only the House voted] houses of congress resolved not to permit the establishment of Maximilian's government in Mexico, Seward immediately notified the [French] Emperor that the foreign relations of the government were exclusively under his charge, adding that congress had no role in them. Under no circumstance, Seward continued, did the United States intend to create difficulties with the French government as a consequence of the establishment of a monarchy in Mexico. Now the resolution, the only resolution regarding Seward which that convention approved: 'Resolved, that we offer our felicitations to William H. Seward for his provident salvation from the assassin's dagger, and that we rejoice that his distinguished service to the nation and to the cause of liberty can still continue.'[34]

The Philadelphia *Press* published a letter . . . claiming President [Juárez] had abandoned the national territory [that] the New York dailies reproduced. . . . Mexico's consul in New York officially, but privately, contradicted that report. . . .

The day before yesterday a Negro regiment from the District of Columbia that had served in the war returned to Washington. Greeting the regiment, the president's . . . remarks left the radical Republicans very complacent because he called the Negroes his countrymen. The president clearly does not consider Negroes as animals as many who call themselves Democrats here have considered them.

A short while ago the question of whether or not to concede the

Negroes the suffrage was submitted to a popular vote in Connecticut, one of the states most antagonistic to slavery. The outcome was negative. This has been taken as proof that the mass of the population is generally opposed to Negro suffrage. . . .

Romero to MRE, 19 October 1865, in Romero, *Correspondencia* V, 710–11

. . . General Grant's order of 13 October directed that the fortifications to the south of Fort Monroe should remain garrisoned with Negro troops. Grant ordered the discharge of all Negro troops when no longer needed for this service. His order also required the discharge of all volunteer cavalry regiments west of the Mississippi River, including Texas of course, and some other regiments in northern states.[35]

. . . From conversations with General Grant with regard to that order and from information from other sources, I have learned that some influential persons in this government have demanded as large a reduction as possible in the army. They wish to demonstrate that no danger of a foreign war exists as well as to introduce more economy into the budget. A cry, especially against the Negro regiments, has been raised in the southern states where they are garrisoned. These influences have dominated the president's thoughts. He has recommended to General Grant that all possible reductions be made. Grant responded with the 13 October order. Thus, several Negro units on the Rio Grande will probably be discharged. In this case, however, this step may be left to the discretion of General Sheridan, who could defer it for as long as he deemed desirable. The volunteer cavalry in the Rio Grande army, which ought to be discharged, will be reduced to two units. Two regular units that General Grant sent to Texas have already replaced the discharged units. After making all the reductions mentioned in the 13 October order, Grant believes the force remaining on the Rio Grande is more than sufficient to expel the French from Mexico if the United States should decide to take that step.

A short while ago, [Hugh] McCulloch, secretary of the treasury, made a speech at Fort Wayne, Indiana. . . . He probably expressed the ideas of the government. . . . He favored reducing the army.

The electoral campaign in New York continues active. The triumph of the Republican party in Pennsylvania, Ohio, Iowa, and New Jersey increased its likelihood for success in New York. The two major parties of this country now present a very curious spectacle. Both claim to be friends of the president, approving his policy and determined to aid him. Both parties believe the president belongs to their side. Each tries to make it appear that the other does not sustain Johnson in good faith. . . .[36]

Romero to MRE, 16 November 1865, in Romero,
Correspondencia V, 792–93

Lately . . . various vague, and at times contradictory, reports from the
[Mexican] Republic have appeared in the Washington dailies. . . . Most
come from persons more or less partial toward the French. . . . One,
which, from its source, merits credit, is the report that [Juárez's] Generals
[Mariano] Escobedo and [Juan N.] Cortina and Colonel [Servando]
Canales continue to besiege Matamoros . . . [and] have occupied the
mouth of the river, seizing a small enemy steamer that had been converted into a gunboat in Clarksville.

Important news has also arrived from Europe. . . . Napoleon will
commence to withdraw his troops from Mexico within a short time, not
leaving any of his soldiers on our territory by August or September of next
year. . . . The French emperor's decision has been attributed to observations made by the U.S. minister in regard to sending Egyptians to
Mexico. Supposedly various economic considerations have also contributed toward inspiring the decision. Although this report might have some
validity, it certainly still lacks a solid foundation of support.

The Spanish queen has decreed the serious prosecution of the slave
trade. Moreover, in certain cases the slaves found in trust should be
liberated. . . . This demonstrates the influence that the abolition of
slavery consummated in this country has begun to exercise in the exterior. . . .[37]

In this country the task of reconstructing the states continues peaceably. South Carolina, the first to rebel against the Union and the place
with more slave interests, has adopted a constitutional amendment permanently abolishing slavery. All the southern states are expected to do the
same, thereby firmly founding this great reform in an incontrovertible
manner. . . .

Romero to MRE, 4 December 1865, in Romero,
Correspondencia V, 862–63

. . . The Republican representatives . . . decided in caucus to present
a resolution to nominate a committee of fifteen people, composed of
nine representatives and six senators, to examine the present condition of
the former rebel states. This Committee on Reconstruction would examine whether it is desirable and upon what terms to admit the representatives and senators of the former rebel states to Congress. Since the
Republicans have an immense majority and all its factions apparently
approved this resolution, Congress will undoubtedly approve it.[38]

In this case, neither house will be occupied with the reconstruction question for several months, leaving them ample time to deal with our affairs.

The House organized today without great difficulty. The Republican candidate Schuyler Colfax remained speaker, obtaining 139 votes against 35 for the Democratic candidate [James] Brooks. This vote revealed the immense imbalance between the parties.

The representatives from Tennessee, one of the insurgent states, solicited admission to the House. Of course, they were denied admission.

Yesterday I had a long conversation with Senator Wade of Ohio. He understands the Mexican question perfectly well and is prepared to do what is necessary for the federal government to assume its proper role in this question. He will be in charge of directing this matter in the Senate. Certainly we could not have found a more appropriate and more capable person.

I have already spoken with a very large number of representatives and senators. In general they are not disposed to do anything that could cause a break with France. This sentiment is very deeply rooted, principally in the New England states. These manufacturing states are located on the Atlantic coast and thus accessible to the attacks of a powerful enemy.

Our affairs are taking such a satisfactory turn, some argue, that the armed intervention of the United States would not be necessary in any event. Others, in my judgment the majority, believe that Congress ought not seriously consider the Mexican question until after the southern representatives and senators have been admitted. Otherwise internal peace cannot be considered completely reestablished, which should be an indispensable prerequisite to accepting a foreign war. [39]

Nevertheless, a very few believe Napoleon will not accept war with the United States for any reason. The interests and honor of this nation demand, these individuals argue, that this government assume a dignified position and request the French forces to withdraw from Mexico. If those believing in this manner were organized and capable of managing the question cleverly, they could obtain a great deal because, whatever might be the desires or the opinions of the others, everyone is decidedly opposed to the French intervention. The force of public opinion is such that very few will dare to oppose any well-presented resolution. . . .

1866

Introduction to 1866

The working class suffered from a marked decline in real wages during the Civil War. It struggled to find an effective means to increase its share of national wealth and to obtain job security and a stable existence. Workers sought strength through the unity of the National Labor Union in 1866. The National Labor Union's chief appeal was the call for an eight-hour day, a measure that would offer job security in a mechanizing economy that was reducing its need for laborers, either as a source of skill or of power.

In the United States, attention focused politically upon the unfolding bitter contest between President Johnson and the radicals. Johnson unflinchingly opposed a radical-directed reconstruction. He fought the radicals over the new Freedman's Bureau Bill, the Civil Rights Act, the Fourteenth Amendment, and a variety of other issues. Since the vision of Johnson and his supporters of the reconstructed union differed in fundamental ways from the radical vision, the president vetoed much congressional legislation. Johnson also built a political base to support the program he proposed.

Romero, initially overjoyed with the rise of Johnson to power, gradually became disillusioned because Johnson retained Seward. Romero had presumed Johnson's commitment to the Monroe Doctrine meant determined resistance to the French in Mexico. Seward, however, continually opposed any form of overt aid to Juárez's government that would upset the French government. Romero wanted to raise forces and purchase arms in the United States to facilitate the overthrow of Maximilian's empire and to drive out the French. As Romero's frustration grew, he fed information to, and cooperated with, the radical efforts to force Seward out of Johnson's cabinet. Later Romero aided the movement to impeach Johnson, in part, to remove Seward's malignant influence from the government.

For some time, Seward had been convinced that the French could be persuaded to withdraw from Mexico. Slowly Johnson accepted Seward's view, arriving at a point in mid-1886 at which he became convinced a

military assault upon the French position was dangerous and not necessary. The alienation between Romero and Grant on one hand, and the
Johnson-Seward team on the other, grew during 1866. Seward objected
to Romero's confidential meetings with Johnson. To end this practice,
Seward issued what became known as the "Romero" circular in
mid-1866. He publicly denied foreign diplomats access to the president
except through his office. Of course, Seward knew before he issued the
circular that he had won the contest between himself and Grant-Romero
for the president's support. Romero salvaged what he could. While
Johnson and Seward were not prepared to enter the confrontational
course towards which Grant and Romero hoped to steer the United
States, they still maintained the public image of uncompromising opposition to the French intervention in Mexico and the puppet Maximilian
empire. Seward and Johnson were patient because they did not view the
French intervention as related to the Civil War and thus did not view it as
an assault upon U.S. sovereignty. Grant and Romero were impatient
because they considered the French intervention as an extension of the
Confederacy's direct challenge to the liberalism and nationalism that
combined to form the laissez-faire social system.

Johnson and Grant moved further away from each other as 1866 wore
,on. Grant resented Johnson's effort to use Romero and himself to support
Johnson's popularity on his 'swing around the circle.' Ostensibly, a non-
political voyage to dedicate a statue of Stephen Douglas in Chicago,
Johnson and Seward converted the trip into a political campaign. The
tour to Chicago represented an attempt to show solidarity with Mexico
and to use Grant's great popularity to bolster Johnson's sagging image.
Grant was presented as a supporter of the administration, and Romero
was introduced prominently at each stop in a form that associated his
goal—ridding Mexico of the French—as linked to the policy of the
Johnson administration. By the later stages of the trip, both Grant and
Romero were trying to avoid the appearance of support for the administration while still milking the large public turnouts for popular support
for getting the French out of Mexico as soon as possible. After the
Chicago ceremony, Romero made an excuse not to continue with the
Johnson party on its return. Grant also lessened his role. During the
return trip, the president increasingly politicized his public appearances
by attacking the radicals.

General Grant also resisted Johnson's efforts to exploit his popularity in
another scheme. When the French evacuated Mexico in late 1866,
Johnson appointed Ohioan Lewis D. Campbell to serve as minister to the
Republic of Mexico and attempted to send Grant along to give Campbell's mission more public attention and to create the impression that the

Johnson administration, in conjunction with Grant, was expelling the French. Grant angrily and categorically refused to accompany the mission. Johnson had been so determined to hitch Grant to the administration's Mexican policy that he actually had his instructions to Grant printed for wider distribution. Thus stymied, Johnson was forced to substitute General William T. Sherman—the second most popular U.S. military leader—as symbol of the strength and correctness of his policy to remove the French. Meanwhile, on the frontier, General Sheridan provided whatever aid he could to the Mexican liberals.

Romero continued his lobbying work with members of Congress and business, military, and media figures. Occasionally, Romero's lobbying encountered significant problems. With the Civil War over and financial and military aid more available in the United States, the number of Mexican liberal agents multiplied. Romero wanted to control the Mexican *caudillos*—Mexican regional military-political strongmen—and agents, but found his task burdensome and difficult. North American speculators, such as popular General John C. Frémont, waited like vultures to fall upon gullible Mexican weapons purchasers. On the cheerier side, Romero found ever larger numbers of congressmen willing to introduce resolutions, make speeches, and cooperate with Romero in other ways. The lobbying campaign he had launched in 1863 was paying fair dividends by 1866. Finally, in late 1866 and 1867, Romero played a peripheral, but not insignificant, role in the impeachment of President Johnson. Beginning in December 1866, Romero was made privy to radical plans, hopes, and aspirations in regard to removing the Johnson-Seward team and thus altering a hated domestic and foreign policy. The plan presented to Romero in December 1866 involved forcing Senator Lafayette Foster of Connecticut to resign, then electing Senator Benjamin Wade as president pro tempore of the Senate, and finally impeaching Johnson in order to make Wade President of the United States.

Political Reviews—1866

Romero to MRE, 24 February 1866, in Romero, *Correspondencia* VII, 205–6

Some Fenians met on 17 February. . . . French agents engaged George Francis Train to persuade that crowd to accept a resolution which, related to the goal of the meeting, declared the Monroe Doctrine a fraud to swindle the American people. Train supported this resolution with a speech using all the French charges against the Mexican people. . . . He also relied upon all the French arguments and inventions to demonstrate that the United States ought to prefer the so-called empire of Maximilian over the Mexican Republic. Attended by two or three U.S. representatives who were ignorant of what was going to happen, this meeting greatly disgusted many members of Congress. Some of these congressmen and other friends of ours consequently decided to hold another meeting in Washington that would be larger and more respectable than that of the Fenians. Our friends sought to counter the effect of the earlier meeting and to strengthen public sentiment in favor of the Monroe Doctrine. They consulted me on the particulars. Our friends, having agreed that this meeting seemed very desirable, are attempting to arrange it for the coming week. . . .

The day before yesterday I attended a funeral ceremony in the anteroom of the House of Representatives dedicated to the memory of Winter Davis. Speaking at the beginning of the ceremony, Speaker of the House Colfax made a brief allusion to the Mexican Republic's cause in these terms: "Inflexibly hostile (he said referring to Winter Davis) to all oppression, whether of slavery on American soil or of republicans struggling in Mexico against monarchical invasion, . . . his death has been lamented throughout the continent."[1]

Some days ago, a rupture was disclosed between Johnson and the Republican members who . . . form a majority in Congress. This split reflects the divergence of opinion on the reconstruction of the former rebel states. Johnson has agreed with the Democratic party. . . . A two-thirds majority of both houses of Congress had approved a bill considerably amplifying the prerogatives and capacity of the "Freedman's Bureau" and extended its existence indefinitely. The president vetoed the project, characterizing it as useless, undesirable, and dangerous for the treasury. Above all, he contended, it was unconstitutional and incompatible with public liberty because, among other reasons, it moved some civil suits from the courts to administrative decision levels and it moved many criminal cases to courts-martial. The bill did not obtain a two-thirds vote in the Senate. Therefore, it remained without effect.[2]

In addition, the bill's fate has produced considerable excitement. The Democratic party immediately held a meeting to express its satisfaction and approval of the presidential policy. The meeting took place the day before yesterday in and around the Grover Theater of Washington with quite heated speeches against the Republicans and the approval of resolutions alluding to the same goal. . . .

The meeting nominated a committee to present these resolutions to Johnson. After completing that work, as agreed, the crowd moved to the park around the president's house. Then the president delivered an improvised speech to the audience. He went so far in the speech as to compare the Republican opponents of his policy with the rebel traitors to the Union. He mentioned Thaddeus Stevens, Sumner, and Wendell Phillips by name. Naturally, this has increased the excitement. To defend his policy in this crisis, Johnson considered it necessary to send two cabinet members, Seward and Dennison, to address a large meeting last night in Cooper's Institute (New York). . . .

This violent rupture between Congress and the executive is undoubtedly very lamentable, especially because it could embarrass the course of [Mexico's] labors and the realization of our hopes in this country. Some believe the dispute could go to the extreme of a civil war. Others classify this evaluation as an exaggeration. . . .

Romero to MRE, 9 June 1866, in Romero, *Correspondencia* VII, 612

. . . It was announced long ago that Fenian expeditions organized in this country would invade Canada. Recently, more than a thousand armed individuals managed to pass clandestinely across the frontier. The Canadian authorities took some prisoners. Because of special instructions emanating from the State Department after the attorney general had heard something about the affair, the authorities of this country arrested some nine hundred others who were about to cross into Canadian territory as part of the same expedition. Consequently, the [federal authorities] have captured some of the individuals who are considered Fenian leaders. Among the prisoners are two generals of Irish origin who had served in the Union army in the recent war. Moreover, on 6 June the president . . . again charged the civil and military authorities to seek to disband or disperse expeditions that attempt to invade English possessions. . . .[3]

This has been the sad outcome for the Fenian conspirators who believed they could avoid the application of the severe U.S. neutrality laws. Perhaps Mexico's efforts would have suffered the same fate if, forgetting those laws and the existing disposition to apply them to avoid compromising the nation, we would have undertaken to organize expeditions to aid in the defense of the Republic without all the indispensable support. The French minister would have requested the enforcement of the neutrality laws, just as the English minister has in the case of the Fenians. Without hesitation, the United States would have ordered its rigorous application. . . .

Romero to MRE, 25 July 1866, in Romero, *Correspondencia*
VIII, 104

. . . Attorney General James Speed resigned. . . . The president
named Henry Stanbery to succeed Speed. The Senate has already confirmed Stanbery. . . .

Tennessee has already ratified the constitutional amendment [the Fourteenth Amendment] that Congress approved. Congress has declared
ratification [of the Fourteenth Amendment] by the legislatures of each of
eleven ex-rebel states as an indispensable condition for admitting their
respective representatives and senators. As soon as word of ratification was
received here, both houses presented bills declaring Tennessee returned
to the union and stating that its representatives and senators ought to be
admitted. The bill passed at once. Yesterday, the current representatives
from Tennessee were received.[4]

. . . Stevens wanted to authorize the speaker and the president pro
tempore of the Senate to convoke a special session if they judge the step
necessary. The constitution concedes this power to call a special session
to the president. Thus, Congress, holding the proposal unconstitutional,
did not approve the bill. . . .

Romero to MRE, 29 September 1866, in Romero,
Correspondencia VIII, 330–32

My heavy work load has interrupted the periodic and regular submission of political reviews. . . . The president proposes to form a party to
support his reconstruction policy. It will be composed of Democrats and
moderates from the Republican party. Johnson has directed all his administration's patronage and the secret labors of his friends to the formation of the new party. From the beginning, he has counted on the support
of the Democratic party, which he has specially praised. However, he has
not attracted many more than about four or five senators and only one
representative from the Republicans. The reason for this has been the
scant popularity remaining to the Democrats because most of them had
opposed continuing the war that ended in the Union triumph. Furthermore, the Democrats wish to preserve their own organization, admitting
into the party's inner circle only Republicans who would adhere to
Johnson's policy instead of organizing a new party on the basis of equality
between Democrats and Republicans. The president's imprudent conduct
in his informal public speeches and his remarks denouncing Congress as
unworthy of that name, because he claims it has degenerated into a

meeting of conspirators, have also contributed to the disappointment of the president's plan. His excessively harsh characterizations of Congress and, in particular some of its most notable members and the leaders of the Republican party, have further inflamed feelings. He has aroused political passions toward himself and against the Democratic party that defends him.[5]

Johnson's conduct probably played a major role in the resounding Republican triumphs in the Maine and Vermont elections and also in those elections that are considered as certain [victories] in other states. The Democratic convention held in Philadelphia . . . was supposedly to avoid these evils and determine the basis for the party that the president desired to create. However, . . . very soon a Republican convention, including the loyal citizens from the South, also met in Philadelphia, clearly delineating the limits that divide the two parties. At this time, everyone agrees that Johnson's plans have failed and that his policy will not carry him forward. Representative [Henry J.] Raymond, editor of the *New York Times*, was among the few Republicans who had joined Johnson. Raymond has just published a sort of retraction, confessing his error and stating that the evils of the congressional policy are preferable to the return to power of the Democratic party. Other similar defections can be expected.

The hot-headed Republicans have announced that the Senate will use its constitutional authority to impeach the president in its next session. . . . In addition, Johnson's friends say that if the Senate should do such a thing [impeach], the president would not recognize the act because ten states of the Union, those previously in rebellion, are not represented in that body. This [defiance by Johnson] would produce a conflict that could lead to a new civil war. However, presumably the good sense of the people would prevent things from arriving at that extreme, and a means will be encountered of conciliating the rival parties, or at least of reconciling the president and Congress to the peaceful exercise of their respective functions. . . .[6]

The generals and officers of the regular and volunteer armies who support the president's policy convened at Cleveland in the middle of last month to adopt resolutions favorable to [Johnson's reconstruction] policy. The military [leaders] opposed to Johnson's policy, almost all discharged now, met a short while ago in Pittsburgh to neutralize the effect of the Cleveland convention. The Pittsburgh convention approved resolutions strongly condemning the president's conduct and approving the congressional policy. General Grant was invited to attend the Pittsburgh manifestation. He refused and he disapproved the conduct of soldiers [in active service] who did attend.[7]

To conclude, I will recall the principal points in which Johnson's policy on reconstruction of the ex-rebel states differs from those Congress has adopted. Johnson would not demand more of these states as a condition for readmitting their representatives into Congress than the three conditions that he imposed upon them. The former rebel states have already accepted these conditions, namely, the recognition of the constitutional amendment to abolish slavery, the nullification of the so-called secession ordinances, and the repudiation of the Confederate debt. In addition to these conditions, Congress would demand a change in the laws for federal elections. In Congress' election plan, only the number of citizens currently eligible to vote would be considered in fixing representation and not the entire state population, even including the colored people who still have not been conceded the right to vote. This change [in election eligibility] is proposed in the form of a constitutional amendment pending the approval of the state legislatures. . . .[8]

1867

Introduction to 1867

The conflict between Johnson and the radical faction of the Republican party intensified with Johnson's vetoes of the First Reconstruction Act (revised in 1867 and 1868), Command of the Army Act, and the Tenure of Office Act. All three pieces of legislation were passed over the president's veto in March. The radicals instituted military reconstruction in mid-1867 when they perceived that Grant pursued a course similar to the one they followed. The radicals recognized that military reconstruction would protect the fledgling Republican parties in the South from assault by Johnson's political allies who sought to destroy the political organizations loyal to the radicals.

Minister Campbell's mission—to establish contact with the Juárez government and to observe the French withdrawal—had proved an unmitigated disaster. It dragged on into early 1867 before Campbell was forced to resign. Sherman had had the good sense to return to the United States much earlier. Later, the Johnson administration sent Marcus Otterbourg to Mexico as minister. In Romero's view, Otterbourg's mission was to prevent the execution of Maximilian. Romero tried to warn the U.S. government that it should not interfere in Mexican treatment of Maximilian. Above all, Romero advised the government not to seek a compromise that would have Maximilian "abdicate" because that step would imply the legitimacy of his crown, something both the United States and Mexico had denied up to that point. Romero warned that any attempt to aid Maximilian would be considered meddling in the internal affairs of Mexico. He recalled that the United States had rejected friendly Russian mediation offers in 1863 with the charge of interference in its internal affairs. The same rule applied to Mexico in 1867. Finally, Romero reminded Seward that when Juárez had been threatened with capture by the French in 1864 and 1865, the United States had not requested the French to treat Juárez with legal and moral respect. Mexico would resent any indication that it needed to be treated in a manner different from the French. Seward proposed General Antonio López de Santa Anna as an intermediate option between Juárez and the Mexican conservatives around Maximilian. The idea interested no one. Santa Anna was arrested upon his return to Mexico in 1867.

Romero's lobbying efforts remained quite successful as he maintained steady contact with congressional leaders and media sources to urge action to remove the French and to establish close relations with liberal Mexico. Nathaniel P. Banks labored with considerable success to implement Romero's goal of obtaining a House Foreign Relations Committee sympathetic to liberal Mexico. Working with Wade, Romero was unable to overcome the cautious yet powerful Sumner leadership in the Senate Foreign Relations Committee. The piper came to be paid, however. Many of those whom Romero had successfully lobbied to support Juárez's Mexico, for example Banks and Thaddeus Stevens, sought repayment in some form. Banks forged some ill-defined link with the Charles Knapp group, which owned Tehuantepec railroad and transportation interests, while Stevens's nephew, Simon Stevens, associated with the Marshall O. Roberts's Tehuantepec railroad and transportation interests. Given the conflicting pressures—Romero felt obligated to both Banks and Stevens—the best that Romero could do was to urge the contending factions to come to terms and present a joint proposal. However, the profits looked better in one large pile than in two small ones, so the Tehuantepec transit interests remained apart, sniping at each other. Romero's most loyal and effective personal link—his bonds with Grant—remained strong. Grant had lost all influence with Johnson, however. Romero returned to Mexico in late 1867.

The economic and social trend toward concentration of capital and production in corporate institutions continued. These corporations relied upon capital to replace labor power and to drive down the unit price of production. This process left the farmer, especially the small farmer, in an exposed, uncompetitive situation. The farmer in the 1860s could compete poorly in an economic system that distributed rewards with priority to capital-intensive production. One early agrarian response was the formation of an organization to foster social and cultural closeness among rural inhabitants, the Patrons of Husbandry, or Grange, in late 1867. The Grange responded to a growing sense of isolation and alienation among American small- and middle-sized farmers.

Political Reviews—1867

Romero to MRE, 14 January 1867, in Romero, *Correspondencia* IX, 30

. . . As soon as Congress met after the Christmas and New Year's recess, [James] Ashley, representative from Ohio, offered a resolution declaring it the duty of the House to impeach the president. This resolution received more than a two-thirds majority and passed to the judiciary committee for a report. The impeachment of the president will quite likely not be carried through now. Many believe Johnson has not given adequate reason to be destroyed. Moreover, the current Congress is already so near the end that a trial could not possibly be completed within that short period (the coming 4 March); hence, the subsequent Congress, upon uniting, would be required to commence the proceedings from the beginning.[1]

Soon after opening their sessions, a large majority of both houses approved a bill conceding Negroes in the District of Columbia the right to vote. The president exercised his veto, returning the bill to the house of its origin with his objections. . . . Majorities of more than two-thirds in the Senate and in the House overrode the veto.[2]

General Banks presented a resolution in the House prohibiting the importation of Asiatic laborers called coolies into the United States. This resolution was approved unanimously without discussion. It will certainly pass the Senate in the same manner.

The hostility between Congress and the president continues. . . . This conflict will prevent anything being done about our affairs. Any important measure originating in Congress would very probably inspire the president's opposition and vice versa. Since the president's opponents will have more votes in the next Congress than in the current Congress, this [stalemate] is not likely to change. . . .

Romero to MRE, 9 March 1867, in Romero, *Correspondencia* IX, 180–82

. . . The Thirty-ninth Congress approved a bill . . . [to] establish military governments in the southern states until those states are disposed to accept various conditions fixed for their readmission to the Union with their own governments. The chief condition is to concede the colored people the right to vote. What President Johnson might do with that bill was anxiously awaited. His approval of the bill would indicate his disposition to cooperate with Congress in the radical reconstruction policy. His disapproval would indicate he does not wish to compromise his own ideas in this respect in the least. Then the dissention between president and Congress would continue. All doubts dissipated on 2 March when the president interposed his veto to the above bill. Nevertheless, more than two-thirds in both houses approved the bill without delay, and it became law despite the president's objections.[3]

Soon after receiving the veto message, the judiciary committee, charged with the preliminary investigation to determine whether it would be suitable or not to impeach Johnson, reported to the House. Judging from the proceedings to that point, it wished to continue the investigation.

At the last hour, the president vetoed another bill regarding the appointment and removal of civil employees. This act even further embittered existing difficulties between both branches.[4]

The Thirty-ninth Congress closed its session at noon on 4 March. Immediately the Fortieth Congress opened its sessions. Before they could proceed to elect the speaker of the House, the Democratic representatives presented a protest signed by thirty-one congressmen against that meeting of Congress. They considered the meeting unconstitutional, as much because sixteen states were not represented as because the president had not convoked it. In addition to the southern states, five northern states had not elected representatives because they hold elections on 4 March. Without considering that protest, the House organized itself. It elected Colfax speaker, just as he had been in the two preceding houses. At the same time, the Senate met with sixteen newly elected senators taking their seats. At once they selected a president pro tempore. According to prior agreement, . . . this office fell on Wade of Ohio, one of our best friends in this country.[5]

The Republican . . . caucus agreed to adjourn this legislative session on 11 March. They would reconvene on 8 May, thereby allowing the states, where elections still have not been held, time to do so. The caucus also decided that meanwhile the judiciary committee would continue to investigate the charges against President Johnson. The Senate, nevertheless, has not agreed to this adjournment. Everything seems to indicate that the radical Republicans intend to impeach and remove Johnson in order to replace him with Wade, a person who holds their complete confidence.

The day before yesterday [7 March], the Senate organized its different committees. The Foreign Relations Committee was composed of Sumner as chairman, [William] Fessenden, [Simon] Cameron, [James] Harlan, [Oliver] Morton, [James W.] Patterson of New Hampshire, and Reverdy Johnson. This committee is more favorably organized in regard to our affairs than in former years. Harlan, Morton, and Cameron are decidedly our friends. Johnson I consider indifferent. I do not know where Patterson, a new senator, stands. I greatly fear that Fessenden and Sumner would be hostile to us if we attempted to solicit financial aid for Mexico. On 5 March I had visited Wade to recommend that he use his influence to form the Foreign Relations Committee out of Mexico's friends. He told me that his special task would be to arrange it [a committee friendly to Mexico].

The House has decided not to appoint committees now but rather after the recess that will end on 8 May. In yesterday's session, nevertheless, General Banks proposed, and the House approved, the immediate naming of the foreign relations committee. . . . I am attempting to arrange that the House Foreign Relations Committee is composed of more decided friends of Mexico than was the case during the past Congress. General Banks will almost certainly remain chairman.

Under the authority that Congress conceded him, the president admitted the territory of Nebraska into the Union as a state. . . .[6]

Romero to MRE, 19 June 1867, in Romero, *Correspondencia* IX, 641–42

General Sheridan's removal of Governor [J. Madison] Wells of Louisiana and of other New Orleans functionaries made use of the authority that the reconstruction law, approved by Congress in its last session, conceded to the commanders of departments in the establishment of military governments in the former Confederate states. Sheridan's action has prompted the president to submit to the attorney general the question of how far these powers extend.[7]

The attorney general's opinion restricted these powers very considerably. His interpretation of the law did not conform either to its stipulations nor to the goal that Congress proposed upon approving that act. After discussing the attorney general's opinion in the cabinet, all the members except the secretary of war approved that opinion. The president conformed with the opinion of his cabinet. As a consequence of this cabinet meeting, some orders were issued and others were prepared for issuance upon Johnson's return. If these orders are carried out, they would make the proscriptions of the reconstruction law futile.

Thus, to prevent the execution of Johnson's orders, and to give an authentic interpretation to the law, Congress will meet on 3 July. It will probably limit itself to issuing a new law clarifying the first. If the president does not resist and declare the new law unconstitutional, Congress will probably close its session without delay. In this case the session will not last more than one or two weeks. Probably, someone in Congress will also want to undertake Johnson's impeachment. . . .

Romero to MRE, 21 July 1867, in Romero, *Correspondencia* X, 202

Yesterday, Congress adjourned after approving a bill clarifying the reconstruction law. The new law places the government of the southern states in the hands of General Grant and of the military commanders of the five departments into which the states are divided. The president vetoed that clarifying bill, but more than two-thirds of both houses passed it again, thereby giving it the force of law.[8]

During the last days of the congressional session, the representatives wishing to impeach the president made a supreme effort. The majority of the committee conducting the previous investigation judged, nevertheless, that no basis existed to bring him to trial, and the affair remained in that state. They would not likely take this step in the end, since so little time will remain until the end of Johnson's term when Congress reconvenes that he will be allowed to finish the legal term of office.

Some representatives also wanted Congress to meet again at the end of October or the beginning of November to consider this impeachment question. However, the majority of both houses did not agree to this. It was decided not to reconvene until 23 November, which is one week before the day fixed in the constitution for the ordinary session.

Several resolutions regarding Mexican affairs remained pending in both houses. The next session will probably not consider these resolutions because the opportune moment will have passed by then. . . .

Romero to MRE, 11 September 1867, in Romero, *Correspondencia* X, 333–34

. . . On 8 September the president granted amnesty to all the people who took part in the southern insurrection, with very few exceptions. This will probably cause some difficulties when Congress meets again this coming November.[9]

Although rumors of cabinet changes continue, I do not believe Seward's departure very probable. General Grant continues in the War Department although he might well leave that post soon. . . .

Romero to MRE, 23 October 1867, in Romero, *Correspondencia* X, 449–50

. . . [Important] elections were held principally in Pennsylvania and Ohio. These elections were viewed as indications of public opinion on the differences between Congress and the president. In Pennsylvania the election was for a judge of the state supreme court and in Ohio for the governorship. The Democrats won in Pennsylvania, while in Ohio the Republicans won by a small majority, much less than expected. Iowa also had hotly contested elections that the Republicans did not win as clearly and decisively as circumstances there promised. Finally, other local elections have taken place in California, above all in San Francisco. The Democratic party has triumphed there.

These partial [Democratic] victories, the one expected in New York, others expected in elections scheduled for this coming November, and those victories that Johnson's party won not long ago in New England, have greatly animated the president's supporters.

Consequently, they have spoken of rebuilding the cabinet in the direction of the Democratic party and therefore favorable to Johnson's reconstruction policy. The *Intelligencer,* considered Johnson's organ, claimed Seward's services are already no longer needed. Seward asked if the president had seen that article. The president allegedly replied that he had indeed seen it before publication. However, the secretary of state is resolved to continue to the very end, the Associated Press added, as is Stanton. Whatever truth may lie in this report, Johnson will almost certainly not make any change in his cabinet so near to the next session of Congress.

. . . The papers have even made a virtue of a plan to conciliate the two public powers in conflict today. This suggestion consists of a committee of congressmen approaching the president to arrange a reconciliation. Nevertheless, presently an arrangement does not seem possible because the two sides differ so radically in viewpoint. The state election results this coming November might greatly influence one of the two parties to concede.

All the Republican press agrees on General Grant's candidacy for president, and even the Democrats do not offer any opposition. Several Philadelphia clubs have solemnly proclaimed Grant. An allusion to his candidacy in a recent meeting in New York received very enthusiastic applause. Meanwhile the radical Republicans are attempting via various means to obtain an opportunity for Grant to express his ideas publicly and explicitly on the pending [reconstruction] questions. Perhaps, it is said, he will even express his views in a letter to a friend who is authorized to publish that letter. [10]

The opposition most frequently attacks the secretary of the treasury. Most recently this official assumed responsibility for the increase in the public debt during the past month, instead of decreasing it by several millions as had been accomplished in all the previous months.

In the west, it is hoped that treaties with some tribes will conclude the war of the Indian uprising. The press has complained repeatedly about the enormous expenses that the United States lays out in forts and garrisons to protect settlers against the Indians, instead of attempting to civilize the Indians. The press has also scored the attempt to remove or to exterminate the American aborigines, rather than to win their goodwill with human and equitable treatment. New ideas opposed to slavery and racial distinction already influence attitudes to the benefit of the Indians as of the Negroes.[11]

The equality of the Negroes before the law is becoming a practical reality. In the case of a young colored Baltimore girl, Chief Justice of the Supreme Court Chase, acting as judge in the Baltimore district, just declared null certain laws about apprenticeships derived from slavery. New Orleans already has a Negro judge; New Orleans has just called together a grand jury composed of Negroes and whites. . . .[12]

Romero to MRE, 18 November 1867, in Romero, *Correspondencia* X, 464–65

Elections . . . were held on 7 November in New York, Massachusetts, Illinois, Kansas, and Wisconsin. Although the elections were only for state offices, the two national parties, the Republicans and Democrats, [sharply] contested the election in order to measure their respective influence on the reconstruction question and related matters. The Democrats triumphed decisively in New York with a majority of fifty thousand. Although the Republicans triumphed in the other states, the margins were quite narrow, much less than they were accustomed to from past elections. In addition, the three western states already mentioned voted against granting suffrage to Negroes and people of color. . . . Under this perspective, the Republican party's loss has been general. The inopportune demands of this party and certain bad habits of puritan intolerance, observable in New York and Massachusetts, apparently have produced this defeat. The complaints, perhaps exaggerated, of the southern population regarding the treatment under the military regimes of the Republican reconstruction plan have contributed to the defeat. Along with Negro suffrage, no one wants to promote women's suffrage. While everyone advocates liberty, including freedom of religion, the people of New York and Massachusetts are exhorted to observe the Sabbath strictly by not selling a drop of liquor from midnight on Saturday until Monday. This people's great affliction with spirituous drinks, and especially the Germans for beer, is challenged in a fanatic and imprudent manner that has contributed greatly to discrediting the Republicans.[13]

The lesson the Republicans received might make them modify their conduct, some believe, and maybe even alter their plan for reconstructing the South a little in the direction of the president's proposed scheme. Allegedly, one of the leaders of the party, Chase, is not inclined to permit Negroes to exercise the suffrage until they are citizens for the length of time required for white immigrants. Nevertheless, other leaders like Wade and Thaddeus Stevens certainly do not wish to make any concessions. . . .

There has been another attempt to defer the trial of Jefferson Davis until Chase is scheduled to preside in Richmond, which would be in May. . . . So many influences favor Davis that, quite possibly, he will never be sentenced. . . .[14]

Another presidential proclamation has fixed 28 November as the day for giving thanks to the All Powerful. The late Lincoln introduced this pious custom on a permanent basis. . . .

Romero to MRE, 11 December 1867, in Romero, *Correspondencia* X, 473–74

Congress convened this past 21 November. . . . Since the normal regular session had not even commenced on that date, the president abstained from submitting his annual message. Both houses limited themselves to nominating their permanent committees. In general they elected almost the same personnel as previously. General Banks continues to chair the House Foreign Relations Committee and Sumner, the Senate Committee. The only change in the House involved the important Ways and Means Committee. This committee reports on all matters that will expend public funds, so that a special vote falls to it, even when a resolution or a treaty demanding expenditure of public funds needs approval. General [Robert] Schenck is the new chairman of this committee.

The House special committee on the impeachment of the president presented a report favoring impeachment signed by a majority of five. The minority of four divided on two particular votes. . . . The most common opinion is that the majority report will not be approved. These massive documents have compelled the papers to publish no more than extracts. Only the conclusions appeared completely. . . .

Johnson sent his annual message on 3 December when the regular session should have begun. The president has attracted attention for the tenacity with which he has insisted upon his reconstruction plan for the southern states with all the theories upon which it is founded. That insistence quickly inflamed the Republicans. It is difficult, however, to anticipate if this will animate them to take direct action against Johnson. In financial matters Johnson recommended reducing the paper money now circulating . . . in order to move toward the time when all transactions would be made in metal. He also recommended reforming the current complicated tax system to make taxes less burdensome, above all for the poor. In general, he sought the reduction of public expenses to lessen the burden weighing on the people. . . .[15]

The presidential message undertakes to demonstrate in detail the desirability of the treaty celebrated recently between the United States and Denmark for the purchase of the islands Saint Thomas and St. John. Johnson announced that the treaty will pass the Senate. . . . The rumor is that the United States will pay $7.5 million for the islands.[16]

Johnson's message recommended that the House should approve the purchase price for Russian America. After the Senate approved the treaty, the U.S. government assumed possession of Alaska.

Noteworthy, the message states gruffly and even harshly that no arrangement exists yet for the payment of claims to U.S. citizens for "British depredations" [the Alabama claims for damages done by Confederate commerce raiders]. . . .[17]

Clubs and meetings continue to express favor in General Grant's [presidential] candidacy. On his part, Grant continues to remain silent before the feelers sent out to discover his political opinions. The War department has introduced widely praised economies and reforms to reduce the army to the minimum that the current law permits. As was expected, Jefferson Davis's trial has been deferred until the spring. . . .

Epilogue: Romero, Mexican-American Liberal Lobbyist

Both the United States and Mexico experienced liberal revolutions in the mid-nineteenth century. Both became obsessed with free-market rhetoric extolling growth, development, and a belief that material progress would resolve any social problems. Moreover, as the Civil War erupted in the United States and the French, Spanish, and British intervened in Mexico in 1861, Mexico and the United States looked back upon a brief but warm relationship in the last years of the 1850s. President Buchanan's administration had received the liberal ouster of the conservatives with considerable sympathy and a desire to negotiate commercial and transit agreements with liberal Mexico.

It was against this background that Romero initially presumed Lincoln and the Republican Party shared similar ideology and goals with Mexico's liberal faction under Juárez. Later, after the Lincoln administration's policy proved disappointing, Romero believed Lincoln's assassination had brought a "true" liberal and friend of Mexico to the White House. President Johnson's early conduct during his first year in office stimulated Romero's expectations before again disappointing the Mexican envoy. Romero believed Seward dominated both Lincoln and Johnson and pursued a policy toward French intervention in Mexico that offered little of the assistance Romero desired. Friendship with General Grant during 1865 and 1866 also encouraged Romero. Moveover, Grant delivered considerable moral and material aid to the beleaguered Mexican liberals. In 1867, the contest in the United States between Romero and Seward became moot. The French troops withdrew and several weeks later Maximilian was a prisoner of Juárez's government.

The execution of Maximilian on 19 June 1867 opened the final act of the many-sided Mexican-United States relations during the mid-nine-teenth century. The debate focused upon several questions initially raised during the Civil War and French intervention years. Was the French activity in Mexico foreign interference in the new world, a clear violation of the Monroe Doctrine? Or was the French intrusion merely an effort to achieve stability and order in a society where none existed? Were the two conflicts—the Civil War and the French intervention—linked in some

227

ideological and real form? Or were they two separate struggles that merely happened to occur at the same time? The debate in the U.S. Congress and in the American media supported the conclusion that the French were attempting to undermine U.S. penetration and influence in Mexico and Latin America and that the two wars thus shared the conflict between liberalism, industrial capitalism's ideological and world view, and conservatism, the remnants of mercantilistic, paternalistic, and agrarian institutions supporting monarchical and aristocratic management of society.

Seward also wished to encourage stability in Mexico. The execution of Maximilian disappointed many North American leaders because they feared the act might provoke renewed French or Austrian intervention in the new world. After the liberals regained authority in Mexico City, Seward ordered Otterbourg to relax any pressure to collect claims of U.S. citizens against Mexico, granting the liberals breathing space to straighten out their affairs before the United States sought to aid its citizens. The breathing space was brief, however, since by late 1868 a claims treaty was signed and ratified, and the claims commission was preparing to hear petitioners.

U.S. relations with Mexico blossomed under Romero's influence. While trade between the two nations had risen sharply during the dual crisis of the 1860s and then waned during the shared adjustment years of the late 1860s and early 1870s, trade expansion gained momentum beginning in the late 1870s. U.S. and Mexican commercial exchange rose in absolute amounts and, as a percentage of either Mexican or U.S. foreign trade, rose regularly after the mid-1870s. Moreover, the view that Romero emphasized for forty years, that the two liberal societies shared ideological perspectives and goal orientation with regard to growth, social and economic opportunity, and other liberal objectives, had laid the basis for Mexico to become a chief investment target for the excess capital accumulation occurring in the United States.

An imbalance that Romero recognized, but misjudged, became the basis for future problems. Even in Romero's vision, Mexico was the weaker of the two partners. The United States was the model, the teacher for Mexican social, economic, and political growth and development. Within a liberal framework of competition, individualism, and growth— whether within a national or international framework—such imbalance in relationships between two unregulated, free-market interactors produces exploitation, marginalization, and extraction of wealth. U.S. and other foreign capitalists supplied the controllers of distribution and the development projects for much of the Mexican nation's wealth. After decades of exploitation, antiforeignism and resilient nationalism emerged to pervade Mexico in the twentieth century.

The United States had spent three-quarters of a century as a territorial expansionist power in quest of its continental empire. The liberal revolution, with its links to industrialism, nationalism, and market expansion, launched a new empire. First, the United States passed through a brief period of wound-healing, the creation of new and solidification of existing liberal domestic institutions, and then full development and growth up to the internal limits of market expansion and accumulation that would invigorate the dormant idea of world-scale market expansion. After all, if market expansion and growth produced well-being and security and were the keys to resolving internal problems, how much more the magic of marketplace expansionism and growth could accomplish if they had the whole world as their field for expansion? In liberal ideology, the absence of growth—stagnation—is the beginning of the end if the process is not halted or reversed. Both Mexican liberals and the U.S. liberals expected to parlay their cooperation into a widening of the marketplace. It was not an accident that U.S. capital as well as trade began to penetrate Mexico extensively in the 1870s and 1880s. This was the future that Romero had envisioned and had lobbied for so incessantly for more than forty years.

Romero left his mark upon U.S.-Mexican relations in many ways. For a long time he had urged a free trade zone along Mexico's northern border in order to induce more economic activity in that region and to demonstrate the advantages of closer economic ties. The border incursions that had disturbed U.S.-Mexican relations prior to and during the Civil War continued in the postwar years, but ultimately a mutual border-crossing policy was adopted in the late nineteenth century.

Romero's private correspondence and his official contacts describe his persistent efforts to encourage foreign participation in the development of Mexican railroads, cotton and other agricultural products, steamship lines, and mining enterprises. In 1880 and 1881, he became involved in several railroad schemes with former President Ulysses Grant, Albert K. Owen, Hiram Barney, and others. In addition to Grant, Owen, and Barney, Romero corresponded regularly with George and W. S. Benfield, George W. Clarke, Alfred Conkling, John W. Foster, David Hoadley (of the Pacific Mail Steamship Company), William Henry Hurlbert, John F. Morgan, Joseph Nimmo, William J. Palmer, George H. Penfield, Edward Plumb, Isaac Seligman (of Seligman Brothers bankers), Thomas Sell, John Tifft (of a New York banking firm), James Henry Work, and Drexel, Morgan, and Company. The index to the second volume of the guide to the Romero correspondence (covering the years 1872–81) lists about 3,450 individuals, firms, or organizations. About 550 of the listed partners in Romero's correspondence appear to be Anglo-Saxon. He may have had other correspondents in the United States because some of his correspondence may have been with hispanic North Americans. This acknowledgment of his contacts with North Americans needs to be qualified by the recognition that the decade covered in this second volume was the period in which Romero had the least contact with U.S. dignitaries because he resided in Mexico from 1869 until 1882.

The ties between the U.S. and Mexican political economies increased noticeably in the post–Civil War and French-intervention decades. David Pletcher's *Mines, Rails, and Progress* describes some of the U.S. activity in Mexico after the Civil War and the French intervention. Pletcher records Romero's role in this economic development, which occurred in the late 1860s, 1870s, and 1880s. A U.S. telegraph firm made Mexico a telegraph center in the late 1880s, and a U.S.-funded railroad was built across the Tehuantepec Isthmus in the 1880s. The scheme of U.S. engineer James Eads to build a ship railroad at Tehuantepec never attracted sufficient capital to begin construction. The chief bonds of the two societies in the economic sphere were mines and rail activity. Other customary interchanges between the two societies continued. In addition to traditional border problems involving banditry and rustling, U.S. capital invested in northern Mexico's agricultural, mining, and railroad development produced disputes over water rights of rivers that crossed the border—see Norris Hundley, Jr., *Dividing the Waters: A Century of Controversy Between the United States and Mexico* (Berkeley, Calif.: University of California Press, 1966).

North of the border, the socioeconomic, cultural and political problems of U.S. society that Romero had observed during his service from 1859–68 remained to disturb a society moving deeper into an industrial transformation. Workers remained poorly paid and shared inadequately in the economic growth—see David Montgomery, *The Fall of the House of Labor: The Workplace, the State, and American Labor Activism, 1865–1925* (Cambridge: Cambridge University Press, 1987) and Herbert G. Gutman, *Work, Culture and Society in Industrializing America* (New York, Vintage: 1977). Racism and ethnocentricism that Romero found so pervasive in U.S. society were so imbued in the self-image that they continued to be overlooked or slighted. The story of black Americans during and after reconstruction reflects the values, attitudes, and policies Romero described during the 1861–67 years—see Eric Foner, *Reconstruction: America's Unfinished Revolution, 1863–1877* (New York: Harper and Row, 1988). The mistreatment of Mexican-Americans that Romero protested against continued, as described by Josefina Zoraida Vázquez and Lorenzo Meyer, *The United States and Mexico* (Chicago: University of Chicago Press, 1985). The United States to which Romero returned in the 1880s bore a close resemblance to the country he had left in 1868. Certainly the material progress was evident, but the social and moral state of the United States may have had Romero checking his calendar to assure himself that in fact years, not merely days, had passed.

After resigning in 1867, Romero returned to Washington in 1868 to conclude the claims treaty. In 1868, he returned to Mexico to serve as secretary of the treasury. Juárez's decision to seek reelection in 1872 displeased Romero, prompting him to resign and pursue an activity he had long advocated—coffee culture in southern Mexico. This phase of his life lasted only three years, in part because of the hostility of Guatemalan President Justo Rufino Barrios, who feared that Romero's presence near Guatemala's frontier portended future Mexican expansion into his country, and in part because in 1875 Romero was elected to the Mexican Senate. Romero attached his political star to Porfirio Díaz and Ignacio Mariscal (his secretary at the Mexican legation in the 1864–67 years). In 1877, after serving only two years of his Senate term, Romero accepted Díaz's appointment as secretary of the treasury. Romero's health turned bad in 1879, compelling his resignation. Battling recurring stomach problems, which had plagued him since his youth, Romero traveled to the United States to consult medical specialists. From 1882 until his death, Romero served as Mexican minister to the United States, except for a short period from mid-1892 until early 1893, when he returned to Mexico for a third period as secretary of the treasury. Romero died in Washington on 30 December 1898, at the age of sixty-one, after an attack of appendicitis.

Romero had not envisioned the major social revolution that would occur a decade after his death. This social revolution blamed much of Mexico's misfortune upon foreign exploitation and abuse of Mexico's political economy and people. It was also a revolution that blamed a comprador Mexican elite—that is, an elite of lawyers, businessmen, politicians, intellectuals, and military that drew its wealth, status, and power from ties to the foreign investors and firms—for many of the wrongs and injustices within Mexico. While Romero saw no need to ponder whether liberal social transformations and liberalism as a basis for international exchange promoted revolution and social unrest, the fact that he worked so hard to promote liberalism in Mexico and as a bond to the United States makes this a fitting question to conclude these insights into Romero's career. To what extent did the world Romero sought to build in the 1860s contribute to the Mexico of the 1910s and 1920s?

Notes

Introduction

1. Eric Foner, ed., "Andrew Johnson and Reconstruction: A British View," *Journal of Southern History* 41 (August 1975): 381.

2. Matías Romero, ed., *Correspondencia de la legación mexicana durante la intervención extranjera, 1860–1868,* (México: Imprenta del Gobierno, 1870–92).

3. These two items are in Romero, ed., *Correspondencia,* 5:297, and the Archivo Histórico de la Secretaría de Relaciones, H/110 (73–0)"865"/1.19-C-R-1, pp. 724–27.

4. *El Siglo Diez y Nueve,* 18 July 1867, p. 4, and 19 July 1867, p. 2; and "Comparative Statement of the number of communications made by the Secretary of State, in each year, to twelve of the principle Foreign legations, from March 4, 1860, to March 4, 1866," Miscellaneous, Public Papers, 1861–69, box 62, folder 13, William Henry Seward Papers, University of Rochester Library.

1860

1. On the political campaign of 1860, see Winifred E. A. Bernhard, ed., *Political Parties in American History* (New York: Putnam, 1973); Arthur M. Schlesinger, Jr., ed., *History of U.S. Political Parties,* 4 vols. (New York: Chelsea House, 1973); Arthur M. Schlesinger, Jr., ed., *History of American Presidential Elections* (New York: Chelsea House, 1971); James G. Randall, *Lincoln, the President,* 4 vols. (New York: Dodd, Mead, 1934–55); Stephen B. Oates, *With Malice Toward None: The Life of Abraham Lincoln* (New York: Harper & Row, 1977); G. S. Boritt, "Was Lincoln a Vulnerable Candidate in 1860?" *Civil War History* 27 (1981): 32–48.

2. On the transcontinental telegraph, see Charles Vivier, "The Collins Overland Line and American Continentalism," *Pacific Historical Review* 28 (1959): 237–53.

3. On Texas on eve of secession, see Walter L. Buenger, *Secession and Union in Texas* (Austin: University of Texas Press, 1984). On blacks and slavery on the eve of secession, see Louis Filler, *The Crusade against Slavery. 1830–1860* (New York: Harper, 1960); Herbert Gutman, *The Black Family in Slavery and Freedom, 1750–1925* (New York: Pantheon Books, 1976); James M. McPherson, *The Struggle for Equality: Abolitionists and the Negro in the Civil War and Reconstruction* (Princeton, N.J.: Princeton University Press, 1964).

4. On secession in the South, see Ralph A. Wooster, "Secession in the Lower South: Changing Interpretations," *Civil War History* 7 (1961): 117–27; William J. Donnelly, "Conspiracy or Popular Movement: The Historiography of Southern Support for Secession," *North Carolina Historical Review* 42 (1965): 70–84; Ralph Wooster, *The Secession Conventions of the South* (Princeton, N.J.: Princeton University Press, 1962); William L. Barney, *The Secessionist Impulse: Alabama and Mississippi in 1860* (Princeton, N.J.: Princeton University Press, 1974); James Tice Moore, "Secession and the States: A Review Essay," *Virginia Magazine of History and Biography* 94 (1986): 60–76.

5. On U.S. government finances and loans, see Bray Hammond, *Sovereignty and an Empty Purse: Banks and Politics in the Civil War* (Princeton, N.J.: Princeton University Press, 1970); Bert W. Rein, *An Analysis and Critique of the Union Financing of the Civil War* (Amherst, Mass.: Amherst College Press, 1962).

6. On South Carolina after Lincoln's election, see Steven A. Channing, *Crisis of Fear: Secession in South Carolina* (New York: Simon and Schuster, 1970).

7. On Buchanan's administration in the secession crisis, see Philip C. Auchampaugh, *James Buchanan and His Cabinet on the Eve of Secession* (reprint; Boston: J. S. Canner, 1965).

8. On the U.S. society and economy in 1860–61, see William J. Barney, *Flawed Victory: A New Perspective on the Civil War* (New York: Praeger, 1975); Robert Cruden, *The War That Never Ended* (Englewood Cliffs, N.J.: Prentice-Hall, 1973); David M. Potter, *The Impending Crisis, 1848–1861* (New York: Harper & Row, 1976).

9. On Kansas-Nebraska in the crisis of 1861, see Gerald W. Wolff, *The Kansas-Nebraska Bill: Party, Section, and the Coming of the Civil War* (New York: Revisionist Press, 1977); Roy F. Nichols, "The Kansas-Nebraska Act: A Century of Historiography," *Mississippi Valley Historical Review* 43 (1956): 187–212.

10. On the U.S. Congress in 1860–61, see Potter, *The Impending Crisis, 1848–1861*.

11. On the financial panic and suspension of specie payment, see Don C. Barrett, *The Greenbacks and Resumption of Specie Payments* (Cambridge: Harvard University Press, 1931). On the conditions of laborers, see Norman J. Ware, *The Labor Movement in the United States, 1860–1895* (reprint; Gloucester, Mass.: Peter Smith, 1959); Emerson K. Fite, *Social and Industrial Conditions in the North During the Civil War* (reprinted; New York: Peter Smith, 1930).

12. On the disagreement between border and cotton states in 1860–61, see Wooster, *The Secession Conventions of the South*; William Barney, *The Road to Secession: A New Perspective on the Old South* (New York: Praeger, 1972).

13. On the Mississippi as an outlet for midwestern goods, see Earl J. Hess, "The Mississippi River and Secession, 1861: The Northwestern Response," *Old Northwest* 10 (1984): 187–207.

14. On U.S. west coast in the crisis and separation to form new state, see John J. Earle, "The Sentiment of the People of California with Respect to the Civil War," in *Annual Report of the American Historical Association* (1907), 1:123–35; Benjamin F. Gilbert, "California and Civil War: A Bibliographic Essay," *California Historical Society Quarterly* 40 (1961): 289–307; Royal A. Bensell, *All Quiet on the Yamhill: The Civil War in Oregon* (Eugene: University of Oregon Books, 1959).

15. On abolitionism on eve of the Civil War, see McPherson, *The Struggle for Equality*.

16. On Buchanan's cabinet, see Auchampaugh, *James Buchanan*; Philip S. Klein, *President James Buchanan* (University Park: Pennsylvania State University Press, 1962).

17. On the Crittenden and other plans to deal with secession, see Albert J. Kirwen, *John J. Crittenden: The Struggle for Union* (Lexington: University of Kentucky Press, 1962); David M. Potter, *Lincoln and His Party in the Secession Crisis* (New Haven: Yale University Press, 1942).

18. On the transcontinental railroad, see Robert W. Fogel, *The Union Pacific Railroad: A Case in Premature Enterprise* (Baltimore: Johns Hopkins Press, 1960); James McCague, *Moguls and Iron Men* (New York: Harper & Row, 1964).

1861

1. On the southern seizure of federal property and South Carolina's negotiations with the federal government in January–April 1861, see Richard N. Current, *Lincoln*

and the First Shot (Philadelphia: Lippincott, 1963); Grady McWhiney, "The Confederacy's First Shot," *Civil War History* 14 (1968): 5–14; Channing, *Secession in South Carolina.*

2. On Charleston and Fort Sumter, see Ludwell H. Johnson, "Fort Sumter and Confederate Diplomacy," *Journal of Southern History* 26 (1961): 441–66.

3. On Louisiana's secession, see Wooster, *The Secession Conventions of the South;* Jefferson D. Bragg, *Louisiana in the Confederacy* (Baton Rouge: Louisiana State University Press, 1941); John D. Winters, *The Civil War in Louisiana* (Baton Rouge: Louisiana State University Press, 1963); Charles P. Roland, "Louisiana and Secession," *Louisiana History* 19 (1978): 389–99.

4. On Texas's secession, see Stephen B. Oates, "Texas under the Secessionists," *Southwestern Historical Quarterly* 67 (1963): 167–212.

5. On the Virginia Peace Convention in 1861, see Jesse L. Keene, *The Peace Convention of 1861* (Tuscaloosa, Ala.: Confederate Pub. Co., 1961); Robert G. Gunderson, *Old Gentleman's Convention* (Madison: University of Wisconsin Press, 1961).

6. On the admission of Kansas to statehood, see James A. Rawley, *Race and Politics: "Bleeding Kansas" and the Coming of the Civil War* (Philadelphia: Lippincott, 1969). On the defense of Washington, see Margaret Leech, *Reveille in Washington, 1860–1865* (New York: Harper & Brothers, 1941).

7. On the Montgomery Congress, see Wilfred B. Yearns, *The Confederate Congress* (Athens: University of Georgia Press, 1960).

8. On the Morrill tariff, see Reinhard H. Luthin, "Abraham Lincoln and Tariff," *American Historical Review* 49 (1944): 609–29.

9. On the use of force to compel compliance with federal law, see Kenneth M. Stampp, *And the War Came: The North and the Secession Crisis, 1860–1861* (Baton Rouge: Louisiana State University Press, 1950); Current, *Lincoln and the First Shot;* McWhiney, "The Confederacy's First Shot," 5–14.

10. On the federal revenue, expenses, and the budget, see Rein, *Union Financing of the Civil War;* Bray Hammond, "The North's Empty Purse," *American Historical Review* 67 (1961): 1–18.

11. On Lincoln's trip to Washington in February 1861, see Victor Searcher, *Lincoln's Journey to Greatness* (Philadelphia: Winston, 1960); William E. Baringer, *A House Divided* (Springfield, Ill.: The Abraham Lincoln Association, 1945); Allan Nevins, *The Emergence of Lincoln*, 2 vols. (New York: Scribner, 1951); Daniel J. Elazar, "The Constitution, the Union and the Liberties of People: Abraham Lincoln's Teaching about the American Political System . . . on his Tour from Springfield to Washington in February 1861," *Publius* 8 (1978): 141–75; Jean H. Baker, *Mary Todd Lincoln: A Biography* (New York: Norton, 1987).

12. On Lincoln's inauguration, see Reinhard H. Luthin, *The First Lincoln Campaign* (reprint; Gloucester, Mass.: Peter Smith, 1964); David M. Potter, *Lincoln and his Party in the Secession Crisis* (New Haven: Yale University Press, 1942); Leech, *Reveille in Washington.*

13. On Lincoln's cabinet, see Burton J. Hendrick, *Lincoln's War Cabinet* (Boston: Little, Brown and Company, 1944).

14. On Jefferson Davis's cabinet, see Rembert W. Patrick, *Jefferson Davis and His Cabinet* (Baton Rouge: Louisiana State University Press, 1944); Burton J. Hendrick, *Statesmen of the Lost Cause* (Boston: Little, Brown and Company, 1939); Jon L. Wakelyn, *Biographical Dictionary of the Confederacy* (Westport, Conn.: Greenwood Press, 1977).

15. On the Thomas Corwin resolution in 1861, see Daryl Pendergraft, "Thomas Corwin and Conservative Republican Reaction, 1858–1861," *Ohio Archeological and Historical Quarterly* 57 (1948): 1–23.

16. On General David Twiggs and the surrender of U.S. forces in Texas, see James G. Randall and David Donald, *The Civil War and Reconstruction* (Lexington, Mass.: Heath,

1969), 170; Allan Nevins, *The War for the Union, 1861–1862* (New York: Scribner, 1959), 18.

17. On the Confederate constitution, see Charles R. Lee, *The Confederate Constitution* (Chapel Hill: University of North Carolina Press, 1963); Curtis A. Amlund, *Federalism in the Southern Confederacy* (Washington, D.C.: Public Affairs Press, 1966).

18. On Arkansas secession, see Jack B. Scraggs, "Arkansas in the Secession Crisis," *Arkansas Historical Quarterly* 12 (1953): 179–224.

19. On Sam Houston and Texas secession, see Edward Maker, Jr., "Sam Houston and Secession," *Southwestern Historical Quarterly* 55 (1952): 448–58; Marion Karl Wisehart, *Sam Houston, American Giant* (Washington, D.C.: R. B. Luce, 1962); Thomas Schoonover, "Documents Concerning Lemuel Dale Evans' Plan to Keep Texas in the Union in 1861," *East Texas Historical Journal* 12 (1974): 35–38.

20. On expeditions to relieve U.S. forts in the South, see Virgil C. Jones, *The Civil War at Sea*, 3 vols. (New York: Holt, Rinehart, Winston, 1960–62).

21. On the U.S. census of 1860, see Nevins, *The Emergence of Lincoln*, vol. 2; Gilbert C. Fite and Jim E. Reese, *An Economic History of the United States* (Boston: Houghton Mifflin, 1973).

22. On raising U.S. armies, see Fred A. Shannon, *The Organization and Administration of the Union Army, 1861–1865*, 2 vols. (Cleveland: The Arthur H. Clark Company, 1928).

23. On commerce raiding and privateers, see George W. Dalzell, *The Flight from the Flag* (Chapel Hill: University of North Carolina Press, 1943); William Morrison Robinson, *The Confederate Privateers* (New Haven: Yale University Press, 1928); Kenneth J. Blume, "The Flight from the Flag: The American Government, the British Caribbean, and the American Merchant Marine, 1861–1865," *Civil War History* 32 (1986): 44–55.

24. On Virginia's secession, see Henry T. Shanks, *The Secession Movement in Virginia, 1847–1861* (Richmond: Garrett and Massie, 1934).

25. On Baltimore in early 1861, see William J. Evitts, *A Matter of Allegiances: Maryland from 1850 to 1861* (Baltimore: Johns Hopkins Press, 1974).

26. On raising Confederate armies, see Albert B. Moore, *Conscription and Conflict in the Confederacy* (New York: The Macmillan Company, 1924).

27. On the U.S. base at Fort Monroe in Virginia, see Robert W. Daly, *How the Merrimac Won* (New York: Crowell, 1957); William C. and Ruth White, *Tin Can on a Shingle* (New York: E. P. Dutton, 1957).

28. On Maryland in secession and war, see Jean H. Baker, *The Politics of Continuity: Maryland Political Parties from 1858 to 1870* (Baltimore: Johns Hopkins Press, 1973); Charles B. Clark, "Suppression and Control of Maryland, 1861–1865," *Maryland Historical Magazine* 54 (1959): 241–71.

29. On foreign mediation efforts in the Civil War, see Donald P. Crook, *The North, the South, and the Powers, 1861–1865* (New York: Wiley, 1974); Brian Jenkins, *Britain and the War for the Union* (Montreal: McGill-Queen's University Press, 1974); Kinley J. Brauer, "British Mediation and the American Civil War: A Reconsideration," *Journal of Southern History* 38 (1972): 49–64.

30. On U.S. blockade proclamations, see Virginia Jean Loar, "Sleepless Sentinels: The North Atlantic Blockading Squadron, 1862–1864," *Civil War History* 31 (1985): 24–38; John B. Hefferman, "The Blockade of the Southern Confederacy, 1861–1865," *Smithsonian Journal of History* 2 (1967–68): 24–44; Stuart Anderson, "1861: Blockade Vs. Closing the Confederate Ports," *Military Affairs* 41 (1977): 190–94.

31. On war and peace Democrats, see Joel Silbey, *A Respectable Minority: The Democratic Party in the Civil War Era* (New York: Norton, 1977).

32. On French recognition of the Confederacy, see Lynn M. Case and Warren F. Spencer, *The United States and France: Civil War Diplomacy* (Philadelphia: University of Pennsylvania Press, 1970).

33. On Tennessee's secession, see Mary E. R. Campbell, *The Attitude of Tennessee Toward the Union, 1847–1861* (New York: Vantage, 1961).

34. On Kentucky neutrality in the crisis, see William H. Townsend, *Lincoln and the Bluegrass: Slavery and Civil War in Kentucky* (Lexington: University of Kentucky Press, 1955); Lowell Harrison, *The Civil War in Kentucky* (Lexington: University of Kentucky Press, 1975).

35. On Missouri in the crisis, see William E. Parrish, *Turbulent Partnership: Missouri and the Union, 1861–1865* (Columbia: University of Missouri Press, 1963); Michael Fellman, *Inside War: The Guerilla Conflict in Missouri During the American Civil War* (New York: Oxford University Press, 1989).

36. On moving the Confederate capital to Richmond, see Jarrell Shofner and William W. Rogers, "Montgomery to Richmond," *Civil War History* 10 (1964): 155–66.

37. On General Winfield Scott as commander of the U.S. army, see Charles W. Elliott, *Winfield Scott: The Soldier and the Man* (New York: The Macmillan Company, 1937).

38. On Fort Pickens and Pensacola Bay, see James M. Merrill, *The Rebel Shore* (Boston: Little, Brown, 1957); George F. Pearce, *The U.S. Navy in Pensacola: From Sailing Ships to Naval Aviation (1825–1930)* (Pensacola: University of West Florida, 1980)

39. On Cairo and control of the Ohio and Mississippi River conflux, see Bruce Catton, *Grant Moves South* (Boston: Little, Brown, 1960). On North Carolina's secession, see Joseph Carlyle Sitterson, *The Secession Movement in North Carolina* (Chapel Hill: University of North Carolina Press, 1939); Paul D. Escott, *Many Excellent People: Power and Privilege in North Carolina, 1850–1900* (Chapel Hill: University of North Carolina Press, 1985).

40. On Virginia joining the Confederacy, see Shanks, *The Secession Movement in Virginia, 1847–1861.* On Colonel Ellsworth in Arlington and Alexandria, see Ruth Painter Randall, *Colonel Elmer Ellsworth: A Biography of Lincoln's Friend and First Hero of the Civil War* (Boston: Little, Brown, 1960); Shofner and Rogers, "Montgomery to Richmond," 155–64.

41. On the war in West Virginia, see Richard O. Curry, *A House Divided: A Study of Statehood Politics and the Copperhead Movement in West Virginia* (Pittsburgh: University of Pittsburgh Press, 1964).

42. On Harper's Ferry in 1861, see Kenneth P. Williams, *Lincoln Finds a General,* 5 vols. (New York: Macmillan, 1949–59).

43. On the Elias Merryman incident, see Walker Lewis, *Without Fear or Favor: A Biography of Chief Justice Roger Brooke Taney* (Boston: Houghton, Mifflin, 1965); Carl B. Swisher, *Roger B. Taney* (New York: Macmillan, 1935).

44. On the death of Stephen Douglas, see Damon Wells, *Stephen Douglas: The Last Years, 1857–1861* (Austin: University of Texas Press, 1971).

45. On the Confederate capture of prizes, see Robinson, *The Confederate Privateers;* Jones, *The Civil War at Sea.*

46. On speaker Galusha Grow, see James T. Dubois and Gertrude S. Mathews, *Galusha A. Grow: Father of the Homestead Law* (Boston: Houghton, Mifflin, 1917).

47. On General Nathaniel Lyon in Missouri, see Jay Monaghan, *Civil War on the Western Border, 1854–1865* (Boston: Little, Brown, 1955); William E. Parrish, "General Nathaniel Lyon, a Portrait," *Missouri Historical Review* 49 (1954): 1–18.

48. On West Virginia's politics, see Curry, *A House Divided.*

49. On the treatment of Mexicans during the secession crisis, see Barry M. Cohen, "The Texas-Mexican Border 1858–1867: Along the Lower Rio Grande Valley During the Decade of the American Civil War and the French Intervention in Mexico," *Texana* 6 (1968): 153–65; Robert W. Delaney, "Matamoros, Port for Texas During the Civil War," *Southwestern Historical Quarterly* 58 (1955): 473–87.

50. On the U.S. budget, see Hammond, *Banks and Politics in the Civil War.*

51. On U.S. naval strength in 1861, see Bern Anderson, *By Sea and by River: The Naval History of the Civil War* (New York: Knopf, 1962); Howard P. Nash, Jr., *A Naval History of the Civil War* (New York: A. S. Barnes and Co., 1972).

52. On early enthusiasm for the war in U.S. Congress, see Robert P. Sharkey, *Money, Class and Party* (Baltimore: Johns Hopkins Press, 1959).

53. On Colonel Richard Taylor's mission in 1861, see Richard Taylor, *Destruction and Reconstruction: Personal Experiences of the Late War* (New York: Appleton, 1879).

54. On McClellan's victories in West Virginia, see Warren W. Hassler, *George B. McClellan: The Man Who Saved the Union* (Baton Rouge: Louisiana State University Press, 1957); Stephen W. Sears, *George B. McClellan: The Young Napoleon* (New York: Ticknor & Fields, 1988).

59. On first Manassas and the rise of General McClellan, see K. P. Williams, *Lincoln Finds a General;* Warren W. Hassler, *Commanders of the Army of the Potomac* (Baton Rouge: Louisiana State University Press, 1962); William C. Davis, *Battle at Bull Run* (Garden City, N.Y.: Doubleday, 1977).

56. On General Benjamin Butler and the Fort Monroe Campaign, see Hans L. Trefousee, *Ben Butler: The South Called Him Beast!* (New York: Twayne, 1957); Richard S. West, Jr., *Lincoln's Scapegoat General: A Life of Benjamin F. Butler, 1818–1893* (Boston: Houghton Mifflin, 1965).

57. On U.S. tariff laws, see Edward Stanwood, *American Tariff Controversies in the Nineteenth Century,* 2 vols. (reprint; New York: Russell & Russell, 1967); Richard Hofstadter, "The Tariff Issue on the Eve of the Civil War," *American Historical Review* 44 (1938): 50–55.

58. On bills to abolish slavery and punish rebellion, see McPherson, *The Struggle for Equality.*

59. On war objectives, see Stampp, *And the War Came;* T. Harry Williams, *Lincoln and the Radicals* (Madison: University of Wisconsin Press, 1941); Kenneth M. Stampp, ed., *The Causes of the Civil War* (Englewood Cliffs, N.J.: Prentice-Hall, 1959); Phillip Shaw Paludan, *"A People's Contest": The Union and the Civil War, 1861–1865* (New York: Harper and Row, 1988).

60. On the Blair-Scott rivalry and the Bull Run disaster, see William E. Smith, *The Francis Preston Blair Family in Politics,* 2 vols. (reprint; New York: Decapo Press, 1969); Davis, *Battle at Bull Run.*

61. On Prince Napoleon's visit to the United States, see Henry Blumenthal, *France and the United States: Their Diplomatic Relations, 1789–1914* (Chapel Hill: University of North Carolina Press, 1970).

62. On New York state politics, see James A. Frost, "The Home Front in New York during the Civil War," *New York History* 42 (1961): 237–97; Robert J. Rayback, "New York State in the Civil War," *New York History* 42 (1961): 56–70.

63. On U.S. loans in Europe, see Rein, *Union Financing of the Civil War.*

64. On the U.S. victory at Cape Hatteras, see Robert S. Holzman, *Stormy Ben Butler* (New York: Macmillan, 1954).

65. On Frémont in Missouri, see Allan Nevins, *Frémont: Pathmarker of the West* (New York: D. Appleton-Century, 1939).

66. On Confederate operations in Arizona and along the Texas-Mexican border, see Ray C. Colton, *The Civil War in the Western Territories* (Norman: University of Oklahoma Press, 1959); LeRoy H. Fisher, ed., *The Western Territories in the Civil War* (Manhattan, Kans.: Journal of the West, 1977); Ronnie C. Tyler, *Santiago Vidaurri and the Southern Confederacy* (Austin: Texas State Historical Association, 1973).

67. On Union mutinies, see Shannon, *The Organization and Administration of the Union Army 1861–1865;* Eugene C. Murdock, *Patriotism Limited: The Civil War Draft*

and Bounty System, 1862–1865 (Kent, Ohio: Kent State University Press, 1967); Bell Ervin Wiley, *The Life of Billy Yank* (Indianapolis: Bobbs-Merrill, 1952).

68. On declining northern enthusiasm for the war, see Brian Holden Reid and John White, "A Mob of Stragglers and Cowards: Desertion from the Union and Confederate Armies, 1861–1865," *Journal of Strategic Studies* 8 (1985): 64–77; Judith Lee Hallock, "The Role of the Community in Civil War Desertion," *Civil War History* 29 (1983): 123–34.

69. On Confederate espionage in Washington, see Leech, *Reveille in Washington, 1860–1865*, 94–96 and chap. 8.

70. On Democratic peace factions, see Jean H. Baker, "A Loyal Opposition: Northern Democrats in the Thirty-Seventh Congress," *Civil War History* 24 (1979): 139–55.

71. On northern confiscation of southern property, see Henry D. Shapiro, *Confiscation of Confederate Property in the North* (Ithaca, N.Y.: Cornell University Press, 1962); Patricia M. L. Lucie, "Confiscation: Constitutional Crossroads," *Civil War History* 23 (1977): 307–21.

72. On northern banks and federal war finances, see Hammond, *Banks and Politics in the Civil War;* David M. Giscke, "The New York City Banks and the Development of National Banking System, 1860–1870," *American Journal of Legal History* 23 (1979): 21–67.

73. On Confederate confiscation of property of U.S. citizens, see Yearns, *The Confederate Congress,* 132, 135, 191, 196.

74. On Confederate currency and finance, see Richard C. Todd, *Confederate Finance* (Athens: University of Georgia Press, 1954); Eugene M. Lerner, "The Monetary and Fiscal Problems of the Confederate Government," *Journal of Political Economy* 62 (1954): 506–72, and 63 (1955): 20–40.

75. On the Russian mediation offer of 1861, see Frank Golder, "The Russian Fleet and the American Civil War," *American Historical Review* 20 (1915): 801–12; Frank Golder, "Russo-American Relations during the Civil War," *American Historical Review* 26 (1921): 454–63; N. S. Kiniapina, "Russia; Grazhdanskaia Voina V SSHA" (Russia and the Civil War in U.S.A.), *Vestrik Mosouskogo U., Seriia 8: Istoriia,* 8 (1980).

76. On Frémont's antislavery conduct in Missouri, see Parrish, *Turbulent Partnership.*

77. On Cuban friendliness to Confederate vessels, see Kinley J. Brauer, "The Appointment of Carl Schurz as Minister to Spain," *Mid America* 56 (1974): 75–84; James W. Cortada, "The Abolition Movement and the Relations between Spain and the United States," *Lincoln Herald* 81 (1979): 27–33.

78. On California's 1861 elections, see Gilbert, "California and Civil War," 289–307.

79. On the capture of Lexington, Mo., in late 1861, see Albert Castel, *General Sterling Price and the Civil War in the West* (Baton Rouge: Louisiana State University Press, 1968).

80. On the New Mexico campaign of 1861–62, see Martin H. Hall, *Sibley's New Mexico Campaign* (Austin: University of Texas Press, 1960).

81. On William H. Russell's reporting, see William H. Russell, *My Diary North and South* (Boston: T. O. H. P. Burnham, 1863).

82. On the Duke of Paris and Count of Chartres, see Ella Lonn, *Foreigners in the Union Army and Navy* (Baton Rouge: Louisiana State University Press, 1951).

83. On Charles Sumner and abolitionism in 1861, see David Donald, *Charles Sumner and the Coming of the Civil War* (New York: Knopf, 1960); Laura A. White, "Charles Sumner and the Crisis of 1860–61," in Avery O. Craven, ed., *Essays in Honor of William E. Dodd* (Chicago: University of Chicago Press, 1935), 131–93.

84. On the first prize cases of the Civil War, see Stuart L. Bernath, *Squall Across the*

Atlantic: American Civil War Prize Cases and Diplomacy (Berkeley: University of California Press, 1970).

85. On efforts to raise forces in Canada, see Robin Winks, *Canada and the United States: The Civil War Years* (reprint; Montreal: Harvest House, 1971). On Garibaldi's offer of service, see Raimondo Luraghi, "Garibaldi egli State Uniti" (Garibaldi and the United States), *Rassegna degli Archivi de Stato*, 42 (1982): 285–89; Herbert Zettl, ed., "Garibaldi and the American Civil War," *Civil War History* 22 (1976): 70–76.

86. On British-U.S. diplomatic hostility, see Norman Ferris, *Desperate Diplomacy: William H. Seward's Foreign Policy, 1861* (Knoxville: University of Tennessee Press, 1976). On Russian-U.S. diplomatic goodwill, see Golder, "Russo-American Relations," 454–63; Kiniapina, "Russia."

87. On a Portuguese decree against privateering and prohibition against armed vessels in Portuguese harbors, see U.S. Department of State, *Papers Relating to Foreign Affairs, 1861*, many volumes—1861–present, 408–11.

88. On the Charles Stone-Edward Baker incident, see Harry C. Blair and Rebecca Tarshis, *Lincoln's Constant Ally: The Life of Colonel Edward D. Baker* (Portland: Oregon Historical Society, 1960).

89. On naval battles at the mouth of the Mississippi, see Clarence E. Macartney, *Mr Lincoln's Admirals* (New York: Funk & Wagnalls, 1956).

90. On rebel batteries blocking passage of Potomac, see E. B. and Barbara Long, *The Civil War Day by Day: An Almanac, 1861–1865* (Garden City, N.Y.: Doubleday, 1971), 130.

91. On the Mason and Slidell mission, see Beckles Willson, *John Slidell and the Confederates in Paris, 1862–65* (New York: Minton, Balch & Company, 1932).

92. On paroling prisoners of war, see James M. McPherson, *Ordeal By Fire: The Civil War and Reconstruction* (New York: Knopf, 1982), 450–56.

93. On the Cherokee Indians in treaty with the Confederates, see Wiley Britton, *The Civil War on the Border: A Narrative of Operations in Missouri, Kansas, Arkansas, and the Indian territories during the Years 1861–65*, 2 vols. (New York: P. G. Putnam's Sons, 1890–1904); Wilfred Knight, *Red Fox: Stand Watie and the Confederate Indian Nations During the Civil War Years in Indian Territory* (Glendale, CA: Arthur H. Clark Company, 1988).

94. On the Wise-Floyd dispute in West Virginia, see Douglas S. Freeman, *Lee's Lieutenants*, 3 vols. (New York: Charles Scribner's Sons, 1942–44); Craig Simpson, *A Good Southerner: The Life of Henry A. Wise of Virginia* (Chapel Hill: University of North Carolina Press, 1985).

95. On activity in U.S. naval yards, see Richard S. West, Jr., *Gideon Welles: Lincoln's Navy Department* (Indianapolis: Bobbs-Merrill, 1943).

96. On Negro colonists for Haiti, see Willis D. Boyd, "The Île à Vache Colonization Venture, 1862–1864," *The Americas* 16 (1959): 45–62; Tinsley L. Spraggins, "Economic Aspects of Negro Colonization during the Civil War (Ph.D. diss., American University, 1957); Gary Planck, "Abraham Lincoln and Black Colonization: Theory and Practice," *Lincoln Herald* 72 (1970): 61–77; Willis D. Boyd, "James Redpath and American Negro Colonization in Haiti, 1860–1862," *The Americas* 12 (1955): 169–82.

97. On transcontinental telegraph, see Vivier, "The Collins Overland Line," 237–53.

98. On McClellan succeeding Scott, see Hassler, *Commanders of the Army of the Potomac*; Herman Hattaway and Archer Jones, "Lincoln as Military Strategist," *Civil War History* 26 (1980): 293–303.

99. On Frémont's removal from command in Missouri, see Nevins, *Frémont*. On William Sherman in Kentucky, see Lloyd Lewis, *Sherman, Fighting Prophet* (New York: Harcourt, Brace, 1932).

100. On the cotton blockade, see Robert H. Jones, "Long Live the King?" *Agricultural History* 37 (1963): 166–71; Crook, *The North, the South, and the Powers*, 257–82; Stephen R. Wise, *Lifeline of the Confederacy: Blockade Running During the Civil War* (Columbia: University of South Carolina Press, 1989).

101. On Beauregard and the defense of Charleston, see T. Harry Williams, P. G. T. *Beauregard: Napoleon in Gray* (Baton Rouge: Louisiana State University Press, 1955).

102. On Memminger advising corn rather than cotton, see Paul W. Gates, *Agriculture and Civil War* (New York: Knopf, 1965).

103. On unionism in North Carolina, see Georgia Lee Tatum, *Disloyalty in the Confederacy* (Chapel Hill: University of North Carolina Press, 1934); Phillip S. Paludran, *Victims: A True Story of the Civil War* (Knoxville: University of Tennessee Press, 1981); Marc W. Kruman, "Dissent in the Confederacy: The North Carolina Experience," *Civil War History* 27 (1981): 293–313.

104. On the seizure of the *Soledad Cos* (Mexican vessel), see Delaney, "Matamoros," 473–87.

105. On the Union victory at Port Royal, see Willie Lee Rose, *Rehearsal for Reconstruction: The Port Royal Experiment* (New York: Vintage, 1964); Rowena Reed, *Combined Operations in the Civil War* (Annapolis: Naval Institute Press, 1978).

106. On the *Trent* affair, see Norman Ferris, *The Trent Affair* (Knoxville: University of Tennessee Press, 1977); Gordon H. Warren, *Fountain of Discontent: The Trent Affair and Freedom of the Seas* (Boston: Northeastern University Press, 1981).

107. On the seizure and transport of William Gwin over Panama, see the *New York Times* 16 November 1861, 4–5.

108. On the Thurlow Weed and Hughes mission to Europe, see Glyndon G. Van Deusen, *Thurlow Weed: Wizard of the Lobby* (Boston: Little, Brown, 1947).

109. On the battle at Paducah, see Catton, *Grant Moves South*, 48–51; Bruce Catton, *U.S. Grant and the American Military Tradition* (Boston: Little, Brown, 1954), 65–66; Peter Parish, *The American Civil War* (New York: Holmes & Meier, 1975), 118.

110. On Kentucky counties declaring neutrality, see Harrison, *The Civil War in Kentucky*; Townsend, *Lincoln and the Bluegrass*.

111. On the condemnation to death of captured southern privateers, see Robinson, *Confederate Privateers*; Nevins, *The War for the Union, 1861–1862*, 208–10.

112. On the elections under the Confederate constitution, see Frank E. Vandiver, *Jefferson Davis and the Confederate States* (Oxford: Clarendon Press, 1964); Amlund, *Federalism in the Southern Confederacy*.

113. On Colonel John Cochrane on arming slaves, see Mary Frances Berry, *Military Necessity and Civil Rights Policy: Black Citizenship and the Constitutions 1861–1868* (Port Washington, N.Y.: Kennikat Press, 1977).

114. On the incident at Guaymas, Mexico, see Thomas Schoonover, *Dollars over Dominion: The Triumph of Liberalism in Mexican-United States Relation, 1861–1867* (Baton Rouge: Louisiana State University Press, 1978), 37–42.

115. On Lincoln as defender of labor over property, see Manoj K. Joshi, "Lincoln, Labour and the Civil War," *Indian Journal of American Studies* (India) 9 (1979): 44–53.

116. On industrialization in the Confederacy, see Raimondo Luraghi, "The Civil War and the Modernization of American Society: Social Structure and the Industrial Revolution in the Old South before and during the War," *Civil War History* 18 (1972): 230–50; Emory M. Thomas, *The Confederacy as a Revolutionary Experience*, Englewood Cliffs, N.J.: Prentice-Hall, 1971).

117. On slavery in the Union, see McPherson, *The Struggle for Equality*. On the split radicalism vs. conservatism in the Republican party, see Hans L. Trefousse, *The Radical Republican: Lincoln's Vanguard for Racial Justice* (New York: Knopf, 1969).

118. On sinking stone-filled boats to seal southern ports, see Virgil Jones, *The Civil War at Sea*, 2:322–31.

119. On the Beauregard-Davis dispute over pursuit of U.S. forces after Manassas, see Davis, *Battle at Bull Run;* Thomas L. Connelly and Archer Jones, *The Politics of Command: Factions and Ideas in Confederate Strategy* (Baton Rouge: Louisiana State University Press, 1973).

120. On a federal election in Hatteras, North Carolina, see Herman Belz, *Reconstructing the Union: Theory and Policy During the Civil War* (Ithaca, N.Y.: Cornell University Press, 1969).

121. On a fire in Charleston, South Carolina, in December 1861, see Long and Long, *The Civil War Day by Day*, 148.

122. On a Union victory at Galveston, Texas, see Parish, *The American Civil War*, 429.

123. On Butler's capture of Ship Island, see Holzman, *Stormy Ben Butler;* Ben R. Poore, *The Life and Public Services of Ambrose E. Burnside* (Providence, R.I.: J. A. and R. A. Reid, 1882).

124. On U.S. funding for iron-clad steam vessels, see James P. Baxter, 3rd, *The Introduction of the Ironclad Warship* (Cambridge: Harvard University Press, 1933).

125. On the seizure of Thomas Roget and J. W. Zacherie from *Victoria* off Matamoros, see Long and Long, *The Civil War Day by Day*, 147.

1862

1. On Stanton replacing Cameron, see Benjamin P. Thomas and Harold M. Hyman, *Stanton: The Life and Times of Lincoln's Secretary of War* (New York: Knopf, 1962); Erwin S. Bradley, *Simon Cameron, Lincoln's Secretary of War: A Political Biography* (Philadelphia: University of Pennsylvania Press, 1966). On Cameron replacing Cassius Clay as minister to Russia, see David L. Smiley, *Lion of White Hall: The Life of Cassius M. Clay* (Madison: University of Wisconsin Press, 1962); Joseph E. Suppiger, "Cassius Clay's Embassy to Imperial Russia," *Lincoln Herald* 77 (1975): 42–47.

2. On foreign protests of the U.S. seizure of *Trent*, see Ferris, *The Trent Affair;* Donaldson Jordan and Edwin J. Pratt, *Europe and the American Civil War* (Boston: Houghton-Mifflin, 1931); A. R. Tyrner-Tyraner, *Lincoln and Emperors* (London: R. Hart-Davis, 1962). On Seward's assertion that Britain had adopted the U.S. view on neutral rights, see Crook, *The North, the South, and the Powers.*

3. On complaints of Welles's management of naval department, see Richard S. West, Jr., *Mr. Lincoln's Navy* (New York: Longmans, Green, 1957); West, *Gideon Welles;* John Niven, *Gideon Welles: Lincoln's Secretary of the Navy* (New York: Oxford University Press, 1973).

4. On British movement of forces to Canada, see Kenneth Bourne, "British Preparation for War with the North, 1861–1862," *English Historical Review* 76 (1961): 600–632.

5. On the Committee on the Conduct of the War, see Hans Trefousee, "The Joint Committee on the Conduct of the War: A Reassessment," *Civil War History* 10 (1964): 5–19.

6. On Confederate newspaper censorship, see J. Cutler Andrews, *The South Reports the Civil War* (Princeton, N.J.: Princeton University Press, 1970).

7. On Lincoln and European intervention in Mexico, see Schoonover, *Dollars over Dominion;* José Fuentes Mares, *Juárez y la intervención* (Mexico: Jus, 1962).

8. On arbitrary imprisonment of blacks in Washington, D.C., see Leech, *Reveille in Washington*, 252–53.

9. On Indiana Senator Jesse Bright's correspondence with Jefferson Davis, see Allan Nevins, *The War for the Union, 1862–1863* (New York: Scribner's, 1960), 2–3.

10. On Kansas Senator and General James H. Lane's expedition to liberate slaves, see Dudley Cornish, *The Sable Arm: Negro Troops in the Union Army, 1861–1865* (New York: Longmans, Green, 1956).

11. On Virginia Governor Letcher's proposal to pursue the war with great vigor, see F. N. Boney, *John Letcher of Virginia: The Story of Virginia's Civil War Governor* (University, Ala.: University of Alabama Press, 1966).

12. On Butler's expedition to Albemarle Sound, North Carolina, see Reed, *Combined Operations in the Civil War*; Jones, *The Civil War at Sea*; John G. Barrett, *The Civil War in North Carolina* (Chapel Hill: University of North Carolina Press, 1963).

13. On Admiral Foote's victory at Fort Henry and Grant's at Fort Donelson, see James J. Hamilton, *The Battle of Fort Donelson* (1968); Edwin C. Bearss, "Unconditional Surrender: The Fall of Fort Donelson," *Tennessee Historical Quarterly* 21 (1962): 47–65; Benjamin F. Cooling, *Forts Henry and Donaldson: The Key to the Confederate Heartland* (Knoxville: University of Tennessee Press, 1987).

14. On the arrest of General Charles Stone, see T. Harry Williams, "Investigation: 1862," *American Heritage* 6 (1954): 16–21.

15. On the law making U.S. Treasury notes legal tender, see Leonard P. Curry, *Blueprint for Modern America: Non-Military Legislation in the First Civil War Congress* (Nashville: Vanderbilt University Press, 1968).

16. On recognition of Liberia and Haiti, see Charles H. Wesley, "The Struggle for the Recognition of Haiti and Liberia as Independent Republics," *Journal of Negro History* 2 (1917): 369–83; Rayford W. Logan, *The Diplomatic Relations of the United States with Haiti, 1776–1891* (Chapel Hill: University of North Carolina Press, 1941).

17. On the abolition of slavery in the District of Columbia and Delaware, see Hans L. Trefousse, ed., *Lincoln's Decision for Emancipation* (Philadelphia: Lippincott, 1975); McPherson, *The Struggle for Equality*.

18. On the Confederate evacuation of Tennessee and Andrew Johnson's appointment as provisional governor, see Clifton R. Hall, *Andrew Johnson, Military Governor of Tennessee* (Princeton, N.J.: Princeton University Press, 1916); Ralph W. Haskins, "Internecine Strife in Tennessee: Andrew Johnson versus Parson Brownlow," *Tennessee Historical Quarterly* 24 (1965): 321–40; Stephen V. Ash, "Sharks in the Angry Sea: Civilian Resistance and Guerilla Warfare in Occupied Middle Tennessee, 1862–1865," *Tennessee Historical Quarterly* 45 (1986): 217–29.

19. On the Curtis, Price, and McCullough campaign in Arkansas, see Monaghan, *Civil War on the Western Border, 1854–1865*.

20. On Burnside's campaign in North Carolina, see Hassler, *Commanders of the Army of the Potomac*; John G. Barret, *The Civil War in North Carolina*.

21. On unionism in the Confederacy, see Tatum, *Disloyalty in the Confederacy*; William C. Harris, "The Southern Unionist Critique of the Civil War," *Civil War History* 31 (1985): 39–56; Paul D. Escott, *After Secession: Jefferson Davis and the Failure of Confederate Nationalism* (Baton Rouge: Louisiana State University Press, 1977); Daniel W. Crofts, *Reluctant Confederates: Upper South Unionists in the Secession Crisis* (Chapel Hill: The University of North Carolina Press, 1989); Drew Gilpin Faust, *The Creation of Confederate Nationalism: Ideology and Identity in the Civil War South* (Baton Rouge: Louisiana State University Press, 1988).

22. On the *Merrimac*, see William C. Davis, *Duel Between the First Ironclads* (Garden City, N.Y.: Doubleday, 1975); William N. Still, *Iron Afloat: The Story of the Confederate Armorclads* (Nashville: Vanderbilt University Press, 1971).

23. On the battle at Valverde, New Mexico, see Colton, *The Civil War in the Western Territories*.

24. On Union government control over telegraph lines to protect campaign secrecy, see Long and Long, *The Civil War Day by Day*, 164–65.

25. On Congress conceding executive financial authority to adopt compensated emancipation, see John Hope Franklin, *The Emancipation Proclamation* (Garden City, N.Y.: Doubleday, 1963); Trefousse, ed., *Lincoln's Decision for Emancipation*.

26. On sentencing Nathaneal Gordon to death for slave trading, see William S. Fitzgerald, "Make Him an Example," *American History Illustrated* 17 (1983): 40–45.

27. On the Sugar Creek, Arkansas, battle, see Robert G. Hastje, *Van Dorn: The Life and Times of a Confederate General* (Nashville: Vanderbilt University Press, 1967).

28. On conflict between the radicals and McClellan, see Trefousee, "The Joint Committee on the Conduct of the War: A Reassessment," 5–19; T. Harry Williams, *Lincoln and the Radicals*.

29. On Admiral Dupont's Florida operations, see Merrill, *The Rebel Shore*; West, *Mr. Lincoln's Navy*.

30. On the Corinto campaign, see Wiley Sword, *Shiloh: Bloody April* (New York: Morrow, 1974); James Lee McDonough, *Shiloh: In Hell before Night* (Knoxville: University of Tennessee Press, 1977); Archer Jones, *Confederate Strategy from Shiloh to Vicksburg* (Baton Rouge: Louisiana State University Press, 1961).

31. On the peninsula campaign of McClellan, see Clifford Dowdey, *The Seven Days: The Emergence of Lee* (Boston: Little, Brown, 1964).

32. On Congressman Albert White's concern with gradual emancipation and emigration projects for blacks, see V. Jacque Voegli, *Free but Not Equal: The Midwest and the Negro during the Civil War* (Chicago: University of Chicago Press, 1967); Forrest G. Wood, *Black Scare: The Racist Response to Emancipation and Reconstruction* (Berkeley: University of California Press, 1968); Thomas Schoonover, "Misconstrued Mission: Expansionism and Black Colonization in Mexico and Central America during the Civil War," *Pacific Historical Review* 49 (1980): 607–20.

33. On north-south trade during the Civil War, see Ludwell H. Johnson, "The Butler Expedition of 1861–1862: The Profitable Side of War," *Civil War History* 11 (1965): 229–36; L. H. Johnson, "Northern Profit and Profiteers: The Cotton Rings of 1864–1865," *Civil War History* 12 (1966): 101–15; L. H. Johnson, "Trading with the Union: The Evolution of Confederate Policy," *Virginia Magazine of History and Biography* 78 (1970): 308–25; L. H. Johnson, "Contraband Trade During the Last Year of the Civil War," *Mississippi Valley Historical Review* 49 (1963): 635–53.

34. On the fall of New Orleans, see Trefousse, *Ben Butler*.

35. On the Yorktown campaign, see Dowdey, *The Seven Days*; Nevins, *The War for the Union, 1862–1863*; Freeman, *Lee's Lieutenants*.

36. On the fall of Fort Pulaski, see Randall and Donald, *The Civil War and Reconstruction*, 444–45.

37. On the income tax, see Sidney Ratner, *Taxation and Democracy in America* (New York: Wiley, 1967).

38. On Confederate abandonment of Norfolk and the *Merrimac*, see Dowdey, *The Seven Days*.

39. On the transcontinental railroad bill, see Leonard P. Curry, *Blueprint for Modern America*, chap. 6.

40. On the proposal to use Negro troops and sailors in the U.S. military, see Berry, *Military Necessity and Civil Rights Policy*.

41. On General Hunter granting freedom to slaves in his department, see T. Harry Williams, *Lincoln and the Radicals*, 136–38; Howard C. Westwood, "Generals David

Hunter and Rufus Saxton and Black Soldiers," *South Carolina Historical Magazine* 86 (1985): 165–81.

42. On the Confederate evacuation of Pensacola, see Pearce, *The U.S. Navy in Pensacola*.

43. On the Homestead Act, see Leonard P. Curry, *Blueprint of Modern America*, chap. 5.

44. On the Seven Days' battle, see Dowdey, *The Seven Days*; Freeman, *Lee's Lieutenants*; Douglas S. Freeman, *R. E. Lee*, 4 vols. (New York: Scribner's, 1934–35).

45. On the fall of Memphis and the value of Vicksburg, see James M. Merrill, *Battle Flags South: The Story of the Civil War Navies on Western Waters* (Rutherford, N.J.: Fairleigh Dickinson University Press, 1970); John D. Milligan, *Gunboats Down the Mississippi* (Annapolis: U.S. Naval Institute, 1965); H. Allen Gosnell, *Guns on the Western Waters: The Story of River Gunboats in the Civil War* (Baton Rouge: Louisiana State University Press, 1949); Lawrence Lee Hewitt, *Port Hudson, Confederate Bastion on the Mississippi* (Baton Rouge: Louisiana State University Press, 1987).

46. On U.S. recognition of Haiti and Liberia, see Wesley, "The Struggle," 369–83; Logan, *The Diplomatic Relations of the United States with Haiti*.

47. On the emancipation of slaves belonging to Confederate employees, see Randall and Donald, *The Civil War and Reconstruction*, 373. On colonization of blacks in Central America or the Caribbean, see Schoonover, "Black Colonization in Mexico and Central America," 607–20.

48. On the U.S.-British treaty to abolish the slave trade, see Conray W. Henderson, "The Anglo–American Treaty of 1862 in Civil War Diplomacy," *American Historical Review* 38 (1932): 511–25.

49. On McClellan's defeat at the Seven Days' battle, see Dowdey, *The Seven Days*; Hassler, *George B. McClellan*.

50. On the Vicksburg's campaign, see Samuel Carter, *The Final Fortress: The Campaign for Vicksburg* (New York: St. Martin's Press, 1980); Earl Schenck Miers, *The Web of Victory: Grant at Vicksburg* (New York: Knopf, 1955).

51. On General Forrest's campaign to Murfreesboro and Nashville, see Virgil Carrington Jones, *Ghosts and Rebel Raiders* (reprint; Atlanta: Mockingbird Books, 1976); Richard S. Brownlee, *Gray Ghosts of the Confederacy: Guerilla Warfare in the West, 1861–1865* (Baton Rouge: Louisiana State University Press, 1958); Robert S. Henry, *"First with the Most" Forrest* (Indianapolis: Bobbs-Merrill, 1944).

52. On declining popular support for military service and for Negro troops, see Jacob Metzer, "The Records of the U.S. Colored Troops as a Historical Source: An Exploratory Examination," *Historical Methods* 14 (1981): 123–32.

53. On arms scandal involving U.S. senators, see the *New York Times*, 11 July 1862, 4.

54. On Butler's problems with European consuls in New Orleans, see Manfred C. Vernon, "General Butler and the Dutch Consul," *Civil War History* 5 (1959): 263–75; Howard P. Johnson, "New Orleans under General Butler," *Louisiana History Quarterly* 24 (1941): 434–536.

55. On the lottery or draft in the North, see Murdock, *The Civil War Draft and Bounty System*; James W. Geary, "Civil War Conscription in the North: A Historiographical Review," *Civil War History* 32 (1986): 208–28.

56. On U.S. budget and finances, see Rein, *Union Financing of the Civil War*; Hammond, "The North's Empty Purse."

57. For the law authorizing commodores and rear admirals, see the *Congressional Globe*, 37th Cong., 2d sess. 1862, 32, pt. 4: 410–11.

58. On the battle of Cedar Mountain, see Edward J. Stackpole, *From Cedar Mountain to Antietam* (Harrisburg, Pa.: Stackpole Co., 1959).

59. On resistance to the U.S. draft or lottery, see Eugene C. Murdock, *The Civil War Draft in the North* (Kent, Ohio: Kent State University Press, 1971); Peter Lenine, "Draft Evasion in the North during the Civil War," *Journal of American History* 67 (1981): 816–34.

60. On the reaction to Pope's order to live off the land, see Freeman, *R. E. Lee,* 2:263–64.

61. On Confederate modification of conscription laws, see Escott, *Jefferson Davis and the Failure of Confederate Nationalism;* William Harris Bragg, *Joe Brown's Army: The Georgia State Law, 1862–1865* (Macon, Geo.: Mercer University Press, 1987); Kenneth Radley, *Rebel Watchdog: The Confederate States Provost Guard* (Baton Rouge: Louisiana State University Press, 1989).

62. On Lincoln and the colonization of Negroes in Central America, see Schoonover, "Black Colonization in Mexico and Central America," 607–20.

63. On the Greeley-Lincoln correspondence about slavery, see Harlan H. Horner, *Lincoln and Greeley* (Urbana: University of Illinois Press, 1953).

64. On the second battle of Manassas, see Stackpole, *From Cedar Mountain to Antietam.* On the court martial of Fitz John Porter, see Otto Eisenschiml, *The Celebrated Case of Fitz John Porter: An American Dreyfus Affair* (Indianapolis: Bobbs-Merrill, 1950).

65. On the Confederate march into Maryland and Pennsylvania, see Freeman, *Lee's Lieutenants.*

66. On the capture of Frankfort, Kentucky, see Joseph H. Parks, *General Edmund Kirby Smith* (Baton Rouge: Louisiana State University Press, 1954); James A. Ramage, *Rebel Raider: The Life of John Hunt Morgan* (Lexington: The University Press of Kentucky, 1986).

67. On gold-paper prices, see Don C. Barrett, *The Greenbacks;* Wesley C. Mitchell, *A History of the Greenbacks* (Chicago: University of Chicago Press, 1903).

68. On the Emancipation Proclamation, see Franklin, *The Emancipation Proclamation;* Trefousse, ed., *Lincoln's Decision for Emancipation.*

69. On the southern reaction to the Emancipation Proclamation, see Harold D. Moser, "Reaction in North Carolina to the Emancipation Proclamation," *North Carolina Historical Review* 44 (1967): 53–71.

70. On northern governors meetings at Altona, Pennsylvania, see William B. Hesseltine, *Lincoln and the War Governors* (New York: Knopf, 1948).

71. On the battle of Antietam, see James V. Murfin, *The Gleam of Bayonets: The Battle of Antietam* (New York: Thomas Yoseloff, 1965); Stephen W. Sears, *Landscape Turned Red: The Battle of Antietam* (New Haven: Tichnor & Fields, 1983).

72. On legislative elections for 38th Congress, see Edward C. Boykin, *Congress and the Civil War* (New York: McBride Co., 1955).

73. On J. E. B. Stuart's raid into Pennsylvania, see Burke Davis, *Jeb Stuart: The Last Cavalier* (New York: Rinehart, 1957); Emory M. Thomas, *Bold Dragoon: The Life of J. E. B. Stuart* (New York: Harper & Row, 1986).

74. On the battle of Perryville, see Richard O'Connor, *Sheridan the Inevitable* (Indianapolis: Bobbs-Merrill, 1953); Joseph H. Parks, *General Leonidas Polk, C. S. A.: The Fighting Bishop* (Baton Rouge: Louisiana State University Press, 1962).

75. On the *Alabama,* see Edward C. Boykin, *Ghost Ship of the Confederacy: The Story of the "Alabama" and Her Captain* (New York: Funk & Wagnalls, 1957); Frank Merli, *Great Britain and the Confederate Navy: 1861–1865* (Bloomington: Indiana University Press, 1970).

76. On Gladstone and British recognition of the Confederacy, see Donald Bellows, "A Study of British Conservative Reaction to the American Civil War," *Journal of Southern History* 51 (1985): 505–26; Kinley J. Brauer, "British Mediation and the American Civil War: A Reconsideration," *Journal of Southern History* 38 (1972): 49–64.

77. On Burnside, see Poore, *The Life of Ambrose E. Burnside*.

78. On the French mediation offer, see Daniel B. Carroll, *Henry Mercier and the American Civil War* (Princeton, N.J.: Princeton University Press, 1971); Warren Spencer, "The Jewett-Greeley Affair: A Private Scheme for French Mediation in the American Civil War," *New York History* 51 (1970): 238–68.

79. On the battle of Fredericksburg, see Poore, *The Life of Ambrose E. Burnside*; Bruce Catton, *Glory Road* (Garden City, N.Y.: Doubleday, 1952); Nevins, *The War for the Union*; Vorin E. Whan, Jr., *Fiasco at Fredericksburg* (University Park: Pennsylvania State University, 1961).

1863

1. On the battle of Murfreesboro, see Thomas L. Connelly, *Autumn of Glory: The Army of Tennessee 1862–1865* (Baton Rouge: Louisiana State University Press, 1971); James Lee McDonough, *Stones River: Bloody Winter in Tennessee* (Knoxville: University of Tennessee Press, 1980).

2. On the minor Union disaster at Galveston, see Parish, *The American Civil War*, 429.

3. On Banks replacing Butler, see Fred H. Harrington, *Fighting Politician: Major General N. P. Banks* (Philadelphia: University of Pennsylvania Press, 1948).

4. On Hooker replacing Burnside, see Walter H. Hebert, *Fighting Joe Hooker* (Indianapolis: Bobbs-Merrill, 1944).

5. On Fitz John Porter being found guilty and dismissed from the service, see Eisenschiml, *The Celebrated Case of Fitz John Porter*.

6. On factional discord in the North, see David Donald, *The Politics of Reconstruction 1863–1867* (Baton Rouge: Louisiana State University Press, 1965); T. Harry Williams, *Lincoln and the Radicals*.

7. On Missouri and U.S. financial aid for emancipating slaves, see Bill R. Lee, "Missouri's Fight over Emancipation in 1863," *Missouri Historical Review* 45 (1951): 256–74; Parish, *Turbulent Partnership*.

8. On state legislatures regarding turning a war to preserve the Union into one against slavery, see Victor Hicken, *Illinois in the Civil War* (1966); Charles M. Knapp, *New Jersey Politics during the Period of the Civil War and Reconstruction* (1924); Earl Schenck Miers, ed., *New Jersey and the Civil War* (1964).

9. On Confederate finances and budgets, see Richard C. Todd, *Confederate Finance* (Athens: University of Georgia Press, 1954); Lerner, "Monetary and Fiscal Problems of the Confederate Government, 1861–65," 506–22.

10. On the U.S. reception of Haitian Minister Ernest Roumain, see Logan, *Diplomatic Relations of the United States with Haiti*.

11. On Cassius Clay replacing Cameron in Russia, see Benjamin P. Thomas, *Russo-American Relations, 1815–1867* (Baltimore: Johns Hopkins Press, 1930); Suppiger, "Cassius Clay's Embassy to Imperial Russia," 42–47.

12. On the Committee on the Conduct of the War blaming McClellan, see William W. Pierson, Jr., "The Committee on the Conduct of the Civil War," *American Historical Review* 23 (1918): 550–76; Trefousse, "The Joint Committee on the Conduct of the War: A Reassessment," 5–19.

13. On the spring 1863 elections, see James A. Rawley, *The Politics of Union: Northern Politics during the Civil War* (Hinsdale, Ill: Dryden Press, 1974); T. Harry Williams, *Lincoln and the Radicals*.

14. On the state of U.S. workers, especially in New York, see Ware, *The Labor*

Movement in the United States, 1860–1895; David Montgomery, Beyond Equality: Labor and the Radical Republicans, 1862–1872 (New York: Knopf, 1967); Herbert G. Gutman, "Work, Culture, and Society in Industrializing America, 1815–1919," in Work, Culture, and Society in Industrializing America (New York: Knopf, 1977), 3–78; Basil L. Lee, Discontent in New York City, 1861–1865 (Washington, D.C.: Catholic University of America Press, 1943); Albon P. Man, Jr., "Labor Competition and the New York Draft Riots of 1863," Journal of Negro History 36 (1951): 375–405.

15. On Kasson's diplomatic service, see Edward Younger, John A. Kasson: Politics and Diplomacy from Lincoln to McKinley (Iowa City: State Historical Society of Iowa, 1955).

16. On Blair's reaction to British and French policies, see the New York Times, 12 April 1862, 8.

17. On Governor Morton's view that the U.S. government should control the Mississippi, see Emma Lou Thornbrough, Indiana in the Civil War Era, 1850–1880 (Indianapolis: Indiana Historical Bureau, 1965); Kenneth M. Stampp, Indiana Politics during the Civil War (Indianapolis: Indiana Historical Bureau, 1949).

18. On popular resistance in Reading, Pennsylvania, see Stanton L. Davis, Pennsylvania Politics, 1860–1863 (Cleveland: The Bookstore, Western Reserve University, 1935); Ervin S. Bradley, The Triumph of Militant Republicanism: A Study of Pennsylvania and Presidential Politics, 1860–1873 (Philadelphia: University of Pennsylvania Press, 1964); David Montgomery, "Radical Republicanism in Pennsylvania, 1866–1873," Pennsylvania Magazine of History and Biography 85 (1961): 439–57; William F. Hanna, "The Boston Draft Riot," Civil War History 36 (1990): 262–73.

19. On the battle of Chicamauga, see Fairfax Downey, Storming of the Gateway: Chattanooga, 1863 (New York: McKay, 1960).

20. On the fall 1863 elections, see Rawley, The Politics of Union; Trefousse, The Radical Republicans; Hesseltine, Lincoln and the War Governors.

1864

1. On Confederate finances and budgets, see Eugene M. Lerner, "Inflation in the Confederacy, 1861–1865," in Studies in the Quantity Theory of Money, ed. Milton Friedman (Chicago: University of Chicago Press, 1956); Todd, Confederate Finance.

2. On the campaign to win the presidential nominations in 1864, see Edward C. Kirkland, The Peacemakers of 1864 (reprinted; New York: AMS Press, 1969); William F. Zornow, Lincoln and the Party Divided (Norman: University of Oklahoma Press, 1954); Ludwell H. Johnson, "Lincoln's Solution to the Problem of Peace Terms, 1864–1865," Journal of Southern History 34 (1968): 576–86; Arthur C. Cole, "Lincoln and the Presidential Election of 1864," Transactions of the Illinois State Historical (1917), 130–38; Frederick J. Blue, Salmon P. Chase: A Life in Politics (Kent, Ohio: Kent State University Press, 1988); Samuel T. McSevency, "Re-electing Lincoln: The Union Party Campaign and the Military Vote in Connecticut," Civil War History 32 (1986): 139–58.

3. On Gillmore's campaign in Florida, see Long and Long, The Civil War Day by Day, 462.

4. On Kirkpatrick's cavalry raid into Virginia, see Samuel Carter, The Last Cavaliers: Confederate and the Union Cavalry in the Civil War (New York: St. Martin's Press, 1980); Stephen G. Starr, The Union Cavalry in the Civil War, 2 vols. (Baton Rouge: Louisiana State University Press, 1979).

5. On the Monroe Doctrine in the 1864 election, see Dexter Perkins, The Monroe Doctrine, 1826–1867 (Baltimore: Johns Hopkins Press, 1933).

6. On Sherman's campaign toward Selma, Alabama, see Basil H. Liddell Hart, *Sherman: Soldier, Realist, American* (reprint; New York: Praeger, 1929); Lloyd Lewis, *Sherman, Fighting Prophet* (New York: Harcourt, Brace, 1932); James M. Merrill, *William Tecumseh Sherman* (Chicago: Rand-McNally, 1971).

7. On Grant being given command of the U.S. Army, see J. F. C. Fuller, *Grant and Lee: A Study in Personality and Generalship* (Bloomington: Indiana University Press, 1957); Bruce Catton, *Grant Moves South* and *Grant Takes Command* (Boston: Little, Brown, 1969). On Sherman and McPherson being given the armies on the Mississippi and in Tennessee, see Elizabeth J. Whaley, *Forgotten Hero: General James B. McPherson* (New York: Exposition Press, 1955).

8. On U.S. gold sales and gold-paper dollar ratios, see Paul Studenoski and Hermann E. Krooss, *Financial History of the United States* (2nd ed.; New York: McGraw-Hill, 1963); Margaret G. Myers, *A Financial History of the United States* (New York: Columbia University Press, 1970).

9. On congressional effort to expel two representatives who favored recognizing southern independence, see Wood Gray, *The Hidden Civil War: The Story of the Copperheads* (reprint; New York: The Viking Press, 1964).

10. On Fort Pillow, see John L. Jordan, "Was There a Massacre at Fort Pillow?" *Tennessee Historical Quarterly* 6 (1947): 99–133; John Cimprich and Robert C. Mainfort, Jr., eds., "Fort Pillow Revisited: New Evidence about an Old Controversy," *Civil War History* 28 (1982): 293–306.

11. On the Wilderness campaign, see Edward Steere, *The Wilderness Campaign* (Harrisburg, Pa.: Stackpole Co., 1960); Freeman, *Lee's Lieutenants*; Noah Andre Trudeau, *Bloody Roads South: The Wilderness to Cold Harbor, May–June 1864* (Boston: Little, Brown, 1989).

12. On the Arguelles trial for slave trading, see Gideon Welles, *The Diary of Gideon Welles*, 3 vols. (Boston: Houghton-Mifflin, 1909–1910), 3:36–45; *New York Times*, 12 April 1864, 4.

13. On German radicals in the United States, see Earl J. Hess, "Sigel's Resignation: A Study in German-Americanism and the Civil War," *Civil War History* 26 (1980): 5–17.

14. On Butler and Sigel failing in campaigns coordinated with Grant's, see Bruce Catton, *A Stillness at Appomattox* (Garden City, N.Y.: Doubleday, 1953); William C. Davis, *The Battle of New Market* (Garden City, N.Y.: Doubleday, 1975); Hess, "Sigel's Resignation," 5–17; William Glen Robertson, *Back Door to Richmond: The Bermuda Hundred Campaign, April–June 1964* (Newark: University of Delaware Press, 1987).

15. On Grant on the Chickahominy, see Catton, *A Stillness at Appomattox*; William C. Davis, *The Battle of New Market*.

16. On Frémont's nomination at the radical Republican convention, see T. Harry Williams, *Lincoln and the Radicals*.

17. On Lincoln's renomination at the Baltimore convention, see Cole, "Lincoln and the Presidential Election of 1864," 130–38.

18. On Hunter versus Jones in east Virginia, see Freeman, *Lee's Lieutenants*.

19. On Grant attacking Petersburg, see Richard J. Sommers, *Richmond Redeemed: The Siege of Petersburg* (Garden City, N.Y.: Doubleday, 1981).

20. On the investigation into fraudulent dispatching of goods to Texas from New York, see James W. Daddysman, *The Matamoros Trade: Confederate Commerce, Diplomacy, and Intrigue* (Newark: University of Delaware Press, 1984).

21. On Ewell fighting Hunter, see Frank E. Vandiver, *Jubal's Raid* (New York: McGraw-Hill, 1960); Benjamin Franklin Cooling, *Jubal Early's Raid on Washington* (Baltimore: The Nautical & Aviation Publishing Company of America, 1989).

22. On Grant's refusal to follow Lee's diversion with Early, see J. F. C. Fuller, *The Generalship of Ulysses S. Grant* (New York: Dodd, Mead, 1929); Fuller, *Grant and Lee*.

23. On Hood and Sherman at Atlanta, see Samuel Carter, *The Siege of Atlanta, 1864* (New York: St. Martin's Press, 1973); John P. Dyer, *The Gallant Hood* (Indianapolis: Bobbs-Merrill, 1950); Richard O'Connor, *Hood: Cavalier General* (New York: Prentice-Hall, 1949).

24. On Confederates at the Canada side of Niagara, see Ludwell H. Johnson, "Beverly Tucker's Canadian Mission, 1864–65," *Journal of Southern History* 29 (1963): 88–99.

25. On Copperheads and other peace factions, see Gray, *The Hidden Civil War*; Frank L. Klement, *The Copperheads in the Middle West* (Chicago: University of Chicago Press, 1960).

26. On the mine assault at Petersburg, see Burke Davis, *To Appomattox* (New York: Rinehart, 1959); Philip Van Doren Stern, *An End to Valor, the Last Days of the Civil War* (New York: Bonanza Books, 1958).

27. On McCook's expedition into Georgia, see Carter, *The Siege of Atlanta, 1864*; Liddell Hart, *Sherman*.

28. On the Wade-Davis manifesto, see Bernard C. Steiner, *Life of Henry W. Davis* (Baltimore: John Murphy Company, 1916); Hans L. Trefousee, *Benjamin Franklin Wade: Radical Republican from Ohio* (New York: Twayne, 1963).

29. On Farragut's attack of Mobile, see Charles L. Lewis, *David Glasgow Farragut*, 2 vols. (Annapolis: U.S. Naval Institute, 1941–43); Howard C. Westwood, "After Vicksburg, What of Mobile?" *Military Affairs* 48 (1984): 169–73.

30. On Confederate attempts to cut Sherman's communications, see Thomas R. Hay, *Hood's Tennessee Campaign* (New York: Walter Neal, 1929).

31. On *Tallahassee* raiding off the U.S. coast, see Norman C. Delaney, "Cruisers for the Confederacy," *American History Illustrated* 8 (1982): 38–46 and 9 (1983): 10–14, 19–21.

32. On Grant's attack of the Weldon railroad, see Bruce Catton, *Never Call Retreat* (Garden City, N.Y.: Doubleday, 1965); Sommers, *Richmond Redeemed*.

33. On raids of Wheeler and Forrest, see John P. Dyer, *"Fightin' Joe" Wheeler* (Baton Rouge: Louisiana State University Press, 1941); Carter, *Confederate and Union Cavalry in the Civil War*; Henry, *"First with the Most" Forrest*.

34. On McClellan as the Democratic nominee, see Randall and Donald, *The Civil War and Reconstruction*, 474–75; Charles R. Wilson, "McClellan's Changing Views on the Peace Plank," *American Historical Review* 38 (1933): 498–505; Stephen W. Sears, "McClellan and the Peace Plank of 1864: A Reappraisal," *Civil War History* 36 (1950): 57–64.

35. On Sheridan's success against Early, see Edward J. Stackpole, *Sheridan in the Shenandoah* (Harrisburg, Pa.: Stackpole Co., 1961).

36. On Montgomery Blair's resignation from Lincoln's cabinet, see Hendrick, *Lincoln's War Cabinet*; Rawley, *The Politics of Union*.

37. On Lincoln's reelection, see Kirkland, *The Peacemakers of 1864*; Zornow, *Lincoln and the Party Divided*; Ludwell H. Johnson, "Lincoln's Solution to the Problem of Peace Terms, 1864–1865," 576–86; Cole, "Lincoln and the Presidential Election of 1864," 130–38; Blue, *Salmon P. Chase*; McSevency, "Re-electing Lincoln," 139–58.

38. On Confederate consideration of arming the negroes, see Bell I. Wiley, *Southern Negroes, 1861–1865* (reprint; Baton Rouge: Louisiana State University Press, 1974); Robert F. Durden, *The Gray and the Black: The Confederate Debate on Emancipation* (Baton Rouge: Louisiana State University Press, 1972).

39. On Sherman's march to the sea, see Burke Davis, *Sherman's March* (New York: Random House, 1980); Merrill, *William Tecumseh Sherman*.

40. On Thomas vs. Hood in Tennessee, see Stanley F. Horn, *The Decisive Battle of Nashville* (reprint; Knoxville: University of Tennessee Press, 1968); Hay, *Hood's Tennessee*

Campaign; Wilbur Thomas, *General George H. Thomas: The Indomitable Warrior* (New York: Exposition Press, 1964); Francis F. McKinney, *Education in Violence: The Life of George H. Thomas and the History of the Army of Cumberland* (Detroit: Wayne State University Press, 1961).

41. On the U.S. vessel attacking the *Florida* in Brazilian waters, see Frank L. Owsley, Jr., *The C. S. S. "Florida": Her Building and Operations* (Philadelphia: University of Pennsylvania Press, 1965).

42. On Sherman's arrival at the Atlantic coast, see Josef C. James, "Sherman at Savannah," *Journal of Negro History* 39 (1954): 127–36.

43. On Thomas's victory at the battle of Nashville, see Horn, *The Decisive Battle of Nashville.*

1865

1. On the fall of Fort Fisher, see Merrill, *The Rebel Shore.*

2. On Francis Blair, Sr., visiting Jefferson Davis, see Smith, *The Francis Preston Blair Family in Politics.*

3. On Lee being named commanding general, see Freeman, *R. E. Lee*; Frank E. Vandiver, *Rebel Brass: The Confederate Command System* (Baton Rouge: Louisiana State University Press, 1956).

4. On Seward and Lincoln meeting with Alexander Stephens, Judge Campbell, and R. M. T. Hunter, see James P. McPherson, "The Career of John Archibald Campbell: A Study of Politics and Law," *Alabama Review* 19 (1966): 53–63; James Z. Rabun, "Alexander H. Stephens and the Confederacy," *Emory University Quarterly* 6 (1950): 129–46; James Z. Rabun, "Alexander H. Stephens and Jefferson Davis," *American Historical Review* 58 (1953): 290–321; John R. Brumgardt, "The Confederate Career of Alexander H. Stephens: The Case Reopened," *Civil War History* 27 (1981): 64–81; Thomas E. Schott, *Alexander H. Stephens of Georgia: A Biography* (Baton Rouge: Louisiana State University Press, 1987).

5. On the constitutional amendment to abolish slavery, see James G. Randall, *Lincoln the President.*

6. On Sherman in South Carolina, see John G. Barrett, *Sherman's March Through the Carolinas* (Chapel Hill: University of North Carolina Press, 1956); Marion Brunson Lucas, *Sherman and the Burning of Columbia* (College Station: Texas A & M University Press, 1976).

7. On the fall of Wilmington, see Merrill, *The Rebel Shore.*

8. On Lee soliciting authority to organize Negro troops, see Durden, *The Gray and the Black.*

9. On Lincoln's second inauguration, see Kirkland, *Peacemakers of 1864*; Zornow, *Lincoln and the Party Divided.*

10. On cabinet changes in the Lincoln administration, see Hendrick, *Lincoln's War Cabinet*; T. Harry Williams, *Lincoln and the Radicals.*

11. On Lee's inability to prevent Schofield, Sherman, and Terry from combining their armies, see Davis, *To Appomattox*; Barrett, *The Civil War in North Carolina.*

12. On the fall of Richmond, see Rembert W. Patrick, *The Fall of Richmond* (Baton Rouge: Louisiana State University Press, 1960).

13. On Lee's surrender, see Clifford Dowdey, *Lee's Last Campaign* (Boston: Little, Brown, 1960); Freeman, *R. E. Lee.*

14. On closing all southern ports, see Frank J. Merli and Robert H. Farrell, "Blockades and Quarantines," in *Encyclopedia of American Foreign Policy,* ed. Alexander

DeConde (New York: Scribners, 1978), 1:90–103; Stuart Anderson, "1861: Blockade vs Closing the Confederate Ports," *Military Affairs* 41 (1977): 190–94.

15. On Davis's flight from Richmond, see David R. Barbee, "The Capture of Jefferson Davis," *Tyler's Quarterly Historical and Genealogical Magazine* 29 (1963): 1–19; Howard T. Dimick, "The Capture of Jefferson Davis," *Journal of Mississippi History* 9 (1947): 238–54.

16. On Lincoln's assassination, see Albert Castel, *The Presidency of Andrew Johnson* (Lawrence: Regents Press of Kansas, 1979).

17. On Johnston's surrender to Sherman, see Gilbert E. Govan and James W. Livingood, *A Different Valor: The Story of General Joseph E. Johnston, C. S. A.* (New York: Bobbs-Merrill, 1956).

18. On the surrender of Richard Taylor and E. Kirby Smith, see Joseph H. Parks, *General Edmund Kirby Smith, C. S. A.* (Baton Rouge: Louisiana State University Press, 1954); Taylor, *Destruction and Reconstruction*; Jackson B. Davis, "The Life of Richard Taylor," *Louisiana History Quarterly* 24 (1941): 49–126.

19. On General Weitzel's removal from command, see Patrick, *The Fall of Richmond*; Richard Lowe, "Another Look at Reconstruction in Virginia," *Civil War History* 32 (1986): 56–75.

20. On criticism of Sherman's surrender terms to Johnston, see Harry W. Pfanz, "The Surrender Negotiations between General Johnston and General Sherman, April 1865," *Military Affairs* 16 (1952): 61–70; George C. Rable, "William T. Sherman and the Conservative Critique of Radical Reconstruction," *Ohio History* 93 (1984): 147–63.

21. On Confederate officers eager to fight against Maximilian, see Alfred Jackson Hanna and Kathryn T. Hanna, *Napoleon III and Mexico* (Chapel Hill: University of North Carolina Press, 1971); Schoonover, *Dollars over Dominion*, 98–99, 192–94.

22. On Lincoln's body returned to Illinois, see James G. Randall, *Lincoln the President*.

23. On Johnson's appointment of a governor for Florida, see Eric McKitrick, *Andrew Johnson and Reconstruction* (Chicago: University of Chicago Press, 1960); Jerrell Shofner, *Nor Is It Over Yet: Florida and the Era of Reconstruction* (Gainesville: University Presses of Florida, 1974).

24. On Spain's turning over the *Stonewall*, see Rafael Gonzales Echegaray, "España y la marina confederada" (Spain and the Confederate Navy), *Revista General de Marina* (Spain) 197 (1979): 293–303; Cortada, "The Abolition Movement," 27–33.

25. On the U.S.–Canadian business convention in Detroit, see Winks, *Canada and the United States: The Civil War Years*.

26. On amnesty and pardons, see Jonathan Dorris, *Pardon and Amnesty under Lincoln and Johnson* (Chapel Hill: University of North Carolina Press, 1953).

27. On the trial of Henry Wirz, see Ovid L. Futch, *History of Andersonville Prison* (Gainesville: University of Florida Press, 1968); Darrell B. Rutman, "The War Crimes and Trial of Henry Wirz," *Civil War History* 6 (1960): 117–33.

28. On reconstructing southern states, see La Wanda and John H. Cox, *Politics, Principle and Prejudice, 1865–1866* (New York: Atheneum, 1969); Robert J. Kaczorowski, "To Begin the Nation Anew: Congress, Citizenship, and Civil Rights after the Civil War," *American Historical Review* 92 (1987): 45–68; Otto H. Olsen, ed., *Reconstruction and Redemption in the South* (Baton Rouge: Louisiana State University Press, 1979); William R. Brock, *An American Crisis: Congress and Reconstruction, 1865–1867* (New York: Harper & Row, 1963); David Donald, *The Politics of Reconstruction, 1863–1867* (Baton Rouge: Louisiana State University Press, 1965); William C. Harris, *The Day of the Carpetbagger: Republican Reconstruction in Mississippi* (Baton Rouge: Louisiana State University Press, 1979); Francis B. Simkins and Robert H. Woody, *South Carolina during*

Reconstruction (reprint; Gloucester, Mass.: Peter Smith, 1932); Richard H. Abbot, *The Republican Party and the South, 1855–1877: The First Southern Strategy* (Chapel Hill: University of North Carolina, 1986).

29. On the U.S. rejection of any payment of Confederate loans, see McKitrick, *Andrew Johnson and Reconstruction*, 161; Randall and Donald, *The Civil War and Reconstruction*, 584, 596; McPherson, *Ordeal by Fire*, 499, 502–3, 516–18.

30. On Fenian activity in the immediate post–Civil War era, see Brian Jenkins, *Fenian and Anglo-American Relations during Reconstruction* (Ithaca, N.Y.: Cornell University Press, 1969).

31. On Alabama, South Carolina, and Mississippi reconstruction, see Brock, *An American Crisis*; Donald, *The Politics of Reconstruction*; Harris, *The Day of the Carpet-bagger*; Simkins and Woody, *South Carolina during Reconstruction*.

32. On North Carolina reconstruction, see W. McKee Evans, *Ballots and Fence Rails: Reconstruction on the Lower Cape Fear* (Chapel Hill: University of North Carolina Press, 1967); E. Merton Coulter, *The South during Reconstruction* (Baton Rouge: Louisiana State University Press, 1947); William C. Harris, *William Woods Holden: Firebrand of North Carolina Politics* (Baton Rouge: Louisiana State University Press, 1987).

33. On New York state elections, see James C. Mohr, *The Radical Republicans and Reform in New York during Reconstruction* (Ithaca, N.Y.: Cornell University Press, 1973).

34. On Maximilian and antimonarchical views of U.S. politicians, see Hanna and Hanna, *Napoleon III and Mexico*; Schoonover, *Dollars over Dominion*.

35. On reducing Negro troops in U.S. service, see Cornish, *The Sable Arm*; Robert Cruden, *The Negro in Reconstruction* (Englewood, N.J.: Prentice-Hall, 1969); David Warren Bowen, *Andrew Johnson and the Negro* (Knoxville: University of Tennessee Press, 1989).

36. On Johnson's position between the two parties in 1865, see Howard K. Beale, *The Critical Year: A Study of Andrew Johnson and Reconstruction* (reprint; New York: F. Ungar, 1958); J. Michael Quill, *Prelude to the Radicals: The North and Reconstruction during 1865* (Washington, D.C.: University Press of America, 1980); Hans L. Trefousse, *Andrew Johnson: A Biography* (New York: Norton, 1989).

37. On Spain abolishing the slave trade, see James W. Cortada, *Two Nations over Time: Spain and the United States, 1776–1977* (Westport, Conn: Greenwood Press, 1978).

38. On the congressional committee on reconstruction, see John G. Clark, "Historians and the Joint Committee on Reconstruction," *Historian* 23 (1961): 348–61; John G. Clark, "Radicals and Moderates on the Joint Committee on Reconstruction," *Mid-America* 45 (1963), 79–98.

39. On the Mexican question in U.S.–French relations and in reconstruction, see Schoonover, *Dollars over Dominion*; Hanna and Hanna, *Napoleon III and Mexico*; Thomas Schoonover, "The Mexican Minister Describes Andrew Johnson's Swing around the Circle," *Civil War History* 19 (1973): 149–61.

1866

1. On the death of Henry Winter Davis, see Steiner, *Henry W. Davis*.

2. On the rupture between Johnson and the Republican majority, see James Sefton, *Andrew Johnson and the Uses of Constitutional Power* (Boston: Little, Brown, 1980); Abbott, *The Republican Party and the South*; McKitrick, *Andrew Johnson and Reconstruction*.

3. On the Fenian invasion of Canada from U.S. soil, see Arthur H. De Rusier, Jr.,

"Importance in Failure: The Fenian Raids of 1866–1871," *Southern Quarterly* 3 (1985): 181–97; W. S. Niedhardt, "We've Nothing Else to Do: The Fenian Invasions of Canada, 1866," *Canada: A Historical Magazine* 1 (1973): 1–20.

4. On Tennessee's readmission to the U.S. Congress, see Thomas B. Alexander, *Political Reconstruction in Tennessee* (reprint; New York: Russell & Russell, 1968).

5. On difficult party realignment, see A. V. House, "Northern Congressional Democrats as Defenders of the South during Reconstruction," *Journal of Southern History* 6 (1940): 46–71; Michael Perman, *Reunion without Compromise: The South and Reconstruction, 1865–1868* (Cambridge: Cambridge University Press, 1973).

6. On the first calls for impeachment of Johnson, see Michael Les Benedict, *The Impeachment and Trial of Andrew Johnson* (New York: Norton, 1973); Hans L. Trefousse, *Impeachment of a President: Andrew Johnson, the Blacks, and Reconstruction* (Knoxville: University of Tennessee Press, 1975).

7. On soldiers conventions in Cleveland and Pittsburgh, see McKitrick, *Andrew Johnson and Reconstruction*, 446–47.

8. On Johnson and radical or congressional reconstruction plans, see McKitrick, *Andrew Johnson and Reconstruction*; Patrick W. Riddleberger, *1866: The Critical Year Revisited* (Carbondale: Southern Illinois University Press, 1979); Quill, *Prelude to the Radicals*; Brock, *An American Crisis*; Donald, *The Politics of Reconstruction 1863–1867*; Harris, *The Day of the Carpetbagger*; Simkins and Woody, *South Carolina during Reconstruction*.

1867

1. On James Ashley's call for impeachment, see Maxine B. Kahn, "Congressman Ashley in the Post–Civil War Years," *Northwest Ohio Quarterly* 36 (1964): 116–33, 194–210.

2. On blacks in D.C. getting the vote over Johnson's veto, see James M. McPherson, *The Struggle for Equality*; William Gillette, *The Right to Vote: Politics and the Passage of the Fifteenth Amendment* (Baltimore: Johns Hopkins, 1965).

3. On military reconstruction passed over Johnson's veto, see James Sefton, *The United States Army and Reconstruction* (Baton Rouge: Louisiana State University Press, 1967); Martin E. Mantell, *Johnson, Grant, and the Politics of Reconstruction* (New York: Columbia University Press, 1973).

4. On the Johnson-radicals fight over civil appointments and removals, see Michael Les Benedict, *A Compromise of Principle: Congressional Republicans and Reconstruction* (New York: Norton, 1974).

5. On organizing the 40th Congress without a presidential call, see Brock, *An American Crisis*; Benedict, *A Compromise of Principle*.

6. On admitting Nebraska to the Union, see Randall and Donald, *Civil War and Reconstruction*, 608–42; Schoonover, *Dollars over Dominion*, 246–48.

7. On Louisiana's reconstruction, see Peyton McCrary, *Abraham Lincoln and Reconstruction: The Louisiana Experiment* (Princeton, N.J.: Princeton University Press, 1978); C. Peter Ripley, *Slaves and Freedmen in Civil War Louisiana* (Baton Rouge: Louisiana State University Press, 1976).

8. On Congress overriding Johnson's veto on the bill to clarify military reconstruction, see Randall and Donald, *Civil War and Reconstruction*, 598–600; James M. McPherson, *Ordeal by Fire*, 522–23.

9. On Johnson granting broad amnesty to southerners, see Perman, *Reunion without Compromise*; Dorris, *Pardon and Amnesty under Lincoln and Johnson*; Harold Hyman, *The Era of the Oath* (Philadelphia: University of Pennsylvania Press, 1954).

10. On a popular call for Grant as president, see Mantell, *Johnson, Grant, and the Politics of Reconstruction.*

11. On an Indian policy that seeks to protect settlers rather than "civilize" the Indians, see Wilcomb E. Washburn, *The Indian in America* (New York: Harper & Row, 1975); William T. Hagan, *American Indians* (Chicago: University of Chicago Press, 1961); Henry E. Fritz, *The Movement for Indian Assimilation, 1860–1890* (Philadelphia: University of Pennsylvania Press, 1963).

12. On the equality of the Negro before the law in 1867, see Cruden, *The Negro in Reconstruction;* Berry, *Military Necessity and Civil Rights Policy.*

13. On a narrow margin of radical victory in the fall 1867 elections, see James C. Mohr, ed., *Radical Republicans of the North* (Baltimore: Johns Hopkins University Press, 1976).

14. On the trial of Jefferson Davis, see Hudson Strode, *Jefferson Davis,* 3 vols. (New York: Harcourt, Brace, 1955–64).

15. On Johnson's annual message, see Castel, *The Presidency of Andrew Johnson.*

16. On the U.S. offer to purchase the Danish Virgin Islands and the acquisition of Alaska, see Charles C. Tansill, *The Purchase of the Danish West Indies* (Baltimore: Johns Hopkins Press, 1932); Halvdan Koht, "The Origin of Seward's Plan to Purchase the Danish West Indies," *American Historical Review* 50 (1945): 762–67; Ronald J. Jensen, *The Alaska Purchase and Russian-American Relations* (Seattle: University of Washington Press, 1975).

17. On the *Alabama* claims, see Adrian Cook, *The Alabama Claims, American Politics and Anglo-American Relations, 1865–1872* (Ithaca, N.Y.: Cornell University Press, 1975).

Bibliographical Essay on Matías Romero's View of the Civil War and Early Reconstruction

Matías Romero's interpretation of the Civil War era has special attraction because it represents an outsider's perspective on the Civil War. Outsiders like Romero were usually less personally, culturally, and emotionally involved in the issues that divided the United States than most of the hundreds of domestic participants and witnesses who left histories, diaries, reminiscences, and autobiographies. U.S. historians have not eagerly sought to acquire the scores of perspectives from foreign observers on the mid-nineteenth-century crisis, yet they should do so. The different hypotheses regarding the broad social meaning of the Civil War era have led observers to gather and emphasize somewhat different bodies of data. The real value of writings by foreign observers of the middle period lies not in the facts that they provide us but rather in the altered conceptions, new arrangements of data, unusual insights, startling analyses, and fresh conclusions they offer us. Precisely these uncommon perspectives, insights, and analyses present us the opportunity to rethink our set vision of the Civil War.

Both contemporary foreign observers and foreign scholars can achieve a fresh, invigorating analysis. Recently, the Italian Raimundo Luraghi offered a stimulating perspective in "The Civil War and the Modernization of American Society: Social Structure and Industrial Revolution in the Old South before and during the War," *Civil War History* 18 (September 1972): 230–50, and in *Storia della Guerra Civile Americana* (Turin: Giulio Einaudi, 1966). Other stimulating modern works by foreign scholars in the U.S. mid-nineteenth-century crisis are Donald P. Cook, *The North, The South, and the Powers, 1861–1865* (New York: Wiley, 1973), and William R. Brock, *Conflict and Transformation: The United States, 1844–1877* (Baltimore: Penguin, 1973). Several contemporary foreign accounts are rather well known: British journalist William Howard Russell, in *My Diary North and South* (Boston: T. O. H. P. Burnham, 1863), and the German soldier and historian Heros von Borcke, in *Memoirs of the Confederate War for Independence*, 2 vols. (reprint; New York: Peter Smith, 1938), both described a wide range of occurrences. Justus Scheibert, *Seven Months in the Rebel States during the North American War, 1863* (Tuscaloosa, Ala.: Confederate Pub. Co., 1958), focused upon military events. Several historians have drawn upon the accounts of foreign diplomats in the United States to reveal private views and interpretations on the meaning and significance of mid-nineteenth-century events. Eric Foner used British materials to shed light upon "Andrew Johnson and Reconstruction: A British View," *Journal of Southern History* 41 (August 1975): 381–90. Kinley Brauer drew upon the Spanish minister's dispatches to offer us a Spanish view of the Civil War in "Gabriel García y Tassara and the American Civil War," *Civil War History* 21 (March 1975): 5–27; Gerald D. Homan, "Netherlands-American Relations during the Civil War," *Civil War History* 31 (1985): 353–64; David C. Rankin, ed. and trans., "Political Parades and American Democracy: Jean-Charles Houzean on Lincoln's 1864 Reelection Campaign," *Civil War History* 30 (1984): 324–29. Finally, Thomas Schoonover used Mexican material in "The Mexican Minister Describes Andrew Johnson's 'Swing Around the Circle,'" *Civil War History* 19 (June 1973): 149–61. He drew upon Costa Rican and Spanish diplomatic documents to describe the impact of the Kansas debate upon Central American and Caribbean societies in "Foreign Relations and Bleeding Kansas in 1858," *The Kansas Historical Quarterly* 42 (Winter 1976): 345–52, and in Thomas and Ebba Schoonover, eds., "Bleeding Kansas and Spanish Cuba in 1857: A postscript," *Kansas History: A Journal of the Central Plains* 11 (Winter 1988–89): 240–42. The author has also translated and edited *The Mexican Lobby: Matías Romero in Washington, 1861–1867* (Lexington: University Press of Kentucky, 1986).

Since Romero had a significant role in the history of Mexico and in U.S.-Mexican relations between 1858 and 1898, it is surprising that little attention has been given to his life from either side of the Rio Grande. The surprise increases with the realization that a large body of his personal and public papers are readily available to the researcher. Romero published about two scores of books and a large number of essays and articles. A list of his publications is found in *Mexican Lobby*. His most imposing publication, which supplied the documents translated in this book, is *Correspondencia de la legación mexicana en Washington durante la intervención extranjera, 1860–1868*, 10 vols. (México: Impresa del Gobierno, 1870–1892). It consists of almost all the dispatches and their annexes that he sent to his government during the 1860–68 years. The originals are available in the Archivo de la Secretaría de Relaciones Exteriores, México. This same archive also possesses a personal file on Romero's diplomatic career. María de la Luz Topete published a brief selection of Romero's correspondence from the 1860s for the Mexican Secretaría de Relaciones Exteriores under the title *Labor diplomática de Matías Romero en Washington, 1861–1867* (México: Secretaría de Relaciones Exteriores, 1976).

The record of Romero's official correspondence with the U.S. government can be followed in the National Archives, Notes to Foreign Legations (Microfilm 99) and Notes from Foreign Legations (Microfilm 54) for the years he was chargé d'affaires, minister, or ambassador. Moreover, much of Romero's formal correspondence relating to his meetings and exchanges with Secretary of State Seward can be found either in U.S. Department of State *Papers Relating to the Foreign Relations of the United States*, various volumes (Washington, D.C.: Government Publishing Office, 1861–present), or in Senate or House Documents, for example: Senate Executive Document 1, 37th Cong., 1st sess.; House Exec. Doc. 100, 37th Cong., 2d sess.; House Exec. Docs. 1 and 54, 37th Cong., 1st sess.; House Exec. Doc. 1, 39th Cong., 2d sess.; House Exec. Doc. 29, 40th Cong., 1st sess.; House Exec. Doc. 1, 40th Cong., 1st sess.; Senate Exec. Doc. 20, 40th Cong., 1st sess. These and other government publications, often appearing with Romero's connivance, present much of the interchange between Romero and the Department of State or his foreign ministry.

The official side of Romero's life can be supplemented by a truly amazing body of private correspondence. In 1952, the Banco de México purchased Romero's private papers, a collection of well over one hundred thousand items—about evenly divided between correspondence received and sent. To guide scholars in the use of the Archivo Histórico de Matías Romero, the Banco de México published a multivolume catalog. So far, Guadelupe Monroy Huitrón has edited two volumes, covering the years 1837–84, under the title: *Archivo Histórico de Matías Romero: Catálogo Descriptivo, Correspondencia Recibida.* 2 vols. (México: Banco de México, 1965, 1970). A third volume concluding the correspondence received was prepared, but funding disappeared. If funding for Romero's research aids is restored, work on a projected four-volume catalog of correspondence sent will be resumed. The Banco de México also permitted the publication of the *Diario Personal de Matías Romero, 1855–1865*, edited by Emma Cosío Villegas (México: Colegio de México, 1960). In addition to this collection, dozens of private collections in Mexico and the United States contain Matías Romero materials. For example, two collections of Edward Lee Plumb papers, located in the Library of Congress and at Stanford University, the Hiram Barney papers at the Huntington Library, and the James W. Beeckman papers in the New York Historical Society contain numerous Romero letters and drafts of letters to Romero.

Yet, in spite of this vast body of manuscript and printed source material, no adequate biography of Romero exists, nor have the Romero papers been used extensively to describe U.S.-Mexican relations in the last half of the nineteenth century. The only biography of Romero is the entirely inadequate Harry Bernstein, *Matías Romero, 1837–1898* (México: Fondo de Cultura Económico, 1973). The best introduction to Romero, both as a person and as a diplomat, can be extracted from Daniel Cosío Villegas, *Historia Moderna de México: El Porfiriato. La Vida Política Exterior*, vols. 5 and 6 (México: Editorial Hermes, 1955–1977). Romero's activity as a promoter of U.S. investment is touched upon frequently in David Pletcher's prize winning *Rails, Mines and Progress: Seven American Promoters in Mexico, 1867–1911* (reprint; Ithaca, N.Y.: Cornell University Press, 1958). Romero's briefer contact with Mexico's internal economy during his tenures as secretary of the treasury is described in Francisco R. Calderón, *Historia Moderna de México: La República Restaurada. La Vida Económica*, vol. 2 (México: Editorial Hermes, 1955–1977).

Four doctoral dissertations and one master's thesis have focused upon Romero's diplomatic labors and made use of his papers. These are Robert W. Frazer, Matías Romero, 1861–1868" (Master's thesis, Duke University, 1941); and sity of California, Los Angeles, 1941); John Patton Ogden, "The Labors of Matías Romero, 1861–1868" (Masters thesis, Duke University, 1941); and Robert Ryal Miller, "Mexican Secret Agents in the United States, 1861–1867" (Ph.D. diss., University of California, 1960), which one should compare closely with Robert B. Brown, "Guns over the Border: American Aid to the Juárez Government during the French Intervention" (Ph.D. diss., University of Michigan, 1951), and Thomas Schoonover, "Mexican-United States Relations, 1861–1867" (Ph.D. diss., University of Minnesota, 1970).

Robert W. Frazer and Robert R. Miller have published articles out of their dissertations. These articles are Robert W. Frazer, "Ochoa Bond Negotiations of 1865–1867," *Pacific Historical Review* 11 (December 1942): 397–414; R. W. Frazer, "Trade between California and the Belligerent Powers during the French Intervention in Mexico," *Pacific Historical Review* 15 (December 1946): 390–99; R. W. Frazer, "The United States European and West Virginian Land and Mining Company," *Pacific Historical Review* 13 (March 1944): 28–40; Robert R. Miller, "Gáspar Sánchez Ochoa: A Mexican Secret Agent in the United States," *The Historian* 23 (May 1962): 316–29; R. R. Miller, "Herman Sturm: Hoosier Secret Agent for Mexico," *Indiana Magazine of History* 58 (March 1962): 1–15; R. R. Miller, "Plácido Vega: A Mexican Secret Agent in the United States," *The Americas* 19 (October 1962): 137–48; and R. R. Miller, "Lew Wallace and the French Intervention in Mexico," *Indiana Magazine of History* 59 (March 1963): 31–50.

Some scholarly works that describe aspects of Romero's activity in the United States and his efforts to influence U.S. policy are by Dexter Perkins, *The Monroe Doctrine, 1826–1867* (Baltimore: Johns Hopkins Press, 1933); R. R. Miller, "Matías Romero: Mexican Minister to the United States during the Juárez-Maximilian Era," *Hispanic American Historical Review* 45 (May 1965): 222–45; Marvin Goldwert, "Matías Romero and Congressional Opposition to Seward's Policy toward the French Intervention in Mexico," *The Americas* 22 (July 1965): 22–40; Thomas Schoonover, "Mexican Affairs and the Impeachment of President Andrew Johnson," *East Tennessee Historical Society, Publications* 46 (1974): 76–93; Thomas Schoonover, "Dollars over Dominion: Developing United States Economic Interests in Mexico, 1861–1867," *Pacific Historical Review* 45 (February 1976): 23–45; and Thomas Schoonover, *Mexican Lobby*. The last two articles appear in revised form as part of Thomas Schoonover, *Dollars over Dominion: The Triumph of Liberalism in Mexican-United States Relations, 1861–1867* (Baton Rouge: Louisiana State University Press, 1978). There is also some Romero material in Thomas Schoonover, "European Intervention and the Bond of Central American and Mexican Liberals, 1864–1868," forthcoming. R. R. Miller, *Arms across the Border: United States Aid to Juárez during the French Intervention in Mexico*, vol. 63, part 6, *Transactions of The American Philosophical Society* (Philadelphia: American Philosophical Society, 1973), discusses Romero's role in Juárez's efforts to obtain U.S. arms. However, all of Miller's writing on Mexican-U.S. relations in the 1860s should be compared with Robert B. Brown's dissertation cited above. Two other articles that touch upon Romero's relationship to the United States era are Thomas Schoonover, "Anteproyecto de Thomas Corwin para un tratado comercial en 1861," *Historia Mexicana* 28 (April–June 1979): 596–609, and Thomas Schoonover, "Misconstrued Mission: Expansionism and Black Colonization in Mexico and Central America during the Civil War," *Pacific Historical Review* 49 (November 1980): 607–20.

For the reader who wishes to go beyond the story Romero presents, there are several starting points. James G. Randall and David Donald, *The Civil War and Reconstruction* (Boston: D. C. Heath, 1969); James M. McPherson, *Ordeal by Fire: The Civil War and Reconstruction* (New York: Oxford University Press, 1982); and James M. McPherson, *Battle Cry of Freedom: The Civil War Era* (New York: Oxford University Press, 1988), are the best volumes on this period. The bibliography in Randall and Donald is extensive although somewhat dated now. However, the Randall-Donald and McPherson texts are large, information-filled volumes. There are several smaller studies that can introduce the reader to the mid-nineteenth-century crisis: William L. Barney, *The Road to Secession* (New York: Praeger, 1972); William L. Barney, *Flawed Victory: A New Perspective on the Civil War* (New York: Praeger, 1975); William L. Barney, *The Passage of the Republic: An Interdisciplinary History of the Nineteenth Century* (Lexington, Mass.: D. C. Heath, 1987); William L. Barney, *Battleground for the Union: The Era of the Civil War and Reconstruction, 1848–1877* (Englewood Cliffs, N.J.: Prentice-Hall, 1990); William R. Brock, *An American Crisis: Congress and Reconstruction, 1865–1867* (New York: Macmillan, 1963); William R. Brock, *Conflict and Transformation: The United States, 1844–1877* (Baltimore: Penguin, 1973); Leonard P. Curry, *Blueprint for Modern America* (Nashville, Tenn.: Vanderbilt University Press, 1968); David Herbert Donald, *Liberty and Union* (Lexington, Mass.: D. C. Heath, 1978); Eric Foner, *Free Soil, Free Labor, Free Men: The Ideology of the Republican Party before the Civil War* (New York: Oxford University Press, 1970); Eric Foner, *Reconstruction: America's Unfinished Revolution, 1863–1877* (New York: Harper & Row, 1988); Herman Hattaway and Archer Jones, *How the North Won: A Military History of the Civil War* (Urbana, Ill: University of Illinois Press, 1983); Roy F. Nichols and Eugene H. Berwanger, *The Stakes of Power, 1845–1877* (rev. ed.; New York: Hill and Wang, 1982); Peter J. Parish, *The American Civil War* (New York: Holmes & Meier, 1975); Thomas Schoonover, "The Confederates in the World System: Manifestations in Central America," forthcoming in *The United States in Central America, 1860–1911: Episodes of Social Imperialism and Imperial Rivalry in the World System*; Richard H. Sewell, *A House Divided: Sectionalism and Civil War, 1848–1865* (Baltimore: Johns Hopkins Press, 1988); Emory M. Thomas, *The Confederate Nation: 1861–1865* (New York: Harper & Row, 1979); and Hans L. Trefousse, *The Radical Republicans: Lincoln's Vanguard for Racial Justice* (New York: Knopf, 1969). A good, if European oriented, narrative of Civil War diplomacy is found in Donald P. Crook, *Diplomacy during the American Civil War* (New York: John Wiley, 1975). German historian Hans-Ulrich Wehler offers a challenging, insightful interpretation of U.S. foreign relations that rests upon a sound understanding of U.S. society and the sectional crisis, in *Grundzüge der amerikanischen Aussenpolitik: 1750–1900* (Frankfurt: Suhrkamp, 1983).

Several good general histories of U.S.-Mexican relations deserve mention. They supply general background for understanding the context of U.S.-Mexican relations in the 1860s, alternative interpretations, and bibliographic guidance for further reading. The best one-volume study of U.S.-Mexican relations is Josefina Zoraida Vásquez and Lorenzo Meyer, *México frente a los Estados Unidos: un ensayo histórico, 1776–1980* (México: El Colegio de México, 1982), which the University of Chicago Press translated as *The United States and Mexico* (Chicago: University of Chicago, 1985) in 1985. In addition, one can turn to Karl M. Schmitt, *Mexico and the United States, 1821–1973: Conflict and Coexistence* (New York: John Wiley, 1974); Howard Cline, *The United States and Mexico, 1821–1963* (3d ed.; Cambridge: Harvard University Press, 1963); and Jonathan Oliff, *Reforma Mexico and the United States: A Search for Alternatives to Annexation, 1854–1861* (University, Ala.: University of Alabama Press, 1981). Also useful, although in Spanish, is Luis G. Zorrilla, *Historia de las relaciones entre México y los Estados Unidos de América, 1800–1958*, 2 vols. (México: Editorial Porrua, 1965–66). The impact of liberalism upon Mexican (and Latin American) society can be followed in E. Bradford Burns, *The Poverty of Progress: Latin America in the Nineteenth Century* (Berkeley, Calif.: University of California Press, 1980) and David Bushnell and Neill Macaulay, *The Emergence of Latin America in the Nineteenth Century* (New York: Oxford University Press, 1988), chap. 9. For those wishing to pursue the international aspects of the Mexican-U.S.-French story, two fine recent bibliographies can guide the reader to sources and secondary literature: Richard Dean Burns, ed., *Guide to American Foreign Relations since 1700* (Santa Barbara, Calif.: ABC Clio, 1983) and David Trask, Michael Meyer, and Roger Trask, comps., *A Bibliography of United States-Latin American Relations since 1810*, 1 vol. and supp. (Lincoln, Nebr.: University of Nebraska Press, 1968, 1979).

Index